CASS SERIES: STUDIED IN INTELLIGENCE

ESPIONAGE
and the
ROOTS OF THE
COLD WAR

The Conspiratorial
Heritage

DAVID McKNIGHT
University of Technology, Sydney

With a Foreword by
RICHARD J. ALDRICH

FRANK CASS
LONDON • PORTLAND, OR

First published in 2002 in Great Britain by
FRANK CASS PUBLISHERS
Crown House, 47 Chase Side, Southgate
London N14 5BP

and in the United States of America by
FRANK CASS PUBLISHERS
c/o ISBS, 5824 N.E. Hassalo Street
Portland, Oregon, 97213-3644

Website: www.frankcass.com

British Library Cataloguing in Publication Data

McKnight, David
   Espionage and the roots of the Cold War: the
   conspirational heritage. – (Studies in intelligence)
   1. Espionage, Russian – History – 20th century 2. Cold War
   I. Title
   327.1'247

ISBN 0-7146-5163-X (cloth)

Library of Congress Cataloguing-in-Publication Data

McKnight, David
   Espionage and the roots of the Cold War: the conspirational heritage/
   David McKnight.
      p. cm – (Studies in intelligence, ISSN 1368-9916)
   Includes bibliographical references and index.
   ISBN 0-7146-5163-X (cloth)
      1. Espionage, Soviet. 2. Cold War. 3. World politics–1945 – I. Title. II. Cass
   series–studies in intelligence.

UB271.R9 M35 2002
327.1247'009'041–dc21
                                                                2002071596

Typeset in 10.5/12.5 Sabon by Cambridge Photosetting Services
Printed in Great Britain by MPG Books Ltd, Bodmin, Cornwall

Contents

A Note on the Text

Please note that the name of the Australian Labor Party is rendered throughout with the correct spelling 'Labor' though in original documents it is occasionally rendered as 'Labour'. The term 'labour movement' refers to the network of trade unions and similar organisations outside the party sphere.

To my daughter, Ilse Scheepers

List of Illustrations

8. Asian and Australian delegates at the Fourth Congress of Comintern in 1922. Later the Pan Pacific Trade Union Secretariat united US, British, Chinese and Australian trade unionists to build underground trade unions.

9. Communist work with Western navies began after 1929. A 1931 revolt by Australian sailors prompted this cartoon in *Smith's Weekly*.

10. Harry Pollitt defended British underground work in the army against Comintern criticism that it was inadequate. Seen here addressing the British Battalion during the Spanish civil war.

11. Underground communists led the biggest section of the Australian Labor Party in 1939–40. After a split the left-dominated State Labor Party merged with the Australian Communist Party.

12. Jack Hughes (right) who was an undercover member of the communist party while rising to lead the New South Wales branch of the Labor Party. With him is Lance Sharkey, secretary of the Communist Party of Australia.

13. Osip Piatnitsky, a key figure in the pre-revolutionary Bolshevik illegal apparatus, he headed Comintern underground work until the mid 1930s.

14. One of several false passports carried by OMS worker Jakov Rudnik, who was arrested after a lapse in conspirational rules which also saw Vietnamese communist Ho Chi Minh arrested.

15. American codebreakers unravel a message from Moscow warning KGB resident Semyen Makarov that he is breaching conspirational rules. Such rules were designed to hide the identity of Soviet intelligence workers from their fellow embassy staffers.

16. A surveillance photo of Wal Clayton, who headed the underground work of the Australian Communist Party and was later recruited to work for Soviet Intelligence in 1945.

Acknowledgements

A number of people assisted me greatly in preparing this book. Dr Peter Cochrane provided intelligent and knowledgeable comment while valuable research assistance came from Lena Goreva in Moscow and Nathalie Apouchtine in Australia. Other support came from June Goss.

The staff of a number of public institutions were helpful. The institutions include the Russian Centre for the Preservation and Study of Documents of Recent History (especially Svetlana Rozenthal), the International Institute for Social History in Amsterdam (especially Mieke Yzermans) and the National Archives in Washington, DC. Also of note were the National Archives in Canberra (especially John Pepper and Moira Smythe) and its state branch in Sydney; the Fisher Library at the University of Sydney and the Mitchell Library in Sydney.

Further assistance for which I am grateful came from Barbara Curthoys, Jane Mills, Geoff Curthoys, Hans-Dieter Senff, Ken Mansell, John Haynes and Judy Tonkin and the Coledale gang.

I am grateful to those who agreed to be interviewed or consulted or who helped in other ways. These include Dimitri Moiseenko (Moscow), Laurie Aarons, the late Claude Jones, Eric Aarons, Audrey Blake, Roger Coates, the late Diana Gould, the late Walter Clayton, Jim Henderson, Jack Hughes, Andrew Campbell, Betty Reilly, Len Fox, the late Bill Callen, Rose Creswell, Phillip Deery, Robert Manne, Stuart Macintyre, Edgar Ross, George Bolotenko and Elizabeth Weiss.

Financial assistance for travel to Russia came from the Search Foundation and the History Department at the University of Sydney.

Finally, thanks to my daughter, Ilse Scheepers, who put up with my absences and preoccupations and to my partner, Jane Mills, who was supportive and always a source of wise advice.

Abbreviations

AA(ACT)	Designates a file held by the Australian Archives (now National Archives of Australia), in its branch in the Australian Capital Territory
ACLF	All-China Labour Federation
ACTU	Australian Council of Trade Unions
ALP	Australian Labor Party
CC	Central Committee
Comintern	Communist (Third) International
CPA	Communist Party of Australia
CPC	Communist Party of China
CPGB	Communist Party of Great Britain
CPUSA	Communist Party of the United States of America
ECCI	Executive Committee of the Communist International
FEB	Far Eastern Bureau (of Comintern)
FOSU	Friends of the Soviet Union
GRU	Soviet military intelligence
InPreCorr	*International Press Correspondence*, Comintern publication
IWW	Industrial Workers of the World
KGB	Soviet political intelligence
KIM	Kommunisticheskii Internatsional Molodezhi (Communist Youth International)
KMT	Kuomintang
MI5, MI6	British internal security service; British external intelligence service
ML	Mitchell Library, part of the State Library of New South Wales

MLOH	Mitchell Library, Oral History Collection
MSS	Manuscript section
NARA	National Archives and Records Administration (Maryland and Washington, DC)
NKVD	Narodnyi Komissariat Vnutrennik Del (People's Commissariat of Internal Affairs)
NSA	National Security Agency
NSW	New South Wales
OMS	International Liaison Service of Comintern
PB	Political Bureau
PCF	Communist Party of France
PPTUS	Pan-Pacific Trade Union Secretariat
Profintern	Red International of Labour Unions, the trade union wing of the Comintern
RCE	Royal Commission on Espionage (Australia)
RILU	Red International of Labour Unions (Profintern)
RSDLP	Russian Social-Democratic Labour Party
RTsKhIDNI	Russian Centre for the Preservation and Study of Documents of Recent History (Moscow)
SMH	*Sydney Morning Herald*
SMP	Shanghai Municipal Police
USSR	Union of Soviet Socialist Republics
WW	*Workers Weekly*, newspaper of the CPA
YCL	Young Communist League

Foreword

This study of the relationship between the Comintern and Soviet espionage underlines the extraordinarily international nature of the network enjoyed by the Soviet underground during the first half of the twentieth century. Accordingly, David McKnight's impressive study of his clandestine subject has required a pattern of global research and intellectual investigation that is no less remarkable in its scope.

In the last few years we have seen many new studies of the Cold War that have sought to make use of the latest archival releases. The result has been a growing consensus that 'we now know' a great deal more about the main influences that determined the direction of the Cold War in both the East and the West. At least three important new windows have opened up on the underground activity of the Soviet Union. In the last few years the US National Security Agency and GCHQ have released many of their decrypts of the now famous 'Venona' traffic – the intercepted and partly deciphered traffic of Soviet intelligence agents in the West. Some of these decrypts have been sanitised in what seems an almost deliberately tantalising way, but they do make clear the vast scale of Soviet underground activity in the West, and notably within the United States.

Meanwhile researchers have worked valiantly to increase the flow of material from the gradually opening archives in Moscow, including the Central Party Archive and also some Soviet intelligence material. Finally, we can add to this the story of the Mitrohkin Archive, a remarkable personal hoard of material smuggled out of the Soviet Union by a figure who for many years was the KGB's keeper of secrets.

David McKnight has used all these sources and more. He has deployed them together with records as diverse as the International

Institute for Social History at Amsterdam, the Shanghai Police Files and the archives of other Western security agencies to give us a truly three-dimensional picture of the Comintern and its world-wide activities.

The result of these investigations is deep insight into the nature of *konspiratsya* and its contribution to Stalinism. The complex linkage between the conspiratorial nature of Bolshevism and patterns of Soviet espionage is now becoming clear. David McKnight demonstrates that, if anything, the anxieties about conspiracy and surveillance were greater amongst communists outside the Soviet Union than inside. Yet these underground networks were not mere toys of the Soviet secret service. As this nuanced study shows us, they enjoyed some independent life of their own, reflecting the diverse and unruly individuals that constituted them. Moreover, far from being 'super-spies', the intellectuals of the Comintern were often enthusiastic amateurs when it came to the underground game and so distinguished themselves by their disturbing disregard for good tradecraft.

This is a landmark book that will be essential reading not only for intelligence specialists but also everyone interested in the Cold War.

Professor Richard Aldrich
August 2002

Introduction

In the early years of the Cold War one of the most devastating charges against someone was that they spied for the Soviet Union. Accusations of treachery, while levelled at only a small number of individuals, symbolised a wider challenge to many others whose left-wing ideas were suspect.

To these charges, the left responded with accusations of witch-hunting – the persecution of a minority for the sake of their ideas rather than any actual wrong-doing. The distinction between 'wrong thoughts' and 'wrong actions' divided the left from their anti-communist opponents. In their justifiable opposition to sweeping and often unsubstantiated allegations, the left and their liberal allies scorned the possibility that there could be any truth to the charges of espionage.

But in fact from the 1930s to the 1950s a significant number of men and women in the United States, Britain, Europe, Australia and Canada were recruited to the Soviet intelligence services. Fired by idealism, they believed that the Soviet Union was the prototype of a new society that would lead to human liberation. They believed that conveying confidential material from their own governments to the Soviet Union was part of a world-wide revolutionary struggle against capitalism.

Their activities and the response of Western governments became the focus of an intensifying Cold War. It began immediately after the Second World War when Dr Alan Nunn May became the first of a number jailed for 'atomic espionage'. The succeeding years saw a welter of similar charges. In 1947 loyalty tests began to be administered to US public servants. In 1948, in testimony to the House UnAmerican Activities Committee, Elizabeth Bentley and Whittaker Chambers named several senior US public servants as spies, and by year's end one

1

of them, Alger Hiss, was indicted for perjury. The year 1950 began with the arrest in Britain of an atomic scientist, Klaus Fuchs, and escalated with the arrest in New York of Julius Rosenberg whose trial, along with that of his wife Ethel, became a *cause célèbre*. The following year, two British 'diplomats', Donald Maclean and Guy Burgess, mysteriously disappeared from their embassy in Washington. Many years later a third man, Kim Philby, also fled to Russia.

But these people and the hundreds of scientists, young university graduates and skilled workers who became enmeshed in other enterprises of espionage were amateurs, rather than professional intelligence workers, and the reason for their often successful activities is intriguing. As well, the reasons for the success of the Russian intelligence services, at least in the period 1920–50, have never been satisfactorily explained. No doubt fear and ruthlessness played their part, but no amount of fear can induce a skill where none existed before.

This book seeks to explore the foundations for these successes in the little-known tradition of underground political activity which was part of the communist movement between 1917 and 1945. In this way, this book also examines the social and political origins of what is commonly known as the 'tradecraft' of espionage. It also seeks to contribute to the study of the causes of the early Cold War, by explaining how this underground work led to espionage. The revelations of espionage demonstrated that during the early Cold War, the left, which was a victim of McCarthyism, also had some well-hidden skeletons in its closet.

KONSPIRATSYA

The actions of people such as Philby, Maclean, Chambers, Bentley, Hiss and others were the embodiment of a pre-Tsarist Russian tradition that was turned to good use by the Soviet intelligence services. The Russian word which denoted this tradition is *konspiratsya*. This word evolved under Tsarism to denote the assembly of practices needed to organise a study circle, a meeting, a trade union or a revolutionary party – without being caught by the police. The word originates in the Latin, *conspirare*, literally to 'breathe together' whence 'to accord, harmonise, agree, combine or unite in a purpose, plot mischief together secretly'.[1] In English the connotations are invariably pejorative. First noted in English in the fourteenth century, 'conspiracy' was sometimes associated with the alleged machinations of Jews. In law, the charge of conspiracy developed as one way of repressing collective action and criminalising dissent. In the waning years of the French Revolution, Francois Babeuf was charged with forming a conspiracy to agitate for radical socialism and egalitarianism. His ideas and methods were later credited with influencing the Russian Social-Revolutionaries and Social Democrats.[2] In the eighteenth and nineteenth century in England the laws against conspiracy together with the infamous Combination Acts were used to attack collective action by workers.[3] In Europe in the nineteenth century the Fraternal Democrats, an international organisation opposing monarchism and promoting the then radical notion of democracy, argued that '[t]he conspiracy of kings must be answered with a conspiracy of the peoples'.[4] Similarly, in the Russia of the Tsars, the populist opposition, and later the Marxists, described their methods as 'conspiracy'.

After 1917 these rules of conspiracy – and the habits of mind which flowed from them – were suddenly elevated to a world stage. With the founding of the Communist International (Comintern) in 1919, these practices now travelled to Shanghai, Berlin, New York, London and to Australia. But while this tradition was mainly embodied by political parties, a parallel expression developed in the newly created Soviet intelligence services. Its officers found that their years of underground struggle equipped them with a 'tradecraft' which worked remarkably well for their new role in espionage overseas. Acting as a hunted revolutionary in your own land was a good preparation for acting as a spy in someone else's country.

This common heritage of political and intelligence work can be seen when we examine the language of key terms. The 'rules of conspiracy' as expressed by Lenin spoke in terms of 'legal' work and 'illegal work'. A small, inoffensive workers insurance co-operative was typical of the 'legal' work by pre-revolutionary Social Democrats and others in the labour movement. By contrast, 'illegal' work might be a secret system of distributing radical newspapers using the contacts gained in that same workers' insurance co-operative. In Soviet intelligence, 'legal work' was a term used to denote espionage carried out by a spy operating under the protected status of a diplomatic official of the USSR. 'Illegal work' was that carried out by a spy with no such cover. On these terms, Nollau has said:

> To regard the words 'legal' and 'illegal' as equivalent to 'lawful' and 'unlawful' would be to misunderstand both Bolshevist semantics

3

and Bolshevist practice. It would be more correct to substitute 'overt' for 'legal' and 'clandestine' or 'conspiratorial' for 'illegal' although it must be remembered that not all of the Comintern's overt work was lawful ... not all clandestine Bolshevist activity was unlawful (for example, the financing of 'Sections' which was almost universally done by conspiratorial means; or the transmission of ECCI instructions ... even when the Communist Party was perfectly legal).[5]

Comintern and Soviet intelligence thus both grew in common soil, but as the revolutionary impulse dissolved, replaced by a loyalty to Stalin, the Soviet government increasingly looked upon the Comintern with new eyes, not primarily as a vehicle for world revolution but as an extension of itself, including as a rich source of agents for Soviet intelligence. The systematic use of Comintern militants for espionage was therefore a feature that accompanied the rise of Stalinism. This was recognised as early as 1955, by Dallin who argued that '[a]lthough aid to Russia including the furnishing of confidential information, was a matter of course, systematic espionage for Moscow was not considered a regular duty or preoccupation of Communism abroad and no one wanted the new Communist underground to become a tool of Soviet intelligence operations.'[6] A particular obstacle to this development, according to Dallin, was Leon Trotsky and his defeat in 1926–7, accompanied by the 'Bolshevisation' drive, made the way clear for espionage.

PARTICIPANTS IN THE UNDERGROUND

Those given tasks by Soviet intelligence were often skilled in the political underground. This was the case, for example, with Richard Sorge, a German communist who learnt his 'rules of conspiracy' in his homeland, where the Communist Party was banned briefly in the early 1920s and always had a significant underground. During the Second World War, posing as a 'pro-Nazi' journalist in Tokyo, and in touch with high Japanese and German military circles, Sorge regularly reported to Soviet military intelligence. Of people like Sorge, the defector Walter Krivitsky, noted: 'Out of the ruins of the communist revolution we built in Germany for Soviet Russia a brilliant intelligence service, the envy of every other nation.'[7]

Communist parties in the West offered many opportunities for astute Soviet intelligence officers. The Communist Party of the United States (CPUSA) had a significant underground organisation from the 1920s onwards which provided a number of recruits to Soviet intelligence.[8] The penetration of the Manhattan Project and the dispatch of valuable information on the atom bomb project are now acknowledged by the Russians to have taken place.[9] This espionage was largely dependent on members of the CPUSA such as Julius Rosenberg and Lona Cohen as well as on sympathetic scientists such as Theodore Hall and Klaus Fuchs.[10] As well, the CPUSA leader Earl Browder was used as a source by the KGB[11] while his sister, Margaret Browder, carried out assignments for it.[12] An analysis of the underground work of the CPUSA and a reinterpretation of old and new evidence in the light of the tradition of *konspiratsya*, is set out in chapters 5 and 7.

Elsewhere, the most acceptable face of this phenomenon was the 'Red Orchestra', networks of agents from the Comintern and Soviet military intelligence (GRU) which conducted espionage against the Nazi regime. Some were relatively inexperienced in the rules of conspiracy, but others drew on a long personal experience in underground political organisation. One group was led by Leopold Trepper, a Comintern union militant who joined Soviet military intelligence in 1937.[13] Another group, the so-called 'Lucy Ring', was based in Switzerland and was run by Alexander Rado.[14] Both had a range of contacts who fed valuable intelligence on German military plans and industrial production to the Soviet military intelligence. Trepper's elucidation of tradecraft after his capture paralleled the 'rules of conspiracy' set out in the Comintern manual discussed in chapter 2.[15]

A reference to the Lucy Ring occurred in the first postwar western inquiry into Soviet espionage, the Canadian Royal Commission on the communication of information to a foreign power.[16] This Royal Commission was established after a Soviet code clerk, Igor Gouzenko, defected in September 1945, bringing with him a large number of documents. The inquiry found that the Canadian Communist Party encouraged certain kinds of workers to keep their membership secret, including 'scientific workers, teachers, office and business workers, persons engaged in any type of administrative activity, and any group likely to obtain any type of government employment'.[17] This technique 'seems calculated to develop the psychology of a double life and double standards', it said.

Perhaps the best known Soviet agent was Kim Philby, who penetrated the British Secret Intelligence Service (SIS or MI6). In his autobiography, Philby recalls his year of 'illegal activity' in central Europe in 1933–4. His self-description is telling, for our purposes. His entire career as a spy, he states, was thirty years 'spent underground' as 'an underground worker'.[18] The way in which one of his associates, Guy Burgess, conceived of his activity is revealing. Only a few years after he left university, he blurted out to a friend that he was trying to recruit: 'I want to tell you that I am a Comintern agent and have been ever since I came down from Cambridge.'[19] A great deal is now known about the true events surrounding the Cambridge spies, based on newly opened Soviet archives. In chapter 5 I refer to recent Soviet archival releases and contextualise the early years of Philby and his associates against the background of the underground tradition of the previous decades.

In chapter 7 I examine the link between the political underground and Soviet intelligence in the atomic espionage in the Manhattan Project, in the Red Orchestra and in Australia where undercover members of the Communist Party of Australia (CPA) obtained British Foreign Office documents and cables.

POLARISED SCHOLARSHIP

The context for understanding the tradition of underground work is still deeply affected by the scholarship of the Cold War. Books about the Comintern or its affiliated parties are often highly partisan. Historians of the communist movement tended to divide between sympathisers and opponents of Marxism. As Studer and Unfried note, 'the implicit or explicit intention of the author to pronounce a moral verdict on the history of communism meant that the work could only be read as an apologia or as a sweeping condemnation'.[20]

To the sympathisers, the use of subterfuge by communist activists was embarrassing and best left unsaid. Such historians saw the charges of espionage levelled against some communists as merely frame-ups designed to cover political persecution.[21] As Gaddis notes, 'Because some charges of Soviet espionage were exaggerated there was a tendency to assume that all of them had been, that the spies were simply figments of the right-wing imaginations.'[22] To opponents of communism, charges of espionage were only the most extreme of the faults stemming from Marxist philosophy. Such charges provided useful proof of communism's perfidy and little more needed to be explored about the origins of this phenomenon. In some cases, such literature was highly coloured and inaccurate.[23] The partisan nature of the Cold War did not encourage a necessary scepticism on the part of historians sympathetic with the left, nor did it encourage historians on the right to see clandestinity in the context of repression.

However, with the opening of new archival sources it must be said that a number of the propositions of the scholarly anti-communist school of thought have been validated.[24] These include the systematic use of western communist parties by Soviet intelligence and the willingness of individuals within them to perform those roles.

This must be tempered however by an acknowledgement of other factors. As studies of secret societies, below, demonstrate, methods of secrecy and conspiracy are not solely associated with communist movements or even political causes. Religious and ethnic groups have used these methods for centuries. The common factor is repression, usually by the state. In order to distinguish this book from partisan stances, I describe the development of conspiratorial methods alongside accounts of political repression. In my view, it is not possible to fully understand the first without understanding the second.

In chapter 1 we see the nineteenth-century origins of communism beginning in highly undemocratic and repressive monarchies. In chapter 4 we examine the urban Comintern underground in China, where repression made the need for underground work patently obvious to the Comintern revolutionaries. Whatever one may think of the enterprise undertaken by the Comintern in China, there is no doubt that the conservative government's policy of summary executions encouraged the conspiratorial tradition.

Repression against communists in the West was, of course, nothing like that of China. Legal restrictions, however, existed and were seen by many as a continuation of repression directed at trade unions and radicals of all stripes which had begun before 1917. Thus it provided a fertile soil for the propagation of elements of the political tradition of Russia. The systematisation of conspiracy is examined in chapter 2. But while much of the conspiratorial tradition had a defensive character, it also sometimes projected the offensive thrusts of communist parties. This occurred when communists began political work within the armies and navies of the West, driven by the dream that such work would be crucial in a future socialist insurrection, as outlined in chapter 3. It also occurred in the penetration of social democratic and labour parties (chapter 6), where the use of clandestine methods could not be justified by reference to repression, but by the convenience and utility of the method.

Underground political work is rarely examined in historical accounts of the communist movement, though it was central to the practice and personal experience of communists in most countries. This was not because underground activity was entirely secret. Publicly available primary sources such as *International Press Correspondence* and *Communist International* contain articles on the principles of underground work, but no single book substantially draws on this and shows their meaning. References occur to illegal work in some standard works on the Comintern, such as Nollau, McKenzie and Lazitch, but they are brief.[25] The books which deal most thoroughly with the role of conspiratorial work are highly partisan and stridently anti-communist, such as Selznick's *The Organisational Weapon* or Avtorkhanov's *The Communist Party Apparatus*.[26]

Historical accounts of the field of Soviet espionage are equally bereft. Discounting that part written in an adventure genre, the remaining works say very little about the bridge between the tradition of *konspiratsya* and later espionage. A classic scholarly work on the KGB by Christopher Andrew and Oleg Gordievsky says nothing of the pre-revolutionary heritage of conspiracy although it points to KGB co-operation with the Comintern, including its underground wing.[27] Knight's analysis is similar to that of Andrews and Gordievsky, seeing the significant roots of Soviet intelligence in the Tsarist police, and saying nothing of the underground tradition and its influence on Soviet intelligence.[28] George Leggett's work on the early Cheka notes in passing that 'the nucleus of the apparatus was recruited from the ranks of comrades who had acquired a high degree of proficiency in the conspiratorial arts during the years in the revolutionary underground'.[29] Dziak briefly noted the influence of the underground experience on the KGB, but confines its significance to the experience of 'covert provocational and counter-provocational duels' with the Tsarist secret police.[30] Writers such as Barron and Deacon make no mention of the conspiratorial heritage.[31]

One writer who does mention this aspect clearly, if briefly, is David Dallin. Dallin points unequivocally to the continuity between the Comintern and Russian intelligence and does so without a descent into the highly combative scholarship characterised by the Cold War.

Significantly, Dallin himself witnessed the 1917 revolution and was acquainted with underground technique as a Menshevik in the Russian Social Democratic Party. In his study of Soviet espionage he pointed out: 'Many of the terms now in use in the Soviet intelligence system originated in the pre-revolutionary underground: *yavka*, a house or apartment where secret agents come to report; *dubok*, literally, a little oak – a hiding place for messages; "illegal", a person carrying false papers; "hospital", prison; "illness", arrest and so on.'[32]

The most fruitful accounts of the communist underground work are often contained in memoirs of communists who played some role in the Comintern illegal apparatuses.[33] Those who then went on to work with Soviet intelligence organisations, for example in the Red Orchestra in wartime Europe, are very useful.[34] The problem from the point of view of a historian is that these accounts are largely anecdotal and fragmentary. In some cases the motive for revealing underground political work is a loss of faith which can present problems of reliability.[35] In the case of the writings of professional intelligence officers who have defected, these are often guided by the intelligence agency of the host nation and are difficult to rely on alone.[36] An exception to this rule is Alexander Orlov's *Handbook of Intelligence and Guerrilla Warfare*, which tellingly refers to the espionage milieu as 'the underground'.[37] Orlov was a senior KGB official who defected in the late 1930s and the book, often anecdotal, is based on one he wrote in 1936 for KGB operatives and for the Central Military School.

The problem of all of these historical accounts is that a study of the heritage of conspiracy falls between the two stools of communist history and intelligence history. Although this problem is not caused by the lack of sources, it is a fact that since the opening of the Russian archives some new work has broken this compartmentalisation, notably Klehr, Haynes and Firsov's *The Secret World of American Communism*.[38] Here we see some accounts of the transition of individuals and groups from underground political work to espionage. Similarly, a recent history of the Communist Party of Australia found persuasive evidence that a senior member of the party assisted the KGB.[39]

A third body of writing which has some relevance covers the phenomenon of 'secret societies'. By this is meant bodies as diverse as the Tiandihui ('triads') of Chinese society, the mafia, the masonic movement, the Irish Fenians and the religious Rosicrucians. Some have classified underground political parties as part of this phenomenon, noting the centrality of secrecy.[40] Chinese secret societies seem to share some of the characteristics of underground parties, with most studies noting that they often organised the poor, embodied self-protection and mutual aid, employed notions of equality or brotherhood, and were associated to varying degrees with social rebellion.[41] Such comparisons are useful in showing that 'conspiratorial' organisations have been a widespread social phenomenon and that repression is a key factor in their origins. This in turn helps demonstrate that conspiracy is not a peculiarly communist product. But the usefulness of this comparison is limited to this observation.

THE NEW ARCHIVAL SOURCES

The poor or patchy nature of studies on the political underground and its connection with Soviet intelligence is perhaps not surprising. The nature of conspiratorial work was itself highly secret. Official documents describing the concrete techniques used for underground work are virtually non-existent. Only general principles of organisation were outlined in communist journals, along with guarded studies of underground political activity in countries such as Mussolini's Italy. When underground political work is noted in the minutes of individual parties, it is often cryptic. When it occurred in Comintern conferences safe within Russia, the minutes show that the matter was treated with great caution. Other sources such as police records are often limited because recruits to underground work were chosen precisely on the basis that they were 'cleanskins', that is, having no police record. Recruits were often provided with a new identity and papers and pseudonyms were used even among colleagues. Thus the resulting patchy nature of these records has created difficult circumstances for the historian. This situation has been changed by the opening of a number of new archival sources in recent years.

One of the key sources for examining the extensive use by Soviet intelligence of communists and left-wing sympathisers in the West are the Venona documents.[42] These are a set of partially decoded cables sent between Moscow and Soviet intelligence posts in the USA, Britain, Australia and elsewhere from 1940 to 1948. Released in stages by the US National Security Agency in 1995–6, these records offer a new and detailed window into the daily routines of an intelligence organisation. In particular they offer insights into the contact between communist parties and Soviet intelligence and establish the targets, the nature of the tasks and the methods used. For our purposes they also reveal strong continuities between the strictly political underground methods and those applied to espionage. These include, for example, careful recruitment involving a detailed biography,[43] the need for *konspiratsya*, even within the Soviet embassy,[44] and detailed instructions on meetings and passwords.[45] These records are also valuable because their credibility can be established at several key points by comparing them with previously established (and uncontroversial) facts, for instance in the US espionage trial of the Rosenbergs.[46] This in turn makes them more reliable in areas where corroboration is less certain. As it is, the Venona material on leading Australian communist, Walter Clayton, fits very well with what is already known. This includes, for example, his recruitment of the security officer, Alfred Hughes, which Clayton first admitted to this writer and which is confirmed in the Venona material.[47]

This book makes extensive use of newly released Russian archival sources, notably that of the Russian Centre for the Preservation and Study of Documents of Recent History, referred to in the text by its Russian acronym, RTsKhIDNI. This archive was the former Central Party Archive of the Communist Party of the Soviet Union (also known as the Institute for Marx–Engels–Lenin). In the period 1989 to 1991, this archive gradually became open to overseas scholars. Previously access to it had been reserved for a small number of Russian researchers working on projects approved by the central committee of the CPSU.

RTsKhIDNI holds the entire archives of the Communist International, the international association of communist parties founded in 1919 and dissolved in 1943. As well as documents of Comintern bodies such as its Executive Committee (ECCI), this archive also holds a vast number of documents of individual communist parties. In the case of many communist parties RTsKhIDNI holds documents which were destroyed or not collected in the home country, due to the practice of centralised monitoring of individual parties world-wide. These records offer a window into frank discussions where private views were articulated which often contradicted public stances.

The significant absence in the records of RTsKhIDNI are documents covering the functioning of the Comintern's International Liaison Service (OMS) and its director, Osip Piatinitsky. These records are still barred to scholars, almost certainly because they contain numerous references to Soviet intelligence organisations and personnel. References to OMS, however, exist in some open documents and a brief account of its work is pieced together in chapter 2.

Other sources used in this book include those of the International Institute for Social History in Amsterdam; the Shanghai Municipal Police records in the National Archives in Washington; those of several Australian security intelligence bodies at the National Archives in Canberra; and the records of the Communist Party of Australia in the Mitchell Library, Sydney.

In 1985, Gabriel Garcia Marquez tells us, the Chilean exile Miguel Littin returned illegally to his country. Littin had been exiled by the Pinochet dictatorship but managed to spend six weeks in Chile directing a film aimed at exposing the repression. 'He entered Chile on a false passport', says Marquez. 'Make-up artists had altered his face and he spoke and dressed in the manner of a successful Uruguayan businessman. Protected by underground resistance groups, Littin travelled the length and breadth of the country, directing three European film crews (who had entered Chile legally on various film assignments) as well as six young film crews from the Chilean resistance.'[48] None of the film crews was aware of the existence of the others and each had innocuous cover assignments.

The parallel with the events and methods portrayed in this book is perhaps surprising at first. But on reflection, rather than being a quaint historical curiosity, it is clear that the traditions and methods of underground activity are still used, in spite of the death of the Soviet Union. Moreover they are used in conditions similar to Tsarism and apparently with some success.

NOTES

1. *Oxford English Dictionary*, 2nd ed. Clarendon Press, Oxford, 1989, 783.
2. Julius Braunthal, *History of the International, 1864–1914* (trans. Henry Collins and Kenneth Mitchell), Thomas Nelson, London, 1966, 35.
3. John V. Orth, 'The English Combination Laws Reconsidered', in Francis Snyder and Douglas Hay, *Labour, Law and Crime: an Historical Perspective*, Tavistock Publications, London, 1987, 136–7.
4. Franz Mehring, *Karl Marx: the Story of his Life* (trans. E. Fitzgerald), George Allen & Unwin, London, 1951, 143.
5. Gunter Nollau, *International Communism and World Revolution: History and Methods*, Hollis & Carter, London 1961, 157.
6. David Dallin, *Soviet Espionage*, Yale University Press, New Haven, 1955, 16.
7. W. G. Krivitsky, *I Was Stalin's Agent*, Hamish Hamilton, London, 1940, 64.
8. Harvey Klehr, John Earl Haynes and Fredrikh Igorevich Firsov, *The Secret World of*

American Communism, Yale University Press, New Haven, 1995, see esp. chapters 6 and 8.

9. Pavel and Anatoli Sudoplatov (with Jerrold and Leona Schechter), *Special Tasks: the Memoirs of an Unwanted Witness*, Little, Brown, London, 1994, 436–67.

10. Apart from the decoded Soviet intelligence cables, the Venona decrypts (see chapter 7), one key scientist, Theodore Hall, has admitted his role in detail: Joseph Albright and Marcia Kunstel, *Bombshell: the Secret Story of America's Unknown Atomic Spy Conspiracy*, Times Books, New York, 1997.

11. I have used the designation KGB throughout to denote the wing of the Soviet secret police which worked overseas although the name of the organisation was known variously as the GPU, OGPU, NKVD, NKGB, MGB, the KI and MVD.

12. Klehr *et al.*, *Secret World*, 238–43.

13. Leopold Trepper, *The Great Game: Memoirs of the Spy Hitler Couldn't Silence*, McGraw-Hill, New York, 1977; Gilles Perrault, *The Red Orchestra*, Mayflower, London, 1970.

14. Alexander Foote, *Handbook for Spies*, Museum Press, London, 1964.

15. Perrault, *Red Orchestra*, 245–6.

16. Justice Robert Taschereau and Justice R. L. Kellock, *Report of the Royal Commission to Investigate Facts Relating to the Communication of Secret and Confidential Information to Agents of a Foreign Power*, Government Printer, Ottawa, 1946; section 6 deals with this incident.

17. Ibid., 69–70.

18. Kim Philby, *My Silent War*, Panther, London, 1980, 12, 180.

19. Goronwyn Rees, *A Chapter of Accidents*, Chatto and Windus, London, 1972, cited in Barrie Penrose and Simon Freeman, *Conspiracy of Silence: the Secret Life of Anthony Blunt*, Grafton Books, London, 1987, 211.

20. Brigitte Studer and Berthold Unfried, 'At the Beginning of a History: Visions of the Comintern, After the Opening of the Archives', *International Review of Social History*, No. 42 (1997), 420.

21. Walter and Miriam Schneir, *Invitation to an Inquest: Reopening the Rosenberg 'Atom Spy' Case*, 3rd edn, Penguin Books, Harmondsworth, 1974; Nicholas Whitlam and John Stubbs, *Nest of Traitors: The Petrov Affair*, Jacaranda Press, Milton (Qld), 1974.

22. John Lewis Gaddis, 'The Tragedy of Cold War History: Reflections on Revisionism', in *Foreign Affairs*, 73, 1 (Jan.–Feb. 1994), 147.

23. See for example Charles A. Willoughby, *Shanghai Conspiracy: The Sorge Spy Ring*, E. P. Dutton & Company, New York, 1952.

24. For example, Ronald Radosh and Joyce Milton, *The Rosenberg File: a Search for the Truth*, Vintage Books, New York, 1984; Robert Manne, *The Petrov Affair: Politics and Espionage*, Pergamon, Sydney, 1987.

25. Nollau, *International Communism*, 162–3; Kermit E. McKenzie, *Comintern and World Revolution 1928–1943: the Shaping of a Doctrine*, Columbia University Press, New York, 1964, 97; Branko Lazitch, 'Two Instruments of Control by the Comintern: the Emissaries of the ECCI and the Party Representatives in Moscow', in Milorad M. Drachkovitch and Branko Lazitch (eds.), *The Comintern: Historical Highlights*, Frederick A. Praeger, New York, 1966, 45–7.

26. Philip Selznick, *The Organisational Weapon: a Study of Bolshevik Strategy and Tactics*, Free Press, Glencoe, 1960; Abdurakhman Avtorkhanov, *The Communist Party Apparatus*, Henry Regnery Company, Chicago, 1966.

27. Andrew and Gordievsky discuss a number of such episodes in *KGB: the Inside Story of its Foreign Operations from Lenin to Gorbachev*, Hodder & Stoughton, London, 1990.

28. Amy W. Knight, *The KGB: Police and Politics in the Soviet Union*, Unwin Hyman, Boston, 1988, ch. 1.

29. George Leggett, *The Cheka: Lenin's Political Police*, Clarendon Press, Oxford, 1981, 235–6.

30. John J. Dziak, *Chekisty: a History of the KGB*, Lexington Books, Lexington, 1988, 4, 39–40.

31. John Barron, *KGB: the Secret Work of Soviet Secret Agents*, Hodder & Stoughton, London, 1974. Richard Deacon, *A History of the Russian Secret Service*, Grafton Books, London, 1972.
32. David Dallin, *Soviet Espionage*, Yale University Press, New Haven, 1955, 1. Another scholar to deal with the Comintern-espionage links is Nollau, but he largely follows Dallin.
33. This literature is vast. Two accounts of women who served as Comintern couriers are: Peggy Dennis, *The Autobiography of an American Communist: a Personal View of a Political Life 1925–1975*, Lawrence Hill & Co., Westport, 1977, 74–87; Betty Roland, *Caviar for Breakfast*, Collins Publishers, Sydney, 1989, 115, 126–30.
34. See Trepper, Perrault and Foote.
35. Whittaker Chambers, *Witness*, Andre Deutsch, London, 1953; Jan Valtin (pseudonym for Richard Krebs), *Out of the Night*, William Heinemann, London, 1941.
36. For example the Petrovs' book was ghost written by senior ASIO officer Michael Thwaites. Vladimir and Evdokia Petrov, *Empire of Fear*, Andre Deutsch, London, 1956.
37. Alexander Orlov, *Handbook of Intelligence and Guerrilla Warfare*, University of Michigan Press, Ann Arbor, 1972.
38. See also now Harvey Klehr, John Earl Haynes and Kyrill M. Anderson, *The Soviet World of American Communism*, Yale University Press, New Haven, 1998.
39. Stuart Macintyre, *The Reds: the Communist Party of Australia from Origins to Illegality*, Allen & Unwin, St Leonards, NSW, 1998, 274–6, 394–5, 400–1.
40. Norman MacKenzie (ed.), *Secret Societies*, Aldus Books, London, 1967, 16–17.
41. Dian H. Murray with Qin Baoqi, *The Origins of the Tiandihui: the Chinese Triads in Legend and History*, Stanford University Press, Stanford, 1994, ch. 3.
42. These are available at the website of the National Security Agency: www.nsa.gov. A discussion of the relevance of these records to Australia is: David McKnight, 'The Moscow–Canberra Cables: how Soviet Intelligence Obtained British Secrets Through the Back Door', *Intelligence and National Security*, vol. 13, no. 2 (summer 1998).
43. All references to cables derived from Venona are indicated by date. This corresponds to the chronological organisation of the cables on the homepage of the NSA. Canberra to Moscow, 5 July 1945.
44. Moscow to Canberra, 30 May 1946.
45. Moscow to Canberra, 8 August 1944.
46. Ronald Radosh does this in detail in 'The Venona Files', *New Republic*, 7 August 1995.
47. David McKnight, *Australia's Spies and their Secrets*, Allen & Unwin, St Leonards, NSW, 1994, 30, 99–100; Clayton interview, 26 March 1995.
48. Gabriel Garcia Marquez, *Clandestine in Chile: the Adventures of Miguel Littin* (trans. Asa Zatz), Grantra Books, London, 1989, Introduction.

CHAPTER ONE

The Roots of Conspiracy

Rereading today the correspondence that we carried on with Russia makes one marvel at the naïveté of our secrecy methods. All those letters about handkerchiefs (meaning passports), brewing beer and warm fur (illegal literature).

N. K. Krupskaya

From its pre-history in the first part of the nineteenth century, communism emerged as a philosophical and political force employing the methods of conspiracy. Secret meetings, the use of front organisations, the smuggling of pamphlets, exile and police repression were all part of the formative experience of the founders of communism, Karl Marx and Frederick Engels. Of the Communist League which commissioned Marx and Engels to write what became *The Communist Manifesto*, Engels said '[it was] a working-men's association, first exclusively German, later on international, and, under the political conditions of the Continent before 1848, unavoidably a secret society'.[1] A secret society has enormous difficulties if it wishes to win mass support. It hardly needs saying that the very purpose of the repression directed against it is to prevent the achievement of this goal. When the repression began to lift in Germany in the last years of the nineteenth century, new legal means of rallying support emerged and one of the strongest working-class movements evolved. The dynamic between repression and conspiracy is one we can trace from the earliest days of the Communist League and the 1848 revolutions to the seizure of power in Russia in 1917 and beyond, to the instigation of revolution by the Communist International from 1919 to its dissolution during the Second World War.

Communism emerged in the 1840s from Germans who had gone into self-imposed exile. In Paris in 1834 one group of German refugees founded the 'secret democratic-republican Outlaws League', according to Engels.[2] A split by the most radical and working-class elements resulted in another organisation, the League of the Just, whose aims 'were those of the Parisian secret societies of the time: half propaganda association, half conspiracy'.[3] For reasons of security the core of the League of the Just was based in London, and formed by Germans, many of whom had been subject to censorship and imprisonment in the fortresses of Prussia. One organisational method of the League of the Just was to form what would later be called front organisations and in some European countries the League formed choral societies, athletics clubs and the like. The conspiratorial methods of the Communist League actually distinguished communism very little from trade unionism and other democratic currents which fought feudalism and monarchism. At this time they were part of a broader democratic and republican movement of which one expression was an organisation called the London-based Fraternal Democrats whose motto was 'all men are brothers'. At one meeting which Marx attended, the Fraternal Democrats noted that

> At our last anniversary commemoration we recommended the formation of a democratic congress of all nations, and we are happy to hear that you [Marx] have publicly made the same proposal. *The conspiracy of kings must be answered with a conspiracy of the peoples.* (emphasis added)[4]

In January 1847 the League of the Just invited Marx and Engels to join them, having been convinced of Marx's views as expressed in a series of pamphlets. The two men agreed and during the year the League undertook a 'democratic reorganisation to suit the needs of a propagandist body compelled to work in secret, but eschewing all conspiratorial airs'.[5] According to Engels, this democratisation of the League 'with elective and always removable boards ... barred all hankering after conspiracy, which requires dictatorship, and the League was converted – for ordinary peace times at least – into a pure propaganda society'.[6] As a mark of this, the new statutes were circulated to League committees in Europe for approval at a second congress at the end of 1847. At this congress the League invited Marx and Engels to draw up a statement of principles which became the famous *Communist Manifesto*.

Members of the newly named Communist League took part in the 1848 revolutions across Europe and for a brief time a democratic space opened and conspiratorial methods were dropped. Refugee members of the League returned to Germany and there they participated and led the ferment. Engels said 'the League had been an excellent school for revolutionary activity' and 'everywhere members of the League stood at the head of the extreme democratic movement'.[7]

One consequence of the counter-revolution of 1848 was the arrest and trial of a group of communists in Cologne in October–November 1852 for high treason.[8] The trial was marked by evidence concocted by the police and was largely aimed at intimidating the liberal and workers movement. Savage sentences resulted and the Communist League was dissolved.

Marx never again associated with secret societies which he disliked because they 'attracted people who enjoyed the romantic attitudes of conspiracy'.[9] According to Engels, conspiratorial methods depended on a rigidly centralised internal 'dictatorship' and this militated against open discussion and public advocacy of radical ideas. When Engels later wrote the history of the Communist League the narrative thread he followed was the transformation of a conspiratorial organisation to a democratic, publicly proselytising movement.

This disinclination to conspiracy did not prevent the opponents of the First International from branding it as such. Speaking of the First International, one early writer on secret societies, Charles Heckethorn, saw the roots of the First International lying with 'the Chartists and the French Democratic Society. Out of that friendship sprang the Society of the Fraternal Democrats'.[10] The 'fanatics of the Unions ... are formed, not by the elite, but by the scum of the working classes'. He argued that '[t]hough it protests against being a secret society, it yet indulges in such underhand dealings, insidiously endeavouring to work mischief between employers and employed and aiming at the subversion of the existing order of things that it deserves to be denounced with all the societies professedly secret.'[11]

LENIN AND THE REINVENTION OF THE RUSSIAN CONSPIRATORIAL TRADITION

A similar dynamic between repression and conspiracy had evolved in Russia in the nineteenth century, where conditions were even harsher than Germany and where a revolutionary movement had existed for many years before Marxism took root. Many of the elements of Soviet intelligence practice were grounded in both these revolutionary movements and the underground party which Lenin fashioned. As we trace the ebb and flow of the Bolsheviks' development over time, we see the gradual emergence of a fully fledged tradecraft.

After the assassination of Tsar Alexander II in 1881 by members of this movement, the authorities 'codified and systematised' pre-existing repressive legislation which put at their disposal two legal forms for dealing with subversion.[12] The milder of the two allowed governors of provinces and cities to imprison a resident for up to three months, to forbid all public or private gatherings, to close down temporarily commercial enterprises, to expel individuals from localities and to hand over 'troublemakers' to military justice. Police powers were increased and local police could detain suspicious people for up to two weeks.[13] Under a harsher 'state of siege', a specially appointed official had all of the above powers but in addition could sack elected *zemstvo* (provincial and local government bodies) officials, sack lower ranking public servants, suspend a publication and close institutions of higher learning. Suspects could be jailed for up to three months and police powers were further increased. After the assassination, ten provinces, including the cities of Moscow and St Petersburg, were placed under the milder state of siege. During the 1905 revolution a number of localities were placed under the harsher decree. In 'normal' everyday life a vast number of activities had to be authorised by the police or government, from opening a Sunday school or medical practice, selling newspapers or books, even living more than 15 miles from your home. In addition, oppositional movements had to deal with a police apparatus which made liberal use of agents. While police agents were used in a limited and temporary way in the Austro-Hungarian empire and in France and Prussia, in Russia such a system was 'the cornerstone of political police work'.[14]

In such conditions all parties and movements comprising the Russian anti-Tsarist forces were heavily reliant on conspiratorial methods. Ulam sees a continuity in the use of these methods, which began with the group generally acknowledged as the precursors of this revolutionary tradition in Russia. These were the 'Decembrists', a group of officers who led a mutiny against Tsar Nicholas I in December 1825.[15] The Decembrists 'came without exception from secret officers' societies' which formed an organisational pattern for critics of Tsardom.

The peculiar conditions of Russia in the 1820s, which remained true until 1905, almost inevitably pushed any organisation devoted to the discussion of social and political purposes into the path of illegality and eventually of revolution. The regime did not allow any forum for the discussion of even the mildest reform of the status quo. It viewed with increasing suspicion purely social clubs and organisations. This in turn had the natural result of turning a chess club or a literary discussion circle into a potential source of subversion.[16]

The repression which followed the Decembrist outbreak meant that almost 40 years passed before the opponents of Tsarism began another significant and organised challenge. One of the first indicators of the revival of the movement was the 'Kazan conspiracy', an ill-fated attempt to rouse peasants by a combination of Polish nationalists and university students. Infiltrated by a police agent, its leaders were shot and jailed in 1863.[17] This preceded a broader strand of opposition to autocracy from the groups known as Populists. An expression of this was the Zemlya i Volya (Land and Freedom) group which, in its second incarnation from 1876, also tried to stimulate the peasantry to revolution. The Populist form of organisation was, of necessity, conspiratorial and continued the tradition of 'professional conspirators with no private lives, obeying total discipline'.[18] Frustrated with the passivity of the peasantry, supporters of terrorism split in 1879, forming the Narodnaya Volya (People's Will) which staged the assassination of Tsar Alexander II in 1881. Six years later, the older brother of the future leader of the Russian revolution, Vladimir Illich Ulyanov (Lenin), was executed for plotting a terrorist attack.

The supporters of Narodnaya Volya were influenced by socialism and after being broken up by the police a number drifted towards the Marxist movement. A key figure in both the Zemlya i Volya and Narodnaya Volya was A. D. Mikhailov, who successfully promoted the use of conspiratorial methods, 'safe houses', coded signals and counter-surveillance of police.[19] The methods reflected their populist goal of an elite takeover and the small degree of mass support they needed to carry this out.

After a period of enforced social calm induced by the repression which followed the Tsar's assassination, Marxist socialism began to strike deep roots from the 1890s. The Marxist Social Democrats were distinguished from Narodnaya Volya by their disavowal of terrorism, their propagandist approach and their orientation to organising groups of workers.[20]

When social democracy developed in the 1890s its basic form was that of workers' circles, often led by intellectuals but not yet organised into a conspiratorial party. These were small, localised groups which initially concentrated on reading and discussion. Both the theory discussed by these workers' circles as well as their own conditions in the burgeoning Russian industry impelled them to begin small-scale agitation. Trotsky's account of his first experience at the age of 18 in 1897 of a workers' circle in Nikolayev was typical of young inexperienced groups: 'We knew that any contacts with workers demanded secret, highly "conspiratory" methods. And we pronounced the word solemnly, with a reverence that was almost mystic.'[21] One basic method was to use a false name, even within the circle: 'I called myself by the name Lvov. It was not easy for me to tell this first "conspiratory" lie; in fact it was really painful to "deceive" people with whom I intended to be associated for such a great and noble cause.' Trotsky's group began, like most groups, in distributing leaflets which they printed at night in their own rooms on a hectograph using primitive handwritten stencils. 'One of us would stand guard in the courtyard. In the open stove we had kerosene and matches ready to burn the tell tale things in case of danger. Everything was crude, but the police of Nikolayev were no more experienced than we were.' The group, known as the South Russia Workers Union, was highly successful in distributing illegal literature. But in January 1898, 200 people were arrested and under police beatings at least one broke revealing details of the organisation while others committed suicide or went insane. Trotsky was imprisoned in Odessa, then exiled to Siberia.

Another such circle and its context was described by Cecilia Bobrovskaya who recalled that in 1894 her workers circle was autonomous, self-acting and amateurish.

> I cannot recall that we were united in any kind of centralised group which took definite measures or passed definite decisions. Perhaps such a group did exist … but I, as a rank and file worker, knew nothing of it. I can only recollect that we lived as a commune, discussed all kinds of questions, studied in circles, consistently consulted with one another. Someone would write a manifesto and

the comrades who happened to be near at hand would read and discuss it. Anyone who had some technical skill would undertake to print and distribute it. There was no proper distribution of functions among us.[22]

Above the circle, the next level of revolutionary organisation was the party committee in a city. Bobrovskaya's assessment of the Kharkov committee in 1899 was of a 'well knit nucleus of revolutionary workers, although it had not yet assumed definite organisational shape and did not even have a definite name'.[23] The Kharkov committee was organised, like many other committees, by a small group of active revolutionaries who selected a few capable comrades, who together declared themselves a committee who carried out tasks at its direction. The 'ultra-conspiratorial' methods of the committee were resented by the next concentric circle outside the committee, which consisted of several score of comrades. 'We were obliged to carry out the decisions of the committee blindly, since we had not the slightest share in their making.' A similar account of a conspiratorial workers circle in St Petersburg is given by Leonid Krasin.[24]

A key organisational failing, which affected Bobrovskaya personally, was that the committee, while supporting those in exile, did not financially support its full-time members, resulting in her suffering from malnutrition at one stage. A highly successful strike and demonstration on May Day 1900 was the undoing of the Kharkov committee and 'led to the arrest of the entire organisation and most of the circles'.[25]

A similar fate befell many other Social Democratic committees. After the 1898 founding congress of the new Social Democratic Party in Minsk, which aimed to weld existing circles into a stronger organisation, most participants were arrested and the movement beheaded. In the period 1895 to 1902, one Moscow Social Democrat estimated that the average life of Social Democratic groups was three months.[26] When Bobrovskaya arrived back in Russia from abroad in 1902 she noted that 'The state of affairs in St Petersburg was quite alarming. Arrests were constant in our organisation ... Every night I slept in a different place.' At the same time the Moscow committee was 'non-existent'.[27]

The world of disorganised circles, subject to periodic arrests and police penetration, were the context in which Lenin's ideas on organisation emerged as a significant force in the Russian Social Democratic movement. In 1895 Lenin had been active in a workers' circle in St Petersburg and been arrested for agitating in support of textile workers whose wages had been cut. The police had learned the year before of Lenin's activities in supporting workers, smuggling literature and planning an underground newspaper and had planted an agent in the St Petersburg Union of Struggle for the Liberation of the Working Class.[28] The December 1895 arrests of over 50 people almost completely destroyed this organisation. Eighteen months later Lenin was sentenced to exile in Siberia from which he emerged in 1900.

In this period Lenin began to develop his ideas on organisation. These centred on the interrelated questions of unifying, professionalising and tightening the organisation of the scattered Social Democratic circles into a party and creating a regular all-Russian newspaper which would develop Marxist ideas and be a practical organiser.[29] Both involved the concrete development of an elaborate conspiratorial organisation, something which Lenin along with Martov (Iulii Osipovich Tsederbaum) and others later undertook immediately they were released from exile in 1900.

While still in exile Lenin had written 'The Tasks of the Russian Social Democrats' in which he argued that the 'most urgent question ... is that of the practical activities of the Social Democrats' since the 'theoretical side' of the struggle (largely against the indigenous Russian Populists) was 'now apparently behind us'.[30] He makes clear his respect for the Russian tradition of conspiratorial methods when he concludes by emphasising the 'grim and rigid routine' of underground work and arguing that 'it was only in conditions such as these that the greatest men of revolutionary practice in Russia succeeded in carrying out the boldest undertakings ... and we are profoundly convinced that the Social Democrats will prove no less self-sacrificing than the revolutionaries of previous generations.'[31]

But the key passage in this text occurs when Lenin debates populist theorist P. L. Lavrov and points out a 'fundamental difference' in tactics between the Populists and the Social Democrats.[32] The former 'cannot conceive of political struggle except in the form of political conspiracy'. The Social Democrats, Lenin says, 'are not guilty of such a narrow outlook; they do not believe in conspiracies; they think that the period of conspiracies has long passed away, that to reduce political struggle to conspiracy means, on the one hand, immensely restricting its scope and on the other hand, choosing the most unsuitable methods of struggle.' In place of the tiny elite which organise its terrorist activities remote from the population, Lenin argues that the fight against the autocracy 'must consist not in organising conspiracies but in educating, disciplining and organising the proletariat, in political agitation among the workers which denounces every manifestation of absolutism'.

Lenin had not simply discarded the elite notion of the conspiracy which had grown up in Russia, but had reinvented it by allying it with the needs of mass agitation. This theme, at first glance quite paradoxical, of combining underground work with mass political work, was the key to Lenin's particular contribution to the theory of organisation and it re-emerged in the Comintern's prescriptions on underground political work by communist parties in the 1930s. Thus the Comintern's guidelines, whether applied in Spain or India or the United States or Australia, contained many echoes of Russian conspiratorial techniques from the late nineteenth century.

In spite of Lenin's polemical writings against Populism, many Social Democrats clearly located themselves as part-inheritors of the populist tradition of underground work. The Manifesto which emerged after the abortive first congress of the RSDLP noted that 'considering the winning of political liberty to be the most important of the immediate tasks of the Party as a whole, Social Democracy marches toward the goal that was already clearly indicated by the glorious representatives of the old Narodnaya Volya'. About which Lenin commented:

> The traditions of the whole preceding revolutionary movement demand that the Social Democrats shall at the present time con-centrate all their efforts on organising the party, on strengthening its internal discipline, and on developing the technique for illegal work. If the members of the old Narodnya Volya managed to play an enormous role in the history of Russia, despite the fact that only narrow social strata supported the few heroes, and despite the fact that it was by no means a revolutionary theory which served as the banner of the movement, then Social Democracy, relying on the class struggle of the proletariat, will be able to render itself invincible.[33]

The inheritance was also a directly practical one. Lenin's wife Nadezhda Krupskaya attributed the young Lenin's conspiratorial technique directly to Narodnaya Volya. '[Lenin] taught us how to use invisible ink and to write messages in books by a dotted code and secret ciphers, and invented all kinds of aliases. One felt that he had been well-schooled in Narodnya Volya methods.'[34] She also records that the first person to initiate her into 'illegal work' was a former Narodovoltsi, Nikolai Meshcheryakov, an old friend who eventually became a Social Democrat. Krupskaya herself played a crucial role in developing conspiratorial methods since she was the key figure in the illegal apparatus set up in 1900 to distribute the Social Democrats' newspaper *Iskra* and keep in contact with its Russian supporters.[35] She later recalled this work as 'extremely primitive'.

> Re-reading today the correspondence that we carried on with Russia makes one marvel at the naïveté of our secrecy methods. All those letters about handkerchiefs (meaning passports), brewing beer and warm fur (illegal literature), all those code names for towns beginning with the same letter as the town itself (Osip for Odessa, Terenty for Tver, Peter for Poltava, Pasha for Pskov and so on), all that substituting of women's names for men's and vice versa – the whole thing was so thin, so transparent.[36]

However, having examined the files of the Okhrana, her biographer, Robert McNeal concludes that in spite of her protestations of amateurism 'she succeeded in imparting to the *Iskra* underground organisation a degree of co-ordination that no previous Russian revolutionary organisation had known'.[37]

While exile taught Lenin a lesson in the methods of the autocratic state, his next task as an editor of *Iskra*, taught him and Krupskaya more systematic lessons in the detailed methods of organising illegally as an *émigré*. Based initially in Munich, the circulation of the illegal newspaper was erratic.

> Trusted persons returning legally were provided with double bottomed trunks like those in which Lenin himself had carried forbidden literature on his return from the West in 1895. Or there was an outright smuggling through frontier posts in Austrian Galicia or Prussia. At times, through connections in the international labor movement, a ship docking in Odessa or other Black Sea ports would also carry a consignment of the revolutionary journal.[38]

Between 1900 and 1903 *Iskra* published 51 editions of around 8,000 copies each much of which was smuggled into Russia. In addition the Social Democratic Party also published Plekhanov's *Zarya* (*Dawn*) along with a number of individual pamphlets such as Lenin's *What is to be Done?* In all, it was a substantial operation, illustrating Lenin's reinvention of conspiratorial methods combined with mass agitation.[39]

CENTRALISM AND CONSPIRACY

It was in this context that Lenin worked on one of his most influential works and certainly the most influential from the point of view of this study. The work was a pamphlet called *What is to be Done?*, which was published in Geneva in 1902.[40] Its title was a reference to a famous novel by radical intellectual and writer N. Chernyshevsky (1828–89) and its purpose was to polemicise against the 'economist' trend in social democracy and to advocate an organisational reconstruction of the Social Democratic Party along more centralised and 'professional' lines. Economism was the name given to a trend in social democracy which emphasised the struggle for the immediate, economic goals of the working class, rather than the struggle for political liberty for all classes in Tsarist society. The other main target was spontaneity, a belief that a revolution would emerge spontaneously, that is, as a result of objective conditions. Lenin strongly argued that it would require a subjective, voluntarist element, that is a strong party, to precipitate it.

The usual question debated in the literature is whether Lenin's prescriptions in *What is to be Done?* foreshadow the creation of the one-party state and of Soviet-style communism. The question which concerns this study is related but different. It is rather to examine the influence of this key text (as well as other writings) on the development of the Bolsheviks' conspiratorial methods which later found their way to the West through the Comintern.

The organisational ideas contained in parts IV and V of *What is to be Done?* ('The rustic craftsmanship of the Economists and the organisation of revolutionaries' and 'The "Plan" for an All-Russian Political Newspaper') show that *What is to be Done?* was an immensely practical pamphlet which responded to a loosely organised movement with a ruthless logic that argued that secrecy and centralisation must take precedence over democracy and other considerations. *What is to be Done?* can very easily be read as an exposition of the first main theme of our study: that Lenin reinvented traditional populist conspiratorial methods and combined them with a mass orientation. Instead of conspiring to assassinate officials, the movement would conspire to distribute ideological bombs through a network of party members and supporters across Russia.

Lenin wrote the latter sections of *What is to be Done?* out of a sense of frustration with the amateurism of traditional Social Democratic circle work. Typically, the activism of a circle would go in cycles, sometimes set by police repression, sometimes by something as mundane as university holidays.[41] At one point Lenin states it was his own 'burning sense of shame' that lay behind his polemical attacks on the 'rustic craftsmanship' of social democracy, that is its organisational amateurism. The main problem was a practical one of ensuring the survival and strengthening of the Russian Social Democrats under Tsarism. His principal target, organisational 'rustic craftsmanship', he defined as:

> simply the result of the spontaneous growth of traditional study circle work; because, naturally, the police, in almost every case, knew the principal leaders of the local movement ... and the police waited only for the right moment to make their raid ... and they always permitted several of the persons known to them at liberty 'for breeding'.[42]

This pattern led to 'amazing fragmentation' and the beheading of the working-class movement. Accounts of police repression directed against the Social Democrats show that it was continuous and enormously disruptive of that party. Historian David Lane records that in 1899 the police arrested members of the Moscow Committee in February, April, May, June, October and December.[43] In 1903, the year after *What is to be Done?* appeared, the St Petersburg committee tried to set up subgroups in the Neva, Town and Vyborg districts, according to Lane. All the agitators were arrested in October and November 1903 and those in Vyborg and Town in December and January 1904.[44] All accounts admit that police activity intensified after the 1905–6 uprising.

The core of Lenin's proposition in *What is to be Done?* was twofold. First, that a cadre of full-time revolutionaries should be constructed which would operate all the secret functions of the party, and second, that this should be done concretely around an *émigré* newspaper which would replace the scattered local publications then existing. The 'first and most urgent task' was to build 'an organisation of revolutionaries able to guarantee the energy, stability and continuity of the political struggle'.[45] The need for secrecy had earlier been attacked from several quarters. A Social Democrat, Prokopovich, argued that their programme spoke of a mass movement rather than 'a plot' as the means of struggle. Prokopovich downplayed the need for a secret tightly organised party by rhetorically asking whether the masses could use secrecy. 'Is a secret strike possible?' he asked. In *What is to be Done?* Lenin replied that a strike could well remain a secret from those not directly involved. Spreading the news of the strike and preparing strikes,

> must be organised according to 'all the rules of the art', by people who are professionally engaged in revolutionary activity. The fact that the masses are spontaneously being drawn into the movement does not make the organisation of this struggle *less necessary*. On the contrary, it makes it *more necessary*; for we socialists would be failing in our direct duty to the masses if we did not prevent the police from making a secret of every strike and every demonstration.[46]

The chief argument against Lenin's plan was that it was undemocratic and a throwback to the conspiratorial methods of Narodnaya Volya. In his defence Lenin argued, as he had five years earlier, that while traditional notions of conspiracy meant restricting the political struggle to a tiny secretive elite, this is not what he meant. Conspiratorial methods were necessary because of absolutism. 'Secrecy is such a necessary condition for this kind of organisation that all the other conditions (number and selection of members, functions, etc.) must be made to conform to it.'[47] Democracy entailed at a minimum publicity and elections for office, but these two things were quite impossible in an autocracy, he claimed. It was simply inconceivable that the rank and file of the party 'should control every step of a secret revolutionary' and should elect 'this or that person when a revolutionary is obliged, in the interests of the work, to hide his identity from nine tenths of these "all"'. On this basis such democracy was 'nothing more than a useless and harmful toy' which facilitated widespread police arrests.[48] In place of democracy, Lenin supported a highly centralised party in which the core would direct and appoint local committees.

The other great organisational barrier that Lenin identified was a kind of localism which resisted the creation of an *émigré*-produced centralised newspaper. The emphasis on localism meant irregular, amateurish, costly and parochial Social Democratic newspapers. Lenin argued that the creation of an all-Russian newspaper was the decisive link in a chain which, if grasped, gave the possession of the chain. The newspaper would be written by professional writers and supported by a network of professional revolutionaries ('agents') who would be paid and could be moved around Russia at will.

The degree to which the prescriptions of *What is to be Done?* spring from the exigencies of absolutism or from Lenin's personal desire for control is one which has been widely debated. John Keep considers that while there is 'a certain element of truth in the argument that Lenin's emphasis on strict discipline was necessitated by the practical problems that faced any clandestine revolutionary party in Russia', this was also 'something of a red herring'.[49] Keep's curious reasoning is that Lenin, a man of principle in matters of organisation, could not possibly allow 'so important a question to be determined by considerations of expediency'. Instead of seeing Lenin as a practical revolutionary facing practical problems, Keep attributes his views in *What is to be Done?* to his 'concept of a revolutionary elite' and to his debt to the conspiratorial methods of populism. While the second reason has much truth, the first is ultimately circular and reflects the influence of hindsight coloured by Cold War scholarship. His 'concept of a revolutionary elite' was itself a response to the conditions of struggle against autocracy.

The most telling criticism of Lenin's organisational plans comes from fellow Social Democrats who, after all, had a contemporary knowledge of the difficulties of organisation under Tsarism. One perceptive critic, Vladimir Akimov, argued that Lenin's tactics were unnecessarily close to the old conspiratorial methods of the Narodnaya Volya, referring to Lenin's discussion with Lavrov quoted above.[50] The key word here is 'unnecessarily', because he maintained that in spite of police repression Social Democratic work 'had both continuity and connectivity'.[51] Akimov's main concern was that a contradiction existed between the mass character of political agitation and the conspiratorial methods of the party conducting the agitation. (A central issue as we have noted.) Akimov argued that Lenin's attempt to yoke these elements showed that he was 'midway between the party of socialist conspiracy Narodnaya Volya and the party of proletarian socialism, the Social Democratic party'. A better model, said Akimov, was the Bund. This was a very large, ethnically based union of Jewish workers which combined both mass work with centralism and secrecy.[52]

Another contemporary critic was the Polish Social Democrat, Rosa Luxemburg. Her 1904 article in *Iskra* (by then under Menshevik

28

control) under the original title of 'Organisational Questions of the Russian Social Democracy' acknowledges much of the basis for Lenin's argument. Russian absolutism, she agreed, was quite unlike that recently experienced in Europe or Germany, under Bismarck in 1878–90. Social democracy, she agreed, was a centralist movement and the path of 'a federative conglomerate' was the wrong one for the Russian party. The question really was the degree of centralisation which was required. Her critique was based on the belief that even under Russian absolutism, the spontaneous creativity and consciousness achieved by the working class could go significantly beyond 'trade union consciousness'. In terms of this study her critique was most pointed. Lenin had indeed tried to ally conspiratorial tradition ('Blanquism') with a mass orientation to the working class – but he had failed because he had corrected the weaknesses of social democracy with a larger than necessary dose of conspiratorial technique.

As an aside, it is worth noting that another critic of Lenin, at least in this period, was Feliks Dzierzynski, a leader of the Polish Social Democratic Party and later head of the Cheka, the precursor to modern Soviet intelligence organisations. Dzierzynski helped systematise conspiratorial organisation quite independently of Lenin, whom he accused of 'autocratic centralisation'.[53] One of his biographers, Robert Blobaum, notes that the independent working out of conspiratorial practices arose from 'pragmatic necessity ... to ensure the party's survival'.[54] Dzierzynski's career, from underground organiser to intelligence chief, shows how naturally the heritage of conspiracy flowed into the tradecraft of espionage.

Both Luxemburg and Akimov counted on a certain historical determinism that a revolution would break out spontaneously in Russia and that the working class's creativity would take care of organisational questions. In the event this is just what occurred when workers' councils or soviets were created in the 1905 revolution.

After the failed 1905 revolution Lenin's views on organisation evolved and he declined to endorse as universal all the views he had expounded in *What is to be Done?*, warning those who read it not to do so out of context. In 1907 he said that '[t]he basic mistake made by those who now criticise *What is to be Done?* is to treat the pamphlet apart from its connection with the concrete historical situation of a definite, and now long past period in the development of our Party'.[55] He described the controversy around *What is to be Done?* as 'bitter and destructive' and attributed it to the 'young and immature workers movement'.

In spite of this, the impact of *What is to be Done?* in countries with very different political conditions was great, certainly much greater than Lenin could ever have intended. The Soviet-sponsored cult of Lenin and the awe in which the October revolution was held ensured that the precepts of *What is to be Done?* became a rigid model which governed the political practice of all communist parties formed after 1917. The key Soviet text studied by Comintern-affiliated parties, the *History of the Communist Party of the Soviet Union (Bolshevik): Short Course*, stated that 'the theoretical theses expounded in *What is to be Done?* later became the foundation of the ideology of the Bolshevik Party'.[56] After the founding of the Communist International in 1919 this ideology of the Bolshevik Party based on *What is to be Done?* became the model for all 'sections' of the Comintern, as national communist parties were known.[57] Because of its influence, Keep rightly believes that *What is to be Done?* 'undoubtedly deserves to rank as a major document of twentieth century political thought'.[58]

The significance of this, for our purposes is that the ideas on organisation in *What is to be Done?* clearly bear the imprint of their circumstances, autocratic Russia, where Social Democrats carried out underground political activity. Lenin and the Bolshevik Party in fact later modified their organisational model to the scheme of democratic centralism but even so the ultra-centralised, consciously undemocratic and conspiratorial methods outlined in *What is to be Done?* gave a certain cast to communist parties in advanced capitalist countries like the United States, Britain and Australia where conditions, in spite of varying degrees of repression, were fundamentally different to Tsarist Russia.

The authority which *What is to be Done?* assumed with Soviet sponsorship partly obviates one problem which many have tried to untangle: the degree to which Lenin intended *What is to be Done?* as largely a local prescription versus the degree to which he saw it embodying universal principles. Whatever his intentions, the successful seizure of power in 1917 and the later cult of Lenin ensured that its prescriptions were universally applied in the communist movement for decades.

Akimov's and Luxemburg's critiques were written after one of the most decisive events in the RSDLP, the split between Bolsheviks and Mensheviks at the July–August 1903 Congress. The split revealed the third critic of the implications of conspiracy-mindedness, Julius Martov, who was one of Lenin's closest comrades and someone who agreed with his ideas on strengthening Social Democratic organisation.

For Martov the issue was not whether conspiratorial methods were needed to operate under and ultimately overthrow Tsarism. Nor was it, initially, over the degree of centralisation and top-down methods of the Social Democrats. Both Martov and Lenin broadly agreed on these issues. In 1900 after his four years of prison and exile and in spite of his comrades' warnings, Martov spent almost a year in Russia building a conspiratorial network which was to distribute the planned newspaper, *Iskra*, and be the embryonic party.[59] A centralist, he attacked the Jewish Bund and demanded they join the Social Democratic Party as ordinary members and not as part of a federation. And like most of his contemporaries in social democracy, he believed in the principle of top-down co-option, that is where a local committee had to be reconstituted, it would be done by a higher committee, not by election from the rank-and-file party members.

But in 1903 during the lead up to the Second Congress, Martov began to modify his views. In a different way to Lenin, he wanted to reconcile the urgent need for conspiracy with the long-term aim of producing a mass party. In an article for Rosa Luxemburg's *Social Democratic Review* he argued that the party's ideological strength would allow for a combination of 'centralisation indispensable to a secret, conspiratorial organisation ... with the necessary autonomy, within defined limits, of the integral parts of the party, an autonomy which should secure for them revolutionary self-reliance'.[60] At the well-attended Congress of the RSDLP, Martov began as Lenin's 'junior partner' and ended as an opponent whose differences, above all on organisational matters, had clearly begun to crystalise. For our purposes, the most significant thing at the Congress was a dispute over the constitutional definition of who could be a party member, not because of its definition of a party member but because of its *de facto* definition of *non-members* – the supportive periphery on whom the conspiratorial apparatus heavily depended.

Both Martov and Lenin agreed that the party was composed of, on the one hand, the small conspiratorial core organisation which ran the underground activities and, on the other, a wider group of party members and supporters. Their disagreement was over how many of the latter group were legitimately members of the party. Martov at one point

31

argued somewhat rhetorically that it would be good if 'every striker or demonstrator' could call himself a party member, a point Lenin seized on.[61] More coolly, Martov wanted this second category to consist of 'the sum total of the active advanced elements of the proletariat',[62] which he defined as 'everyone who accepts the party programme, supports the party by material means and affords it regular personal assistance under the guidance of one of its organisations'.[63] Lenin however wanted to confine this group to those who supported the party by 'personal participation in one of its organisations'.

In the end Lenin lost and Martov's wider definition of membership was carried by 28 votes to 22. Again, most commentators on this debate discuss it in terms of Lenin's ruthlessness and elitism, but for our study its significance lies in the fact that the periphery is the crucial link between the professional revolutionaries and the masses.[64] When a party operates under illegal conditions its mass work (e.g. distributing a newspaper) must be conducted in and through this periphery. An overly tight relationship between the periphery and the core risks a loss of contact with the masses, rendering the struggle pointless. An overly loose relationship between them and the periphery risks opening the core of the party to police.

In this period the most specific and practical guide which Lenin wrote about the actual details of conspiratorial work occurs in his *Letter to a Comrade on our Organisational Tasks*.[65] The highest bodies of the party (other than the Congress) were the Central Organ and the Central Committee, the former being the ideological leader and the latter the practical leader. Both were abroad and hence the 'real' organisation was based around major cities where the head of the Social Democratic organisation was the committee.[66] In its region the committee had supreme power. It allocated work and appointed bodies below it. It monitored the work of the party and added to its own membership by co-option. Party members reported in detail to it, even to the extent of providing lists of contacts' names and addresses.

Below the committee were two groups, the first of which was the 'network of executive agents' who would be organised in district and factory subcommittees. These were all party members, primarily concerned with the distribution of *Iskra* and leaflets and, in times of 'war', the organisers of demonstrations, strikes, etc. Just beyond this core were what Lenin referred to as 'circles and groups of all kinds serving the movement (propaganda, transport, all kinds of underground activities, etc.)'. These groups may or may not be members of the party. They formed a kind of reserve for the party and undertook conspiratorial activity. Beyond this again were looser study circles and trade union circles whose members may not even know that among their number were one or two party members.

This assemblage of groups was governed by several conspiratorial practices, Lenin said. First, each group was absolutely separate from the bodies above it through the appointment of a single link person appointed from the committee. This link person had no special privileges and his/her existence was 'a necessary concession to the absolute demands of secrecy'. Second, the whole party was highly centralised. All party members provided detailed reports to the committee This reporting system gave the committee, the Central Organ and the Central Committee the ability to piece together the whole picture of political activity in the compartmentalised units and beyond them in the city at large. It also allowed the Central Committee to rapidly appoint adequate substitutes for local committees when the inevitable police arrests took place. Third, an additional element was needed alongside centralisation and compartmentalisation. This was decentralisation of party activity. Lenin argued that '[w]e must centralise the leadership of the movement. We must also ... as far as possible decentralise responsibility to the Party ... This decentralisation is an essential prerequisite of revolutionary centralisation and an essential corrective to it.'[67]

THE 1905 REVOLUTION

Many of Lenin's assumptions and his conspiratorial practices were turned upside down when the revolution finally occurred. The revolution was largely spontaneous, beginning with a strike over economic demands followed by a demonstration in January 1905 which was fired on by soldiers. A strike wave then broke out which culminated in October when the Tsar relented and a shaky period of legality began, lasting until the crushing of the revolution in December. In this period of freedom many of Lenin's predictions proved false. The working class went far beyond 'trade union consciousness'. Spontaneously it created the 'soviets', councils of workers organised on a city-wide basis which could be seen as an alternative government.[68]

This rapid development of partial political liberty in 1905 showed the inadequacy of the Social Democratic Party built on a conspiratorial basis. After quickly taking stock of events, Lenin's response was surprisingly flexible. The doors of the party had to be thrown open, new members admitted, a Congress called, based on the 'elective principle' and on democracy which had not been possible in the underground.[69] The party had 'stagnated while working underground ... it has been suffocating underground during the last few years. The "underground" is breaking up'.

Before it was bloodily suppressed in December 1905, the revolution created an unstable but quite different situation to Tsarist absolutism. Newspapers and parties became legal and operated openly. The police apparatus continued to function but monitored, rather than arrested, revolutionaries.[70] Krupskaya records that Lenin's strategic view was that '[t]he secret machinery of the party was to be preserved. At the same time it was absolutely essential to set up more and more legal and semi-legal Party and affiliated organs'.[71]

Marcel Liebman argues convincingly that Lenin's ideas of organisation and the actual character of the party changed sharply during the experience of the 1905 revolution. 'The Leninist Party, a tightly knit group of professional revolutionaries, was, in its way, a reflection of the autocratic regime against which it fought. When that regime was obliged to liberalise itself, the organisation that Lenin led took on a new character: one year after the outbreak of the revolution he described this organisation, for the first time, as "a mass party"'.[72] At the April 1905 Congress Lenin moved a resolution which, while acknowledging that the democratic principle was not fully possible under autocracy, nevertheless called for its application 'to a much larger extent'.[73]

But even after the counter-revolution triumphed, certain legal forms continued to exist, principally trade unions and the quasi-parliament, the Duma. While the Bolsheviks urged the boycotting of the initial Duma elections, they soon changed their minds when public interest rose and several independently elected members of the Duma joined the Social Democrats.

The brief blossoming of liberty in 1905 was followed by a period of fierce police repression and the virtual destruction of the party's entire underground structure.[74] Krupskaya describes the period 1908–11 as one in which the

> prisons were full to overflowing, the prisoners were subject to brutal treatment and death sentences followed one after another.

The illegal organisations were driven deep underground, and even so they found it hard to escape detection. During the revolution the composition of the party membership had undergone a change; new members joined the party who had no experience of the pre-revolutionary underground or of secrecy methods of work [sic] ... the government's intelligence service was splendidly organised.[75]

In trying to elude arrest, Lenin himself was nearly killed when ice broke under him as he walked over the frozen Baltic Sea to reach a ferry to take him to Sweden.[76]

The decision to go completely underground was taken towards the end of 1907. At the level of party work in Moscow this meant, for example, that Bobrovskaya as the secretary of the Moscow Regional Committee worked from seven different apartments on each of the seven days of the week. To find her, party members had to go to another apartment, give the correct password and then be handed the address of the apartment for that day. Under such conditions even the simplest task was extraordinarily long and drawn out, frustrating and difficult.

In this period the Social Democrats underwent a significant change in attitude towards the legal forms of organisation which had arisen during the revolution and which later existed in greatly restricted form. These legal forms of organisation covered political work in the Duma and in trade unions, workers' clubs, co-operatives and insurance organisations.

One part of the Menshevik faction of the Social Democrats, led by Martov and Theodor Dan, urged that the party's effort be mainly directed to the legal institutions with the illegal apparatus co-ordinating the work. The party should stay in the background and not compromise the new legal organisations.[77] Another part of the Mensheviks urged as a concomitant of this the abandonment of the reconstruction of the party underground, a position Lenin damned as 'liquidationist'.[78] In fact, the involvement by Social Democrats in legal organisations was quite effective. The police noted in 1910 that most party members 'belong to authentic clubs and societies. Since all meetings are held under a legal guise it is difficult to expose their criminal work'.[79]

One faction of the Bolsheviks, meanwhile, took the opposite approach, demanding the withdrawal of all party workers from the legal institutions, especially the Duma, and the concentration of all work on the underground. These became known as the Otzovists ('recallists') for their demand for the recall of Social Democratic deputies from the Duma.

In this debate Lenin acknowledged that both legal and illegal methods could and should be used. This was not surprising considering, for example, the fate of the party's press. In 1911, according to Krupskaya, censorship was relaxed in Russia and Bolsheviks found they could contribute to legal newspapers. In parallel, their underground newspapers were badly disrupted after their distribution apparatus was penetrated several times by police agents.[80] The distinction between legal and illegal work had its later parallel in intelligence practice. Soviet spies with diplomatic cover were said to be 'legal'. They could use embassy premises for the detailed technical work of espionage while diplomatic couriers could be used for sending communications and transporting money. For 'illegals' who operated in a hostile country no such protection existed.

The Social Democrats' practice of centralism and internal democracy had also changed. The underground Social Democratic Party in the Ukraine from 1911 onwards is far more recognisable to us today as a 'normal' party employing democratic centralism rather than the consciously undemocratic elite of a decade earlier. Elections for higher committees and for officers were democratic except where police conditions made co-option necessary.[81] By 1912 this was endorsed by the Bolshevik Central Committee, which praised this system of 'combining the principle of election by *raion* [district] cells with the principle of co-optation'. This method made 'possible the establishment of the closest and most direct ties between the leading body and the lower level cells and at the same time permits the creation of a highly conspiratorial executive body which is small, very mobile and has the right to speak at all times for the organisation'.[82] In his detailed study of the Russian underground Elwood notes that 'The choice between illegal and legal activity was a matter of pragmatic necessity, not ideological preference, forced on the local Social Democrats by the relative success of the police in combating illegal activity and in infiltrating the illegal organisation. Ironically, even Lenin realised this failure of illegal modes of operation and organisation and consequently placed his emphasis increasingly on utilising legal opportunities to broaden his faction's influence.'[83] By 1913 Lenin actively encouraged the party's activity in legal workers' insurance funds, which he believed would strengthen their ties with the masses.[84]

This period of repression saw the beginnings of a specialised party agency to combat police *agents provocateurs*. The revolution of 1905 had pricked the consciences of some police, one of whom was Leonid Men'shchikov, who defected to the revolutionary camp and turned over a quantity of police documents. In 1909–10 a large number of police agents was uncovered in a number of anti-Tsarist parties, including 90 agents in the Social Democrats.[85] A key figure in this exposure was a member of the Social Revolutionary Party, Burtsev, who began to specialise in exposing agents. This function later became institutionalised in all communist parties as a Control Commission. As well as rooting out informers, the Control Commission disciplined members on matters which might bring the party into disrepute, typically, personal morality, including sexual morality. It also liaised with undercover members and it was often to the head of the Control Commission in western parties which Soviet intelligence looked when it recruited espionage agents.[86]

THE HERITAGE OF CONSPIRACY

In his study of Soviet espionage, David Dallin observes that '[t]echniques, methods and personnel of the new Soviet secret intelligence services were taken over from the underground experience and apparatus of the Russian revolutionary parties ... Two generations of pre-1917 revolutionists had developed underground techniques to an unprecedented degree. "Conspiracy" which in its Russian meaning refers to the totality of rules of clandestine political activity, was habit and hobby to these revolutionists.'[87] Dallin briefly notes some linguistic continuities between conspiratorial work before and after 1917 but does not systematically set out the clandestine heritage. Moreover, his project is to examine one part of that heritage, the practical application of intelligence principles.

It remains to draw out clearly from the preceding account of underground political work the key constitutive elements of this organisational heritage. Each has an application to the practice of espionage. They can be divided into three layers:

1. the overall political and philosophical stances underpinning conspiratorial practice
2. the structural aspects of conspiracy as they affected the model of a vanguard party
3. the repertoire of conspiratorial techniques vital to an underground party

These I shall examine in turn.

The chief factor in the first group of broadly political and philosophical elements was Lenin's 'reinvention' or reconstitution of the Russian tradition of conspiracy. The essence of this was the combination of elite conspiratorial organisation with *mass*-based political activity. The most practical expression of this was the secret production of a revolutionary newspaper for *mass readership*. In *What is to be Done?* Lenin expressed the primacy of this kind of newspaper as a 'collective organiser' which provided a 'basic thread' to guide the building of a revolutionary party. He likened it to the thread (or string) which guides bricklayers to lay bricks in different parts of a large building whose overall structure they were unfamiliar with. In the 21 conditions for membership of the Communist International laid down by its Second Congress (1920), the combination of mass and conspiratorial approach is primary.[88]

While Lenin's privileging of the central role of a newspaper is obvious and has been noted by all commentators, it is worth observing that the conspiratorial techniques involved in distributing copies of the newspaper and in gathering written reports for publication lends itself to the practice of espionage based on clandestine contact and the gathering of information.

The second part of the broadly political aspect of the heritage was the preparedness to use legal opportunities in combination with an illegal practice rather than seeing these as alternatives. This aspect, as we have seen, only developed in the period after 1905 and was accompanied by a division among the Social Democrats. Later the combination of legal and illegal methods not only became a major theme in Comintern guidelines for banned parties, but was also part of the conceptual framework of Soviet intelligence in a foreign country.

The third part is the one most commonly highlighted by Lenin's critics: the subordination of party democracy to wider revolutionary ends. As we have seen, Lenin's position on this varied, especially after 1905, but the promotion of *What is to be Done?* as the key text of communist organisational methods meant that affiliates to the Communist International came to regard democracy as secondary, and even disruptive, particularly after the 'Bolshevisation' of 1928–30. The official organ-isational principle of the Bolsheviks, embodied in point 12 of the 21 conditions of the Comintern, was 'democratic centralism' and this formulation arose as Bolsheviks and Mensheviks cohabited in the decade before 1917.[89] But this principle was hedged by Comintern's principle 12, which stated that '[i]n the present epoch of acute civil war the Communist Party will only be able to fulfil its duty if it is organised in *as centralist a manner as possible*, if *iron discipline* reigns within it, and if the party centre, sustained by the confidence of the Party membership, is endowed with the fullest rights and authority and *the most far-reaching powers*' (emphasis added).[90]

Finally and perhaps less definitely one can speak of a certain ruthlessness and political sectarianism which accompanied the functioning of the illegal Bolshevik Party. To what extent this atmosphere was due to the physical and mental hardships of illegal work, occasional bouts of imprisonment, exile and torture and the like is hard to say.[91] In his analysis of the Russian intelligentsia, Tim McDaniel argues that an autocracy encouraged a tendency toward dogmatism and sectarianism among its opponents. Without open debate and a collision of views, 'ideas, when they took root, became more absolute'.[92] In terms of the wider working class McDaniel notes:

> Worker activists repeatedly attacked the intelligentsia for its hierarchical practices, its failure to become involved in economic struggles, and its sectarianism … [t]he weakness of pressures for reform can be traced to consequences of autocratic repression. First, the need for conspiracy disarmed much of the workers' critique of the party. In the face of tsarist repression, intelligentsia leaders claimed, with considerable justice, that centralisation was a necessary part of underground work. Too much participation would threaten the necessary secrecy of the party's activities and expose the activists to arrest. Bitter experience convinced many workers that this rationalisation was justified, although the issue never ceased to create great resentment.[93]

The second major element of the conspiratorial heritage was its implications for the structure of the party. In terms of espionage, the party parallels the intelligence organisation.

Centralisation was the key here and was valued above democracy by Lenin's faction, as we have seen. The organisational principle embodying this was co-optation, that is, higher bodies would co-opt new members from lower bodies. A key figure in the theory and practice of organisational secrecy, Osip Piatnitsky (1882–1938), explained this in his autobiography while discussing the work of the Odessa party organisation on the eve of the 1905 revolution:

The organisation of that time, in Odessa as well as in the rest of Russia, was built from top to bottom on the principle of co-optation; in the plants and factories and in the workshops, the Bolsheviks who worked there invited (co-opted) workers whom they considered to be class-conscious and who were devoted to the cause ... When a member of the sub-district committee dropped out (if he had been arrested or gone away), the remaining members co-opted another with the consent of the district committee ... When a city committee was arrested as a body, the Central Committee of the Party designated one or two members to form a new committee.[94]

As well, information and control of human resources within the party was centralised. This, paradoxically, entailed a high degree of decentralisation and responsibility by the local and factory committees of the party, a fact recognised by Lenin in his *Letter to a Comrade on our Organisational Tasks* (1904). But for Lenin this decentralisation was necessary to serve the centre, rather than involving any autonomous action by the rank and file. 'The Party centre should always have before it, not only the exact information regarding the activities of each of these [local] groups, but also the *fullest possible information regarding their composition*' (emphasis in original). This is strikingly similar to the subsequent organisational practice of Soviet intelligence, which required minute details of information from its officers overseas, detailed biographies of potential agents and strict control of operational matters.[95] Similarly, the system of *Iskra* agents could be seen, with hindsight, as an organisational precursor to a system of espionage. After the German party was beheaded in 1933 the Comintern adopted a wider notion of decentralisation as a conspiratorial tactic and guidelines stressed the need for 'the creation of an independent leadership in local organisations – leadership which will be able to react immediately to events, without waiting for directives from the centre'.[96]

Another conspiratorial principle affecting the structure of the party involved the specialisation of individuals and groups. Lenin saw this principle as one of the keys to organisational strength and enunciated it very early in his *The Task of the Russian Social Democrats* (1897).[97] 'Without a strengthening and development of revolutionary discipline, organisation and underground activity, struggle against the government is impossible. And underground activity demands above all that groups and individuals specialise in different aspects of work and the job of co-ordination be assigned to the central group of the League of Struggle, with as few members as possible.' He repeated a similar proposition in his *Letter to a Comrade on our Organisational Tasks* when he argued that '[t]he whole art of running a secret organisation should consist in making use of everything possible, in "giving everyone something to do"' and this entailed the local committee supervising groups of 'government officials; transport, printing and passport groups; groups for arranging secret meeting places; groups whose job it is to track down spies; groups among the military; groups for supplying arms; groups for the organisation of "financially profitable enterprises", for example.'[98] Lenin's notion of specialisation when added to his notion of party bodies in contact through a link person shows a striking similarity to the methods of espionage where compartmentalisation and specialisation are crucial for preservation of secrecy. Associated with this was the deployment of certain members as 'reserves'. The 'reserves' played little active part in party activity until new blood was needed. Bobrovskaya noted that '[Reserves] were indispensable because they were seldom arrested and were able, after mass arrests, to weave together the torn threads of the organisation and hand them over to fresh workers.'[99] A system of reserves or alternates was crucial according to later Comintern guidelines for underground work.[100]

The most important single specialisation in the Social Democratic Party was the operation of an illegal printing press.[101] As Elwood has noted, this was strictly segregated from the rest of the party organisation and given a 'semi-autonomous status so as to avoid police observers and provocateurs'.[102] This entailed that '[t]he large and noisy printing presses were usually concealed in dachas, peasant huts, mineshafts and on at least two occasions in monasteries. The apartment of a wealthy sympathiser in an upper-class section of town was also prized as an unlikely hiding place for a revolutionary press.'

Such support from non-party forces is the final aspect of the conspiratorial heritage in connection with the party structure. We have already seen that disagreements over this distinction between members and supporters was the basis for the split between Mensheviks and Bolsheviks. The crucial role of the periphery in providing cover, assistance and reserve forces is hardly recognised in the work of Lenin and others, even though both sides relied heavily on non-party sympathisers. Krupskaya notes the use of sympathetic sailors (for transport) and

41

dentists (for rendezvous in their waiting rooms).[103] Elwood notes the use of a sympathetic doctor's waiting room as a meeting place and the overall problem of the 'room question' for local organisations.[104] Throughout the memoirs of Cecilia Bobrovskaya there are frequent instances of young middle-class sympathisers providing shelter and food, sometimes at great risk, to the Social Democratic revolutionaries.[105] One illegal printshop serving the rural towns around Moscow in 1907 was supported by a 'finance committee [which] consisted largely of the wives of engineers, lawyers, doctors and there was even the wife of a rubber manufacturer on this committee. There were only three of our people on the committee', she noted. Piatnitsky refers warmly to support he received in his early underground work from the Bund.[106] For Soviet intelligence organisations, the sympathetic periphery in any given nation was constituted by the local communist party.

The Bolsheviks developed a range of techniques for clandestinity to evade police surveillance while conducting political work. A great many of these had a direct application to the methods and tools of intelligence organisations.

The use of pseudonyms and false passports was basic to Social Democratic work. 'Lenin' was an assumed name (one of over 50),[107] as was 'Stalin', 'Trotsky', 'Molotov', 'Piatnitsky' and many others. In letters and correspondence, party members were usually referred to by pseudonyms or numbers.[108] In public journals and books (such as the first edition of Lenin's *The Development of Capitalism in Russia*), the Social Democrats used 'Aesopian' or allegorical language at times. In private letters they developed the technique of secret writing or 'chemical letters' where a message in lemon juice or chlorine would be written between the lines of an innocuous letter. Coded letters which involved sender and receiver referring to the same edition of a book (often a common, innocuous story book) were also used. The code consisted of numerical fractions, the numerator and denominator of which as well as their sum would refer variously to specific pages, lines or words. The fraction would be buried among meaningless fractions and the receiver would have to know which of the string of fractions held the key to the message. The code was extremely hard to crack but, needless to say, this method sometimes resulted in an impenetrable message for the intended receiver if there was confusion over which book held the key.[109]

Letters were mailed from neutral countries to addresses of little known members or sympathisers. The underground Bolshevik newspaper

Proletarii (established after the Third Congress to challenge the Menshevik-controlled *Iskra*) printed certain unobtrusive numbers which, to the initiated, denoted which 'cover addresses' were currently active and in use for correspondence.[110] The use of couriers for the personal delivery of letters and copies of propaganda was widespread.[111] Couriers were also used for the distribution of the party press. The autobiography of Piatnitsky reads as a text book on underground work especially the transport of newspapers across borders. Piatnitsky used double bottomed suitcases until customs began to recognise the style which were all made at the same factory, then switched to 'breast plates', a waist-coat which held some hundreds of newspapers printed on onion skin paper. For shifting heavy quantities of literature, Piatnitsky used smugglers of criminal contraband as well as the smugglers of religious tracts.[112]

Elwood considers that the Social Democrats' communication techniques, in the face of mail interception, the revolutionaries' own sloppiness and agent infiltration, were 'a complete waste of time'. No system, of course, can withstand an agent who is privy to codes, addresses, pseudonyms. Greater value seemed to come from the smuggling of literature to Russia, though this too was penetrated by police agents.

By 1917 the Bolshevik faction was numerically weak but organisationally strong because they had developed a coherent outlook, structure and repertoire of techniques for underground political work. After 1917 refinements to this tradition and the lessons from the opening of the Okhrana files ensured that when the 'Russian model' of social democratic political parties began to spread, it was heavily oriented to the outlook and principles of conspiracy. At the same time this organisational heritage became a key foundation for the highly successful Soviet espionage services.

NOTES

1. Frederick Engels, 'Preface to the English Edition of 1888, Manifesto of the Communist Party', in vol. I of Karl Marx and Frederick Engels, *Selected Works*, Moscow, 1958, 25.
2. Frederick Engels, 'On the History of the Communist League', in vol. II of Karl Marx and Frederick Engels, *Selected Works*, Foreign Languages Publishing House, Moscow, 1958, 339.
3. Ibid.
4. Braunthal, *History of the International*, 69.
5. Mehring, *Karl Marx*, 139. Not all 'conspiratorial airs' were eschewed however. In September 1847 the Brussels committee held a banquet of international workers solidarity of which Mehring notes, 'it was customary to choose banquets as a framework for

political propaganda in order to avoid police interference inevitable at public meetings'. Mehring, *Karl Marx*, 140.

6. Engels, 'History of the Communist League', 348
7. Ibid., 351.
8. Karl Marx and Frederick Engels, *The Cologne Communist Trial* (trans. with introduction by Rodney Livingstone), Lawrence & Wishart, London 1971.
9. Ibid., Introduction, 23, 29.
10. Charles William Heckethorn, *The Secret Societies of all Ages and Countries*, George Redway, London, 1897, vol. II, 114–15.
11. Ibid., 113.
12. Richard Pipes, *Russia Under the Old Regime*, Weidenfeld & Nicolson, London, 1974, 305.
13. Ibid. 306–9.
14. Nurit Schleifman, *Undercover Agents in the Russian Revolutionary Movement: the SR Party, 1902–14*, St Martin's Press, New York, 1988, ix.
15. Adam B. Ulam, *Lenin and the Bolsheviks: the Intellectual and Political History of the Triumph of Communism in Russia*, Secker & Warburg, London, 1966, 21–8.
16. Ibid., 22.
17. Franco Venturi, *Roots of Revolution: a History of the Populist and Socialist Movements in Nineteenth Century Russia*, Weidenfeld & Nicolson, London, 1960, 303–15.
18. Isiah Berlin, introduction to Venturi, *Roots of Revolution*, xxv.
19. Deborah Hardy, *Land and Freedom: the Origins of Russian Terrorism, 1876–1879*, Greenwood Press, Westport, CT, 1987, 80–3.
20. Ironically, Marx himself favoured the followers of Narodnaya Volya over those of the 'father of Russian marxism' Georgi Plekhanov according to Norman M. Naimark, *Terrorists and Social Democrats, the Russian Revolutionary Movement Under Alexander III*, Harvard University Press, Cambridge, MA, 1983, 70–1.
21. Leon Trotsky, *My Life: an Attempt at an Autobiography*, Charles Scribner, New York, 1930, 103–14.
22. Cecilia Bobrovskaya, *Twenty Years in Underground Russia: Memoirs of a Rank and File Bolshevik*, 2nd edition, Proletarian Publishers, Chicago, 1978, 23–4.
23. Ibid, 33.
24. Naimark, *Terrorists and Social Democrats*, 165.
25. Bobrovskaya, *Twenty Years*, 43.
26. Cited in David Lane, *The Roots of Russian Communism: a Social and Historical Study of Russian Social Democracy 1898–1907*, 2nd edition, Martin Robertson, London, 1975, 99.
27. Bobrovskaya, *Twenty Years*, 62–5.
28. Ulam, *Lenin and the Bolsheviks*, 123.
29. S. V. Utechin, introduction to *What is to be Done?*, Panther, London, 1970, 22–6.
30. Lenin, *Collected Works* (hereafter *CW*), Progress Publishers, Moscow, 1978 (published in the United Kingdom by Lawrence & Wishart, London), vol. II, 327.
31. Ibid., vol. II, 350.
32. Ibid., vol. II, 340.
33. Lenin, *A Protest by Russian Social Democrats*, in *CW*, vol. IV, 181.
34. N. K. Krupskaya, *Reminiscences of Lenin*, Foreign Languages Publishing House, Moscow 1959, 20. Krupskaya states that Lenin personally held 'the old revolutionaries of Narodnaya Volya in great respect', 83.
35. An interesting and detailed account of aspects of Krupskaya's correspondence can be found in Robert C. Williams, *The Other Bolsheviks: Lenin and his Critics, 1904–1914*, Indiana University Press, Bloomington and Indianapolis, 1986, 5–19.
36. Krupskaya, *Reminiscences*, 76.
37. Robert H. McNeal, *Bride of the Revolution: Krupskaya and Lenin*, Victor Gollancz, London 1973, 101.
38. Ulam, *Lenin and the Bolsheviks*, 167.

39. McNeal, *Bride of the Revolution*, 98.
40. *CW*, vol. V, 347–527.
41. Ibid., vol. V, 462.
42. Ibid., vol. V, 145.
43. Lane, *Roots of Russian Communism*, 98.
44. Ibid., 69.
45. *CW*, vol. V, 446.
46. Prokopovich is referred to in the text as N. N. and the author 'Reply'. *CW*, vol. V, 451.
47. Ibid., vol. V 475–76.
48. Ibid., vol. V, 479.
49. J. L. H. Keep, *The Rise of Social Democracy in Russia*, Clarendon Press, Oxford, 1963, 94.
50. Vladimir Akimov, 'A Short History of the Social Democratic Movement in Russia', in Jonathan Frenkel (translation and introduction), *Vladimir Akimov on the Dilemmas of Russian Marxism, 1895–1903*, Cambridge University Press, Cambridge, 1969, 313ff.
51. Frenkel, *Akimov*, 321.
52. Keep, *Rise of Social Democracy*, 44–5.
53. Robert Blobaum, *Feliks Dzierzynski and the SDKPiL: a Study of the Origins of Polish Communism*, East European Monographs, Columbia University Press, Boulder, 1984, 112–13.
54. Ibid., 112.
55. Lenin, preface to the collection, 'Twelve Years', in *CW*, vol. XIII, 101.
56. Edited by 'A Commission of the CC of the CPSU (B)', *History of the Communist Party of the Soviet Union (Short Course)*, Foreign Languages Publishing House, Moscow, 1943, 38.
57. In Australia a hardback edition of *What is to be Done?* was one of the first substantial, locally published texts by the CPA. The edition is not dated but the imprint, Wright & Baker, was used in the late 1920s and early 1930s.
58. Keep, *Rise of Social Democracy*, 94.
59. Israel Getzler, *Martov: a Political Biography of a Russian Social Democrat*, Melbourne University Press, Carlton, Victoria, 1967, 45–7.
60. Cited ibid., 68.
61. *CW*, vol. VII, 259.
62. Cited in Getzler, *Martov*, 79.
63. Keep, *Rise of Social Democracy*, 127.
64. For example, see ibid., 129ff. Keep concentrates on Lenin's methods and the 'enduring imprint' of the debate 'upon the psychology of Lenin and his followers' (133).
65. In *CW*, vol. VI, 233–50.
66. My summary of Lenin's views is based on *CW*, vol. VI, 244–7
67. Ibid., vol. VI, 246–7.
68. Leon Trotsky, *1905*, Pelican Books, Harmondsworth, 1973, 265–8.
69. Lenin, 'The Reorganisation of the Party', *CW*, vol. X, 29–39.
70. Krupskaya records that after their arrival Lenin and she lived apart 'for reasons of secrecy' and both had to contend with secret police dogging their steps. *Reminiscences*, 139.
71. Ibid., 135.
72. Marcel Liebman, *Leninism Under Lenin* (trans. Brian Pearce), Jonathan Cape, London, 1975, 48.
73. Ibid., 49–50.
74. Ralph Carter Elwood, *Russian Social Democracy in the Underground: a Study of the RSDLP in the Ukraine, 1907–1914*, International Institute for Social History, Amsterdam, 1974, 34–6.
75. Krupskaya, *Reminiscences*, 165.
76. Ibid., 160–1.
77. Much of this discussion is based on Elwood, *Russian Social Democracy*, 27–32.
78. A Menshevik, Eva Broido, noted that 'Some of the Mensheviks ... lost all interest in underground party work and, intent on holding on to the few legal conquests of recent

years, worked only within the narrow legal limits.' Vera Broido (trans. and ed.), *Eva Broido: Memoirs of a Revolutionary*, Oxford University Press, London and Oxford, 1967, 137.

79. Elwood, *Russian Social Democracy*, 95.
80. Krupskaya, *Reminiscences*, 217, 225.
81. Elwood, *Russian Social Democracy*, 89.
82. Ibid., 103.
83. Ibid., ix.
84. Krupskaya, *Reminiscences*, 261.
85. Schliefman, *Undercover Agents*, 134.
86. This was the case in Australia where Soviet intelligence used the secretary of the Control Commission, Walter Clayton, as a talent spotter (see chapter 8 below).
87. Dallin, *Soviet Espionage*, 1.
88. *Theses, Resolutions and Manifestos of the First Four Congresses of the Third International*, trans. Alix Holt and Barbara Holland, introduction by Bertil Hessel, Ink Links, London, 1980, 92–7.
89. Liebman, *Leninism Under Lenin*, 49–53.
90. *Theses, Resolutions and Manifestos*, 95.
91. Liebman attributes these features entirely to the conditions of repression and hopelessness which engulfed the Bolsheviks after 1907, see *Leninism Under Lenin*, 53–61, esp. 61.
92. Tim McDaniel, *Autocracy, Capitalism and Revolution in Russia*, University of California Press, Berkeley, 1988, 220.
93. Ibid.
94. O. Piatnitsky, *Memoirs of a Bolshevik*, Martin Lawrence, London, 1932, 76–7.
95. Examples of the instructions from Soviet intelligence in the 1940s and 1950s are identified in the Venona material issued by the National Security Agency on its home page (http://www.nsa.gov). See for example, in the fifth release of previously classified information, 'The KGB and GRU in Europe, South America and Australia' and the biography supplied of Miss Bernie in cables on 25 April and 5 July 1945.
96. 'On the Question of Illegal Work', *Communist International*, vol. 10, no. 23 (1 Dec. 1933), 857.
97. *CW*, vol. II, 349.
98. Lenin, *CW*, vol. VI, 240.
99. Bobrovskaya, *Twenty Years*, 64.
100. 'On the Question of Illegal Work', 857–8.
101. In the 1920s and 1930s, the Society of Old Bolsheviks published a series of pamphlets one of which was entirely devoted to this. S. Kedrov, *Une Imprimerie Clandestine [A Secret Printery]*, Bureau d'Editions, Paris, 1932.
102. Elwood, *Russian Social Democracy*, 143.
103. Krupskaya, *Reminiscences*, 78, 144.
104. Elwood, *Russian Social Democracy*, 94.
105. Bobrovskaya, *Twenty Years*, 52–3; 69–70.
106. Piatnitsky, *Memoirs*, 25, 28.
107. Albert L. Weeks, *The First Bolshevik: a Political Biography of Peter Tkachev*, New York University Press, New York, 1963, 7.
108. Elwood, *Russian Social Democracy*, 59–60.
109. Ibid., 59.
110. Ibid., 60, footnote 53.
111. Interestingly, the first use of couriers or agents in the communist movement seems to have occurred in Prussia, where journeymen were used as emissaries by the Communist League and played a 'significant part' in its organisation. Marx and Engels, *Cologne Communist Trial*, 16.
112. Piatnitsky, *Memoirs*, 57–8, 139.

CHAPTER TWO

The Communist International and Clandestine Methods: the Conspiratorial Impulse

The essence of illegality does not lie in hiding a small group of people from the enemy; it lies in carrying on uninterrupted mass work, and in having a constant influx of new help from the masses – this with the help of a strongly welded hidden organisation.

'On the Question of Illegal Work'[1]

The decade after the 1917 revolution saw the conspiratorial methods of the Russian Social Democrats spread to all parties affiliated with the Communist International. The resolutions of the first four congresses of the Third International (1919–22) spoke about the need for an underground apparatus, about the mass character of illegal work and about the combination of legal and illegal work. One crucial decision occurred at the Third Congress of the Communist International in 1921, when it was decided to found a Commission on Illegal Work. Its task was to address problems of political work in countries where repression was strong such as Italy, Yugoslavia, Romania, Estonia, Lithuania and Latvia, or where powerful communist parties faced potentially stronger repression such as France, Germany and Czechoslovakia. The commission, for the first time, began to systematise the organisational theories of the RSDLP about underground political work. This deepened following the Fifth Congress in June–July 1924 which announced a drive towards the 'Bolshevisation' of the affiliated parties. This strengthened the attachment of all communist parties to the Russian model, including its conspiratorial elements, although in many cases the preoccupation with conspiratorial work had begun to be misapplied to the work of the communist parties in conditions unlike those of Tsarist Russia. By the time of the the Sixth World Congress of Comintern in 1928 there was a renewed urgency to create illegal structures through its prediction of a new world war, during which communists would face considerable repression.

After the seizure of power by the Bolsheviks in October 1917 and the subsequent military opposition which this aroused both internally and externally, the Bolsheviks became convinced that in order for the new socialist government to survive in Russia they had to spread their form of revolutionary socialism to Europe and beyond.

To achieve this, they reasoned, new revolutionary parties, imbued with a truly revolutionary theory, were needed. The parties of the Second International, which had split when war broke out in August 1914, were clearly unwilling and unable to lead revolutions. So the Russian Social Democrats revived an idea which they had initiated in September 1915: the creation of a Third International.[2] In the wake of the revolt of German workers in November 1918, they called a conference of 'all parties hostile to the Second International' which was held in March 1919.[3] In spite of the reservations of a number of parties the conference was converted into the first congress of a new Third (Communist) International.

The aim of the Bolsheviks was to split existing socialist and Social Democratic parties in order that new revolutionary parties could emerge. But such was the high regard in which the Russian socialists were held that many of these same socialist parties, whom the Bolsheviks described as 'centrist' (that is, not revolutionary), wanted to join the new Communist International. The president of the Communist International, Grigori Zinoviev, spoke in this period of the need to 'lock the Comintern' and 'place a sentry on the gate'.[4] The 'sentry' emerged at the Second Congress of Comintern in August 1920. It consisted of 21 'conditions of admission' to which a prospective party member of the new International had to agree before being accepted.

On 30 July, the revolutionary leader Leon Trotsky presented the conditions to the Communist International.[5] Among them were several references to the need for underground work. The third point read:

> In almost every country in Europe and America the class struggle is entering the phase of civil war. Under such conditions the Communists can place no trust in bourgeois legality. They have

48

an obligation of setting up *a parallel organisational apparatus* which, at the decisive moment, can assist the Party to do its duty to the revolution. In every country where a state of siege or emergency laws deprive the Communists of the opportunity of carrying on all their work legally, it is absolutely necessary to *combine legal and illegal activity*. (emphasis added)

The fourth point stressed the obligation to promote propaganda in the army and noted that when interrupted by law 'it must be continued illegally'. This point was repeated in condition 14 in relation to propaganda against the transport of war material directed to the enemies of the Soviet republics. A separate resolution on parliament noted that

> The Communist deputies must combine their legal work with illegal work if the Central Committee so decides. In those countries where the Communist deputy enjoys a certain immunity from bourgeois law, this should be used to assist the Party's illegal organisational and propaganda work.[6]

A separate document, the Statutes of the Communist International, drafted by Lenin, emphasised the creation of 'illegal communist organisations alongside the legal organisations'.[7] The need to combine legal with illegal methods and the need to 'utilize the slightest possibility allowed by the laws' was also emphasised and illustrated by reference to the experience of the Bolsheviks after the 1905 revolution.[8]

In the period November 1920 to January 1921 three key socialist parties, in Germany, France and Italy, voted on whether to accept the 'twenty one conditions' and significant communist parties were formed in each of these countries.

Following the Second Congress and consonant with its emphasis on the need for illegal organisation, one of the leading figures in the Communist International, the writer Victor Serge, wrote a pamphlet entitled 'The Methods and Procedures of the Russian Police'.[9] Serge explained that after the 1917 revolution a large part of the files of the 'most battle-hardened political police' had fallen into the hands of the revolutionaries. After outlining the elaborate surveillance apparatus of the Okhrana, Serge explained how the revolutionaries managed to survive and triumph:

> The Russian revolutionaries in fact considered that clandestine (illegal) action was the subject to unbending rules. At every turn

they asked themselves: 'Is this in line with the rules of conspiracy? ... Thanks to this science of conspiracy, the revolutionaries were able to live illegally in the main cities of Russia for months or years at a time. They were able to turn themselves, as the case required, into pedlars, coachmen, 'rich foreigners', servants etc.[10]

Serge went on to observe that the outlook and habits of socialists who used these methods inevitably changed. 'Illegal action, over a period creates habits and an outlook which can be considered the best guarantee against police methods', he said. Klehr, Haynes and Firsov make a similar point that 'clandestine habits of mind and behaviour pervaded all levels of the [American] Communist Party'.[11]

While the Second Congress of the Comintern emphasised the need for a clandestine apparatus, the Third Congress, in June–July 1921, emphasised the need to combine illegal work with legal work. The key resolution, 'The Organisational Structure of the Communist Parties, the Methods and Content of their Work', chastised illegal parties for being 'not sufficiently skilful at seizing opportunities to engage in legal activities ... [i]n such cases Party work tends to amount to a Sisyphean labour performed by ineffectual conspirators', it said.[12] Many communist parties, it warned, had equated illegal work with the creation of 'a close knit and exclusively military organisation, isolated from other aspects of party work and organisation'. This was 'undoubtedly a mistaken view', it said.[13] Quite clearly it contradicted Lenin's notion that the purpose of conspiratorial methods was to engage in mass political agitation. On the other hand, legal parties had 'as a whole, not yet grasped fully how seriously they must work to prepare the party for the revolutionary insurrection, the armed struggle and the illegal struggle'. While legal, these parties had to, for example, 'hide addresses with care, develop the habit of destroying correspondence, learn to preserve necessary documents, educate people in conspiracy etc'.

A 'special apparatus', the Congress said, was needed to deal with underground facilities and contacts and it gave the following example of how it might be developed in a legal situation:

A system of secret communication can function reliably and efficiently only if it has been in regular operation for a long time. In all these spheres of special revolutionary activity, every Communist Party needs some secret preparations, if only on a small scale. In most cases a system may be established legally, provided the type of apparatus that may need to be created is kept in view: for example an underground apparatus organising postal and courier services, transport, accommodation, etc. can be developed by the careful distribution of legal leaflets and also legal publications and letters.[14]

Clandestine habits and a certain conspiratorial frame of mind, therefore, developed not only in banned parties but in legal ones.

THE COMMISSION ON ILLEGAL WORK

By the time of the Fourth Congress, in December 1922, political conditions for communists in a number of countries were worsening. Rather than revolution spreading, a counter-revolution was in full swing as European governments took fright at the new Russian order. In October 1922 Mussolini had staged a virtual *coup d'état* and was appointed Prime Minister of Italy. That same month in Romania the new Communist Party was formed as a largely secret organisation and two years later it was banned.[15] In Yugoslavia the Communist Party, which had been the fourth largest party after elections in November 1920, with 65,000 members, had been reduced to 1,000 members after it was taken unprepared by its outlawry in August 1921.[16] In Hungary, the attempted communist revolt of 1919 was followed in 1920 by a counter-revolution which saw the execution of 5,000 communists and the formal banning of the party in 1921.[17] In Bulgaria, the Communist Party, which had won 20 per cent of the vote in elections in 1920 and 1923, staged an abortive uprising in 1923 which was bloodily suppressed and followed by the banning of their party.[18]

To respond to these events the Fourth Congress decided to establish a special Commission on Illegal Work. Until this moment, a number of references to illegal work were routinely contained in public reports of the Comintern. However, in the published papers of the Fourth Congress, the details of the decision to form the Commission were not reported. One small, understated part of a published resolution, 'Thesis on the Reorganisation of the Executive', noted that 'a number of important parties are to all appearances approaching a period of illegality [and therefore] the presidium is instructed to devote greater attention to the preparation of the Parties in question for illegal work. Immediately after the Congress the presidium shall begin discussions on this subject with all parties concerned.'[19]

One month after the Congress decision the Commission on Illegal Work held the first meeting of a series which lasted until 23 May 1923.[20] According to its papers, now available in Moscow, its members consisted of Osip Piatnitsky, Mikhail Trilisser and Emilien Yaroslavsky, with Edward Prukhnyak initially secretary of the Commission but soon replaced by the Lithuanian communist, Vikenti Mitskevich-Kapsukas.

Piatnitsky, as we have seen, was a key figure in the Bolsheviks' pre-revolutionary underground organisation. After the Third Congress Piatnitsky was made head of the Comintern's international liaison service, the OMS (Otdel mezhdunarodnykh svyazey), which organised the transport of letters, personnel and money between Moscow and member communist parties.[21] His work in the Commission on Illegal Work was part of his wider responsibilities as a member of the Organisation Department of the Comintern.[22] Mikhail Abramovich Trilisser worked with Piatnitsky in the initial operation of the OMS. At this time Trilisser had been, according to Andrew and Gordievsky, the head of the foreign section of the Cheka since 1921, an early illustration of the intermingling of political and intelligence tasks of the new Soviet state.[23] (Trilisser remained with Soviet foreign intelligence and at the Seventh Congress of the Comintern in 1935, under the name Moskvin, he was elected to the Presidium of the Executive Committee of the Communist International (ECCI) and also became head of the OMS.) Emilien Yaroslavsky was a member of the central committee of the Russian Communist Party (Bolshevik) and between his time on the Commission on Illegal Work and 1934 was a member of the control commission of the Russian party; Vikenti Mitskevich-Kapsukas, a Lithuanian who briefly headed a revolutionary government in Lithuania at the end of 1918 and the beginning of 1919, then worked underground before returning to Comintern where he became a member of the ECCI in 1924.

The Commission on Illegal Work formally functioned as part of the Organisation Department of the ECCI.[24] It operated under the close supervision of the chairman of the Communist International, Grigori Zinoviev, who had to approve all letters sent by the Commission.[25] One of the first tasks of the Commission was to improve the security of the ECCI itself, since foreign communists, unschooled in the ways of konspiratsya were careless with documents.[26]

A draft resolution on illegal work reflected the Comintern's alarm at the white terror which had broken out in central Europe and was hampering revolutionary work.[27] It warned that many communist parties 'do not look seriously at the prospects of going underground' in the conditions of white terror. In order to make the transition to the structure and practice of underground work, the Commission urged parties to study the experience of Finland and the Baltic countries which, it said, served as a model. 'These parties had worked underground for seven years and had managed to keep guiding the workers' movement from that position.' This resolution reflects a Leninist principle of clandestine work which we have already encountered. In his *Letter to a Comrade on our Organisational Tasks* (1904), Lenin proposed decentralisation in a very weak form which essentially meant that widely scattered local party bodies actively kept the central leadership informed. In this resolution, however, decentralisation is proposed in a stronger sense. Discussing the organisational structure of illegal parties, the resolution states that party branches in enterprises, in villages and in other regions must 'switch over to local cells'; that is, divide into smaller organisations to make illegal work easier. While this form of decentralisation is desirable, the resolution urges that 'the political work within local cells should be based on the centralisation principle, on discipline and conspiratorial rules'. That is, centralisation within the cell, but decentralisation of the party as whole, as a way of avoiding repression. The principle that legal work should be combined with illegal work is also stressed. '[W]hile carrying on mass work under illegal conditions, all opportunities for legal work should be used as well', it says. However, it gives primacy to illegal organisation, describing it as 'the backbone of the workers movement'.[28] The emphasis on legal work occurs in other recommendations of the Commission. For example, its instructions to the Communist Party of Yugoslavia in March 1923 begins with an invocation that while legal work must continue, an illegal cell structure should be set up wherever possible.[29]

The Commission's aims and its role was soon broadened to become more educative and directly supervisory. In August 1923 Zinoviev and Radek approved an expanded 'Instruction on the Work of the Illegal Commission' which gave as its prime purpose: '[to] collect and sum up the experience of work in various countries, *especially the Russian experience*' (emphasis added).[30] It was also to 'supervise' the preparation of underground work in various countries, including work in the army, and workers' and peasants' self-defence units. Delegates from overseas parties based in Moscow were to be instructed in illegal work and acquainted with techniques such as 'the setting up of underground printing shops, the development of codes and the question of passports'. Finally, the Commission was charged with collecting 'material about methods of work used by fascist organisations and preparing measures to combat them'.

The initial activity of the Commission on Illegal Work consisted of examining the situation in Italy and particularly at the possibilities of conspiratorial work in the Italian army and navy; examining the state of underground work in various countries, including Yugoslavia, Hungary, Czechoslovakia, Germany, North America, Lithuania, Latvia and France; and preparing a document of systematic instructions on the conduct of underground work. One document which survives was 'How to behave during interrogation', which urges arrested militants to 'refuse to give out any information concerning the party, its composition, organisational structure, contacts and individuals'.[31] It noted bluntly that 'this kind of tactic may, of course, infuriate the police and they may harass the arrested person even more but the organisation will be left intact'.

The Commission addressed three letters to the Central Committee of the Italian Communist Party (PCI) during 1923, informing them of methods which the Russian party had developed. These dealt with questions of organisational structure, contacts, illegal techniques and actions which might be used in the conditions of the fascist dictatorship. The situation of the newly formed PCI illustrated the worries of the Comintern leadership that hitherto legal parties were badly prepared for the illegality which accompanied regimes such as Mussolini's. One of the first resolutions of the Commission concerned the Italian Communist Party's attempt to purge the party of informers and police agents.[32] The PCI proposed a form of centralised registry for the details of party members. The Commission strongly disapproved of this method and warned the PCI not to implement it. Such a move would 'put the members in great danger, as with all parties, for one can never be sure that these documents will not fall into the hands of the police. The fact that the family names are coded changes very little', the resolution added. Instead the Commission proposed a reorganisation of the party on the basis of *troikas* (groups of three members), along with stricter methods of vouching for new members. The situation in Hungary was also dealt with by the Commission. In April 1923 the Organising Bureau of the ECCI charged the Commission with working out recommendations for financing, printing and distributing illegal publications in Hungary, particularly in factories.[33]

The failed revolt by the German communists in October 1923 was followed by the banning of the German Communist Party. Its underground technique however was inadequate and drew the wrath of the Commission whose attention to detail was striking. In a long letter to the German Communist Party in November 1924, following a police raid and subsequent publicity about that party's bureau for manufacturing false passports, the Commission strongly criticised in the smallest detail the conspiratorial methods of the bureau.[34] The production of false passports took place in a flat owned by a carpenter who was a member of the German Communist Party. It was 'rented' to two 'bachelors' whose cover story was that they were draughtsmen. Yet they did not appear to have clients and the cleaner who entered the flat did not see any draughting activities. 'The Bureau also kept the legal passports of those to whom it supplied illegal passports', said the Commission. 'This allowed the police to identify exactly those who worked underground. As well, the police found photographs of those who worked underground. The Bureau hired premises in a carpenter's flat but this was incorrect because it was in a proletarian part of the city and this part is kept under stricter surveillance than other parts of the city.'

At the Fifth World Congress of the Comintern in June–July 1924, the work of the Commission on Illegal Work was reinforced by the adoption of a new set of statutes. Paragraph 35 stipulated that 'The Communist Parties must be prepared to carry on their work illegally. The ECCI must assist the parties in the preparation of illegal work, and see to it that work is carried out.'[35] In November 1924 the Commission drew up a plan of work which outlined four goals.[36] First, the systematic instruction of communist parties in illegal methods through printed instructions, letters, articles and booklets and through verbal instruction of representatives of communist parties who go abroad to work. Second, supervision of the conspiratorial practices of individual parties and of arrests in their ranks. Third, a study of the actions by fascists aimed against communists and the development of practical measures to combat fascists. Fourth, the summing up of work of the illegal parties, including Russia, and developing this experience for practical use by illegal communist parties.

To teach conspiratorial practice, the Commission relied on special meetings with foreign delegates who regularly came to Russia to attend international gatherings such as enlarged ECCI plenums. Such special meetings seem to have occurred at the Third and Fourth Enlarged ECCI Plenums in 1923 and 1924.[37] In January 1925, after reviewing the situation in Germany, Italy, Romania and France, the Commission decided to call delegates to the Communist International to a full-scale meeting on illegal work.[38] By this stage those participating in the Commission's work included the Swiss communist Jules Humbert-Droz, who later played a role in the *Rote Kapelle* (Red Orchestra), the Soviet espionage groups in Nazi-occupied Europe.[39]

THE RULES FOR PARTY CONSPIRATORIAL WORK

A major product of the Commission was a booklet spelling out in detail the 'rules of conspiracy'. In effect, it was the distillation of 25 years' underground experience of the Russian Social Democrats and of the conspiratorial tradition from which they emerged. The booklet consisted of 19 sections covering such matters as the protocols and precautions for running a 'conspiratorial flat', arrangements for meetings, the storing of archives, the operation of illegal printing presses, the behaviour of an illegal worker who lives in places such as hotels, the correct procedures when under police interrogation or in detention. Entire sections were devoted to party pseudonyms, to preventative measures against penetration by the police and to measures needed after the exposure of a comrade.

Labelled 'Top Secret' *(Sovershenno Sekretno)* and dated 15 February 1925, *The Rules for Party Conspiratorial Work* contained no reference to who wrote or published it, save a note that

> These rules are just draft 'rules' requiring additions and some editing by those who compiled them. However these draft rules may serve as a basis for discussion by comrades who have similar experiences. In our opinion such rules should be a collective effort of all the parties that have the experience of underground work.[40]

The booklet began with series of general principles. Of prime importance was compartmentalisation or the principle of organisational separation:

> The party's illegal apparatus should be organized so that even the heaviest failure or the biggest provocation cannot lead to the destruction of the entire apparatus. To achieve these aims the following principles should be observed:

(a) One and the same person should not be entrusted with several kinds of work such as contacts, illegal printing shops or military organisation.

(b) Extreme caution should be observed during the transfer of one and the same worker from one illegal duty to another, especially if the organisation where this person worked is not liquidated or retains the same structure after the departure of this worker.

(c) Conspiratorial information should not be given even to high ranking officials unless this information is used in their work.

(d) Unfamiliar persons should not be given a chance to work in any illegal organisation.

(e) A person who has just been released from prison or from detention should not be allowed for some time to work in any illegal organisation even though this person had been engaged in such work prior to his arrest.

(f) Illegal workers should not be allowed to work in any of the legal organisations.[41]

Choosing individuals to work in an illegal apparatus was highly selective and based on the principle that 'any person is considered to be unreliable until he proves the opposite'. The normal way in which the party gathered members was based on a person being recommended by a trusted party member. Thus a potential underground worker always had to be 'recommended' by someone but this was not in any way sufficient. The responsible party worker had to examine the potential worker's background, family, physical health and personal habits and morality. Gamblers, those inclined to alcohol, those subject to chronic diseases such as epileptic fits must not be accepted, said *The Rules for Party Conspiratorial Work*. If it was impossible to positively establish reliability, honesty and political soundness, the person had to be rejected. (Such procedures, when carried out by intelligence organisations, are known as 'positive vetting'.)

The *Rules* emphasised that the party always had to have available the necessary resources for underground work, including 'reserves' of cadres whose legal work had never made them known to the police.

The similarities with intelligence tradecraft are apparent when the document discusses the basis of meetings between illegal workers. Workers from different parts of the illegal apparatus should always meet in open places, such as the street or park, and not in restaurants, cafés or in similar public places. Only in exceptional circumstances could they meet in a 'conspiratorial flat' (that is, one used by an underground worker), and in any case, they could never meet in the same place twice. Every arrangement for a meeting should specify 'at least two places, one for meeting, one in reserve'.

Clandestine meetings of party bodies had to be arranged with special care, with each participant unaware of the actual meeting place, only of a rendezvous from which they would be taken to the meeting:

> The participants in meeting are not allowed to leave it before meeting ends or even for a period of time. If a meeting is held in the countryside and this place is not known to the participants, then the participants are brought to meeting and are led away at night, so they cannot see the route. In this event such places can be used for another meeting. In a village, guards are placed and an observation post must be arranged to watch passers-by and the local area. If the meeting is in a forest, the guards should pretend to pick mushrooms or berries. Those present at the meeting should behave in such a way that no other residents should become suspicious. If there is a reason to believe that such a place has become known to a suspicious person, the meeting should be dissolved, without panic.[42]

Also outlined was the interconnection between centralisation and decentralisation which we have already discussed:

> In a workshop, department etc. it is necessary to organise, instead of one large illegal cell, a number of smaller cells from which a bureau is formed with representatives from all the cells. The members of one cell should not know the members of the other cells.

A significant part of the pamphlet was devoted to conspiratorial practice inside military organisations, while another part was devoted to underground work in legal organisations. All party members active in legal trade unions, co-operatives or parliament should 'carefully conceal their illegal activity and their connections with the party', it recommended. The party organisation within a legal trade union was centralised and operated from the top down. Rather than a fraction composed of all party members in a particular field, the correct party structure consisted of 'a bureau of three to five comrades' which led the political work and co-opted, if necessary, other reliable party members from the legal organisation. 'General meetings of all party members in an organisation are never called', it stated flatly. Discussing the problem of how party members themselves would be able to recognise a party proposal put forward under some guise, the *Rules* stated, somewhat obscurely, that 'the bureau puts forward a proposition in such a way that the name of the party is not mentioned but nevertheless party members understand how the proposition arose'.

While *The Rules for Party Conspiratorial Work* was a document which was to be guarded and to be prevented from falling into the hands of the police, other publications that less obviously expounded the 'rules for conspiracy' were openly published. In 1924, while still a member of the Commission on Illegal Work, Piatnitsky concluded the writing of his memoirs, a task he had been fitfully working on since 1921. In an introduction to the work which was published in 1925, the same year as the *Rules*, the Marx–Engels–Lenin Institute noted:

> These memoirs should serve as excellent material for training our younger generation ... In this respect Comrade Piatnitsky's book might serve as a sort of text book, and an excellent text book at that, which would help our comrades abroad, who are carrying on their revolutionary work in capitalist countries, to learn the methods of organising underground work and help them to become model Bolshevik Party workers.[43]

The book was translated into several key languages, German (in two editions, 1927 and 1930), Czechoslovak (two editions, 1927 and 1930), Japanese (1928) and French (1930). English and Spanish editions appeared in 1932. The book is a genuine memoir, in which the recounting of conspiratorial practices is integrated into a narrative of Piatnitsky's lifetime party work. His ability to smuggle literature across borders and to arrange illegal printing workshops clearly made him an invaluable member of the Bolshevik leadership. At one point, while explaining in detail the structure of the Bolshevik Party, Piatnitsky apologises that such detail is necessary 'because a large percentage of our Party members did not participate in those organisations and I think it is useful for them to know this. Besides, our brother parties abroad are in great straits because they cannot find a suitable guise in which to clothe their local organisations under illegal conditions.'

The last surviving documents of the Commission on Illegal Work are dated 1926; however its functions did not cease after this date but were taken over by the Organisation Department of the ECCI, headed by Piatnitsky with Boris Vasilyev as second-in-charge.[44] In this way the functions were integrated with all of the Comintern's organisational work. By 1933, with the growth of fascism obvious in Europe, the Organisation Department was restructured. A 'Party Building' department was created with the duties '(a) to train personnel for the illegal party work and illegal techniques ... and (b) instruct personnel on illegal work in the army.'[45]

The leadership of the Comintern devoted considerable time to questions of underground work. In the period 1924–8, for example, discussions of the Secretariat of the ECCI (after December 1926, the Politsecretariat) on the topic 'questions of parallel organisations' constituted 6 per cent of its agenda items.[46] From the early 1920s, then, the proselytising of conspiratorial methods was an established part of normal Comintern advice to parties whether illegal or legal.

COMINTERN'S INTERNATIONAL NETWORK

The most intense practical application of the conspiratorial work of the Comintern was carried out by its international liaison service, the OMS. This body undertook clandestine courier activities and work which supported underground political activities. These included the transport of money and letters, the manufacture of passports and other false documents and technical support to underground parties, such as managing 'safe houses' and establishing businesses as cover activities. Unlike other Comintern files, those about the OMS are still generally withheld from scholarly research, presumably because the documents would reveal details of its links with intelligence personnel and organisations.

The OMS initially used Soviet diplomatic and commercial establishments for cover, but after the Arcos raid in Britain and the attack by the Kuomintang on the Soviet embassy in Peking in 1927 these no longer provided safe refuge.[47] After this time, the OMS operated mainly 'illegally', outside diplomatically protected premises, with the exception that diplomatic pouches were sometimes used to send money. In order to operate illegally, OMS workers established businesses, particularly import–export firms which normally used commercial cables and money transfers extensively.

One of the most detailed accounts of the work of the OMS concerns its work in Shanghai. Here, after the 1927 split between the communists and Kuomintang, an OMS worker, Jakov Rudnik ('Marin'), set up the China Trading Company as part of his responsibility for administering a clandestine apparatus serving the Far Eastern Bureau (FEB) of the Comintern. The main work of the FEB was liaison with the Chinese Communist Party and the cultivation of contact with countries in East and South-east Asia. The responsibility of the OMS included setting up safe houses and cover addresses for mail; arranging meetings between members of the FEB and the Chinese Communist Party (CPC); couriering mail between the ECCI in Moscow and both the FEB and the CPC; encoding and decoding all communications; couriering and accounting for money to the CPC and the FEB; and finally, arranging for Asian students to travel to Russia to study at the Communist University of the Peoples of the Far East.[48]

To operate all of this with the requisite regard to conspiratorial practice, Rudnik and his wife, Tatania Moiseenko, set up eight different post office boxes and seven different bank accounts and operated under six passports. They also rented ten apartments and two offices in which the FEB could meet and conduct other activities. Rudnik's collaborators were the former head of the OMS, A. E. Abramovich ('Albrecht') and his wife, who were responsible for communications and for supplying the CPC with funds. Rudnik also had the job of travelling to Japan and elsewhere in China.

From its formation in the early 1920s, the OMS co-operated closely (though not without tension) with both Soviet military intelligence and the foreign intelligence wing of the NKVD.[49] By mid-1937, the work of the OMS was largely integrated with that of Soviet intelligence, symbolised by the appointment of Mikhail Trilisser as the head of the OMS.[50] Krivitsky, writing in 1939, after his defection from military intelligence, said that '[i]n recent years the OGPU has gradually taken over many of the OMS functions' but that in the transport of money and certain aspects of co-ordination, the OMS still played the main role.[51]

During the purges of 1937–9 the OMS was named as a key component of counter-revolutionary activity. An October 1937 letter from Comintern leaders Dimitrov and Manuilsky to the Soviet party accused the OMS of being infiltrated by a 'spy organisation' and 'enemies of the people'. For these reasons it had to be 'totally liquidated'.[52] Ironically, perhaps its conspiratorial methods raised suspicion among its accusers about such 'infiltration'.

'BOLSHEVISATION' AND THE SPREAD OF UNDERGROUND METHODS

The proselytising and systematising of the Russian conspiratorial heritage was part of a broader process in which the Russian organisational model of a party was imposed on the non-Russian parties of the Communist International. Again, Piatnitsky was a key figure in driving this process. By 1924 he and other leaders of the Comintern were grappling with the ebb of the revolutionary tide, particularly in Germany. One factor identified by Piatnitsky was the organisational structure of parties, particularly in the work place.[53] The German Communist Party, he argued, institutionalised a division between trade union work at the level of the Central Committee and the work at the level of factories, which was neglected. In Italy, workers in the factory committees in Turin discussed party questions largely in their locality branches. In Czechoslovakia, the party was entirely organised on the basis of electoral districts, rather than work places.

Piatnitsky complained that the party structures of non-Russian Comintern sections 'do not differ in respect to form of organisation from the social democratic parties and organisations existing side by side with them, notwithstanding the fact that the aims of the Social Democrats and the Communists are profoundly different'.[54] This element of competition and ultimately a desire to conquer social democracy and its grip on the working class was a significant factor in the drive to Bolshevisation. The Comintern felt that in a straight contest in the factories, as opposed to parliamentary elections, it could beat social democracy.[55]

The Third and Fourth Congresses of the Comintern had both passed resolutions calling for the reorganisation of the structure of communist parties using the model of the Russian party. By the time of the Fifth Congress in June–July 1924 there was a new determination to carry through this process.

The Fifth Congress's 'Resolution on Reorganisation of the Party on the Basis of Shop Nuclei' noted the largely unfulfilled resolutions of previous Congresses and called for the restructuring of all communist parties on the foundation of 'shop nuclei' or 'factory cells'.[56] Factory cells had existed prior to this point in non-Russian parties but they were not the actual basis of the party to the degree they had been within the Bolshevik Party. Instead, communist party branches were often organised on a suburban and local basis. If a number of party members all worked in the same factory, they usually formed a fraction for the purpose of co-ordinating their political work inside the factory. In essence the 'Resolution on Reorganisation' decreed that the entire structure of the existing communist parties be transformed. The one minor concession to the old structure was what were termed 'street nuclei', which could be set up 'as a temporary measure' for those unable to work in factory nuclei but, the resolution warned, these 'must not be placed on a footing of equality with the factory nuclei'.

The Comintern leadership was aware that this directive relied heavily on the Russian experience and its assumed relevance to other parties. Reviewing the six months following the Fifth Congress, a member of the ECCI presidium, Dmitri Manuilsky, criticised the 'hypocrites of the Second International' who said that Bolshevisation meant a loss of self-determination by individual European parties. Bolshevisation, he said, 'cannot be simply an imitation of the practice of the Russian Bolsheviki'. The Comintern leadership feared adverse consequences 'if we begin to copy blindly Russian experience in other fields'. A blind application of *What is to be Done?*, for example, could lead to the creation of 'closed circles of Party functionaries and intellectuals'. Even though in Poland and the Balkans there were illegal parties whose position most closely resembled that of the Bolsheviks under Tsarism, argued Manuilsky, it would be wrong to establish 'general organisational principles for all the parties of the Comintern, especially those parties working in highly developed capitalist countries with large masses of workers and under more or less legal conditions of existence'.[57] Yet this is ultimately what occurred.

Piatnitsky also realised that significant differences existed between Russia and other countries whose communist parties were members of the Comintern. On the most basic level, workers in Europe and the United States did not necessarily live near their factory, as they often tended to do in Russia. Night-time meetings of the factory nuclei were therefore difficult because there were few late trains.[58] More significantly, in advanced capitalism, large, relatively autonomous trade unions existed side by side with workers' parties. As well, workers' parties had established themselves at the municipal level and in national parliaments. In Russia, a parliament of a sort existed only after 1905. Having pointed out these differences, Piatnitsky simply downplayed or ignored them. The experience of a few selected examples of factory nuclei in France and Germany, he asserted, 'has absolutely proved that these are not something peculiarly Russian, not adaptable to European and American conditions'.[59]

Yet over the next three years, in spite of Manuilsky's and Piatnitsky's stated intentions, the organisational schema of the Russian Bolsheviks became a dogma applicable to all parties, including those in highly developed capitalist countries.[60] Within this process, the conspiratorial heritage of the Bolsheviks was widely spread.

Following the Fifth Congress of the Comintern, the Organisation Department of the ECCI called two special 'organisation conferences' of the Comintern, the first in March 1925 and the second in February 1926. Both debated and reinforced the decision to base the structure of communist parties on the 'factory cell' basis. At the first conference Piatnitsky repeated his argument that because the young communist parties were organised on a local or residential basis, they were reproducing the methods of the Social Democratic parties and this led to a passive membership. The problem was greatest, he said, in parties which were illegal or semi-legal. The membership was divided into local groups, at the head of which was an elected or appointed functionary. Workers at a particular factory might be scattered through a number of local groups. 'Cases have occurred when communists unconsciously have acted against their fellow Party members, owing to the fact that they did not know each other', he said.[61]

The process of Bolshevisation – that is, the imposition of the Russian method of party organisation on all other Comintern parties – was not achieved without considerable resistance. At the Fifth Congress, Muna, a Czech delegate, had argued that the factory cell reorganisation assumed large factories existed in all countries. In Czechoslovakia, smaller enterprises prevailed, he said. The resolution on organisation effectively meant destroying existing local organisation.[62] In the United States a different problem existed. Before 'Bolshevisation' could proceed, the American Workers Party had to restructure itself from a federation of 19 communist groups based on national and language groups to a system of unified central and district committees.[63] As well, the Organisation

Department found out that only 40 per cent of the American communists were members of trade unions.[64] In his closing speech to the 1925 conference, Piatnitsky acknowledged that there had been 'sharp criticism' directed against him from the German party. Elsewhere it is clear that the German communists Ruth Fischer and Werner Scholem, the French communist leader Fernand Loriot and the Italian leader Amadeo Bordiga were part of a minority who opposed 'Bolshevisation'.[65]

In his report on the 1926 Organisation Conference to the Enlarged ECCI, Franz Dahlem noted that at the 1925 Organisation Conference there was still scepticism that a party structure based on factory nuclei was 'a Russian speciality'. By the second conference, he claimed, there were 'no longer any serious opponents' to the plan.[66]

The Bolshevisation campaign both predicted the need for more underground work and promoted a number of the lessons of the Russian underground tradition. The 'Theses on Bolshevisation of the Communist Parties' adopted by the Fifth ECCI Plenum in March–April 1925, contained an addendum on illegal work which was intended to remain secret.[67] It predicted that many legal parties might be forced to work underground in future and that every communist party 'must keep its whole technical apparatus for illegality in readiness'. However, in line with Bolshevik practice it urged that every party defend 'its legality to the bitter end'. Just as the Bolsheviks had learned in the period 1912–14, the ECCI urged every banned party to 'take advantage of every passing opportunity of conducting legal activity and for the extension of such activities'.

Strong echoes of post-1905 Bolshevik practice could also be heard in its warning that the discipline of an illegal party 'must be much more strict than that of the legal parties'. Democratic election could still be practised, but only because 'any unnecessary limitation to this democracy would cause the separation of the party from the masses, would make it pedantic and transform it into a group of conspirators'. The theses thus reinforce the central tenet of underground work that, paradoxically, having mass connections in a conspiratorial party is the key to its survival.

We have already seen that from 1923 to 1926 the Commission on Illegal Work assisted banned communist parties, particularly in the Baltic states, Poland and the Balkans by systematising the lessons from the Russian conspiratorial experience. In 1927 when Piatnitsky reviewed the results of the 'Bolshevisation' campaign, he argued that it helped the illegal parties survive under conditions of White Terror.

Only through the existence of these factory groups and our fractions in the trade unions can the fact be explained that in spite of the terror that our party is subjected to even in Poland proper, the majority of the Polish workers still follow the lead of our party which has no legal press, while the Polish Socialist Party has a press and enjoys the protection of the authorities.[68]

Italy was another case in which 'Bolshevisation' assisted the work of an illegal party, according to Piatnitsky. Although it lost three-quarters of its membership and was neutralised for a time after Mussolini's seizure of power, by 1927 the Italian Communist Party's work within and outside the unions had begun to recover.[69] Whether or not this was so, there is no doubt that conspiratorial methods very similar to those of the Bolsheviks were used in fascist Italy. Some years later at a 1930 conference of trade unions working illegally a leading communist trade unionist, 'Nicolletti' (Guiseppe Di Vittorio) explained that after the destruction of Catholic and reformist trade unions it was only possible to work within fascist unions.[70] Most trade union work took place in local factories although some interunion organisation existed. An illegal monthly publication of the General Confederation of Labour had a circulation of between 5,000 and 20,000 copies. Leaflets were left in toilets and hand delivered to the post boxes of workers at a factory. The most defiant and open form of leaflet distribution took place on May Day at factory gates. To do this, Nicolletti explained, they distributed the leaflets from cars which carried armed guards. On the Day of Anti-War action, 1 August 1929, they distributed leaflets from seven cars although many workers thought they must have had hundreds of cars because of the large number of factories covered in such a short time.

The Italian leader, Palmiro Togliatti ('Ercoli') put this practice into a more general strategic approach in his closing speech to the Thirteenth Plenum of the ECCI (December 1933).[71] By this time fascism was no longer an Italian phenomenon and the Plenum emphasised that going underground had to be combined with mass work. The transition to illegality, argued Togliatti, meant being organised in such a way as to be able to conduct mass work and lead mass struggles under any conditions. As part of this, he said, political work had to be carried out in all mass organisations, including fascist trade unions.

WESTERN COMMUNISTS AND ILLEGAL WORK

However, the application of 'Bolshevisation' to Western Europe, North America and Australia, where communist parties and trade unions were largely legal, was fraught with difficulties. In spite of earlier statements, the Comintern leadership, led on this question by Piatnitsky, imposed on all Comintern parties a 'Russian' form of organisation with all the earmarks of its conspiratorial heritage.

In the Russian experience, Piatnitsky argued, factories were 'the only places where workers could discuss their needs, the political situation of Russia and the tasks of the working class'.[72] Yet the fact was that in democratic countries the relative political freedom enjoyed by the working class only existed *outside* factories and work places. The factories were places of absolutism decreed by employers. This was even acknowledged in a later resolution of the Org. Department:

[I]n capitalist countries the factory nucleus can only work as an illegal organisation. Therefore its work and the work of every member of the factory nucleus must be conducted in a manner to keep any police agency in the factory as much as possible in the dark with regard to the Party membership of the workers ... That is why it is essential to observe essential conspirative rules in the work of the factory nucleus. This applies equally to countries with illegal or legal Communist Parties.[73]

By insisting that the basis for the whole communist party organisation must be the factory nuclei, Comintern leaders forced western communists to carry out much of their political work in a place where they were most vulnerable and, significantly, where they were forced to behave as an illegal group. They were naturally untrained in this technique, a point noted by the 1926 organisational conference, which criticised the serious defect that 'many factory nuclei have not yet learned to adopt the proper invisible methods of work which are conducive to constant and energetic activity on the part of the nucleus members and which save them from falling victims to the terror of the employers and governments ... [t]he employers do not miss such opportunities to clean out communists who have become known to them'.[74]

This imposition of underground methods on legal parties was seen by the Comintern to have a 'silver lining' in the sense that it would force communists to prepare for illegality by teaching them the methods of conspiratorial work. Dahlem noted this virtue in his report on the 1926 Organisation Conference to the Enlarged ECCI:

> Another experience gained through our reorganisation is that the nucleus organisation is the best communist organisation under illegal conditions. Even now, in legal times, our nuclei in the capitalist countries must work underground, carefully, skilfully, and we have seen in all our practical experience that under the compulsion of finding methods against the employers and the police, we are obtaining really good cadres of factory workers whom we know will come up to the scratch [sic] in our revolutionary fights. In the residential organisations, on the contrary, it was revealed that in times of civil war and illegality they are useless to a great extent.[75]

However, Piatnitsky's own analysis, replete with statistics gathered by the Organisation Department of the ECCI, showed that the construction of factory nuclei had major difficulties in countries where parties functioned legally. In the United States, Great Britain, Germany, Czechoslovakia and France factory groups were weak and concentrated in small factories. 'In Chicago out of the 24 groups, only 12, with 96 members, are in large factories ... [o]ut of 300 factory groups in New York, only 12 are in the metallurgical industry and four in the wood-working industry ... 159 (53 per cent) are in the tailoring industry.'[76]

In Britain, the most successful factory groups were based on coal mining communities. There, as in Tsarist Russia, workers lived and worked in the same district where life was centred around a single enterprise. In large factories employers organised espionage systems and communists, such as those in the Vickers and Armstrong enterprises, were routinely sacked. Piatnitsky commented that although the Communist Party of Great Britain was legal, its factory groups 'are nevertheless, compelled to work underground. Just as soon as the employers learn, through their spies in the factories, that any of the workers belong to the Communist Party, they discharge them'.[77]

On top of this, factory groups were not used as the basis for political campaigns partly because many workers preferred to do political work in a locality other than their work place. The 1925–6 Bolshevisation campaign had discouraged organisation based on residential groups and 'street groups' were a compromise. The Communist Party of the United States had 440 factory groups and 400 street groups, yet the former accounted for 26 per cent of the membership while the latter accounted for 60 per cent. In Germany, as well as the USA, many workers preferred to conduct their political work in local areas, and not at their factory. Piatnitsky was forced to conclude: 'Street groups never played any role in the organisational structure of the Communist Party of the Soviet Union. It is impossible to do without them abroad. Facts have proved this.'[78]

In spite of these self-imposed difficulties, the conspiratorial model was reinforced in the Comintern from 1927 onwards. In this year the Russian communists and the Comintern began an ultra-leftist political turn which became known as the 'Third Period'. In this period, it was claimed, capitalist stabilisation would end and the opponents of the Soviet Union in Europe and Great Britain would prepare to make war on the Soviet state. In May 1927 the Eighth Plenum of the ECCI urged that '[b]oth before the outbreak of war and in war-time the communist parties must work persistently to set up an illegal apparatus for the fight against war; they should not however confine themselves to these underground activities'.[79] A report prepared for the Sixth World Congress (1928) by the Organisation Department of the ECCI noted that one of the significant problems of its work was: 'Inadequate utilisation of the organising experience of the CPSU, especially of the experience with underground work, for which the need is steadily growing.'[80]

The Sixth World Congress, held from July to September 1928, deepened this orientation towards illegal work by invoking Lenin who argued that 'the only possible way of continuing revolutionary work after the outbreak of war is the creation of an illegal organisation'.[81] The resolution, 'The Struggle Against Imperialist War and the Tasks of the Communists', chastised the parties where an 'opportunist view prevails that the conduct of anti-war activity is the business only of the youth, or of a special organisation, while activity within the army is regarded as not being absolutely essential'.

Communist political work within the armed forces of Europe and the United States became one of the most secret and little understood aspects of the conspiratorial heritage and is worthy of detailed study on its own.

NOTES

1. 'On the Question of Illegal Work', *Communist International*, vol. 10, no. 23 (1 Dec. 1933).
2. Bertil Hessel, Introduction, *Theses, Resolutions and Manifestos of the First Four Congresses of the Third International*, xiii.
3. Ibid., xv.
4. Cited ibid., xxii.
5. Ibid., 92–7.
6. 'The Communist Party and Parliament', ibid., 104.
7. 'Statutes of the Communist International', ibid., 123–7.
8. 'Theses on the Fundamental Tasks of the Communist International', ibid., 139
9. Victor Serge, *What Everyone Should Know About State Repression* (trans. Judith White), New Park Publications, London, 1979. The section referred to was published in the *Bulletin Communiste* of 10, 17 and 24 November 1921. It subsequently appeared in revised form in 1926 as *Les Coulisses d'une surete generale. Ce que tout revolutionnaire devrait savoir sur la repression*, Faits et Documents, Libraire du Travail, Paris, 1926.
10. Ibid., 41.
11. Klehr, Haynes and Firsov, *The Secret World of American Communism*, 70.
12. 'The Organisational Structure of the Communist Parties, the Methods and Content of their Work: Theses' in *Theses, Resolutions and Manifestos*, 234–61.
13. Ibid., 259.
14. Ibid., 260–1
15. Keith Hitchins, *Rumania: 1866–1947*, Clarendon Press, Oxford, 1994, 399–400.
16. Aleksa Djilas, *The Contested Country: Yugoslav Unity and Communist Revolution, 1919–1953*, Harvard University Press, Cambridge, MA, 1991, 63–4.
17. Bennett Kovrig, *Communism in Hungary: from Kun to Kadar*, Hoover Institution Press, Stanford, 1979, 74–82.
18. Nissan Oren, *Revolution Administered, Agrarianism and Communism in Bulgaria*, Johns Hopkins University Press, Baltimore, 1973, 9–11, 24–5.
19. *Theses, Resolutions and Manifestos*, 364.
20. The papers of the Commission on Illegal Work consist of 17 individual files (*delo*) at RTsKhIDNI, 495-27-(1-17). The files are neither systematic nor complete, like many Comintern files from the period of the early 1920s. The founding of the Commission, its composition and intended functions ('Resolution on Illegal Work', undated) are found in *delo* 2, along with 'Instruction on the Work of the Illegal Commission', signed by Zinoviev and Radek on 25 August 1923.
21. The biographies of members of the Commission are based on Lazitch and Drachkovitch, *Biographical Dictionary of the Comintern*, 311–12. Archivists at the RTsKhIDNI declined to provide a number of biographies, referring this researcher to the Lazitch text, which they said was reliable and which they used themselves.
22. A report on the work of the Org. Department in 1924, giving personnel and responsibilities, is found at RTsKhIDNI, 495-25-5. Files relating to Piatnitsky in the RTsKhIDNI were not available for scholarly research at the time of research for this book (1996–7). It was widely believed that these files, as well as those on the OMS, have been withheld for purging of material related to Soviet intelligence activities and personnel.
23. Andrew and Gordievsky, *KGB*, 56.
24. RTsKhIDNI, 495-18-254.
25. RTsKhIDNI, 495-27-2.
26. Letter from Mitskevich–Kapsukas to Presidium, 28 February 1923, RTsKhIDNI, 495-27-3.
27. This undated document, 'Resolution on Illegal Work' is found in RTsKhIDNI, 495-27-2.
28. Ibid.
29. 'Instructions on the Work of the Yugoslav Communist Party', 5 March 1923, RTsKhIDNI, 495-27-1.
30. 'Instruction on the Work of the Illegal Commission', RTsKhIDNI, 495-27-2.

31. RTsKhIDNI, 495-27-2.
32.. RTsKhIDNI, 495-27-1.
33. See Protocol 16 of the Org Buro, 10 April 1923, RTsKhIDNI, 495-27-3.
34. RTsKhIDNI, 495-27-1.
35. *Communist International*, no. 7 (Dec 1924–Jan. 1925), 57.
36. 'Plan of Work of Commission', 19 November 1924, RTsKhIDNI, 495-27-1.
37. See an undated document on the plan for the work of the Illegal Commission, which speaks about the use of enlarged ECCI meetings. The file covers 1922–24. RTsKhIDNI, 495-27-3.
38. There is no record of the deliberations of this meeting, though this cannot be taken to mean that such a major meeting did not take place. The call for such a meeting is recorded in the minutes of a Commission meeting on 13 January 1925. RTsKhIDNI, 495-27-1.
39. Lazitch with Drachkovitch, 162.
40. *Rules for Party Conspiratorial Work*, RTsKhIDNI, 495-27-2.
41. Ibid.
42. Ibid.
43. Piatnitsky, *Memoirs of a Bolshevik*, 2.
44. No formal mention of the disbandment of the Commission exists in any of the protocols of the Organisation Department; however, in 495-20-955 there is evidence that conspiratorial matters are being handled by the Department's Uzkaya (Narrow or Select) Commission, headed by Piatnitsky. On the structure of the Org. Dept in 1927, see 495-25-110.
45. Letter dated 23 September 1933, RTsKhIDNI, 495-25-231.
46. This can be simply worked out from statistics given in the *The Communist International: Between the Fifth and Sixth Congresses, 1924–28*, Dorrit Press, London, 1928. The Secretariat and Politsecretariat discussed 1,459 questions, of which 'questions of parallel organisations' constituted 92 items.
47. The report of two OMS workers in China in 1927–31 has been made available to this writer by their son, Dimitri Moiseenko. The document, written by Yakov Rudnik, is closed to researchers. 'The Rudnik Report' is found at RTsKhIDNI, 579-1-151. Krivitsky contradicts this but the Rudnik Report is likely to be more accurate.
48. This description is based on the Rudnik Report.
49. Aino Kuusinen, *The Rings of Destiny: Inside Soviet Russia from Lenin to Brezhnev*, William Morrow and Company, New York, 1974, 40.
50. Mikhail Narinsky and Jurgen Rojahn, *Centre and Periphery: the History of the Comintern in the Light of New Documents*, International Institute of Social History, Amsterdam, 1996.
51. Krivitsky, *I Was Stalin's Agent*, 69–70.
52. Kevin McDermott, 'Stalinist Terror in the Comintern: New Perspectives', *Journal of Contemporary History*, vol. 30 (1995), 121–2.
53. O. Piatnitsky, 'Organisational Problems of Comintern Sections', *Communist International*, no. 4 (1924) 99–104.
54. Ibid., 100.
55. See Dahlem's report to the Enlarged ECCI, *International Press Correspondence* (hereafter, *InPreCorr*), vol. 6, no. 28 (15 April 1926).
56. 'Resolution on Reorganisation of the Party on the Basis of Shop Nuclei', *Communist International*, no. 7 (Dec. 1924–Jan. 1925).
57. D. Manuilsky, 'Bolshevisation of the Parties', *Communist International*, no. 10 (1925), 46–50.
58. O. Piatnitsky, 'Party Construction in the Sections of the Communist International', *InPreCorr*, 5 February 1925.
59. Ibid., 126–8.
60. This is also the conclusion of a recent study of Comintern archives. Jakov Drabkin, 'The Idea of the World Revolution and its Transformation', in Narinsky and Rojahn, *Centre and Periphery*.
61. O. Piatnitsky, 'Conference of the Sections of the Comintern on Organisation', *Communist International*, no. 11 (1925), 23–4.

62. *Les Questions d'Organisation au Veme Congres de l'IC.* Libraire de L'Humanite, Paris, 1925, 13.
63. O. Piatnitsky, 'Achievements and Immediate Tasks in Organisation', *Communist International*, 30 May 1927, 152.
64. O. Piatnitsky, 'Achievements and Tasks in Factory and Trade Union Work', *Communist International*, 15 June 1927, 178.
65. 'Report on the Organisation Conference' (Comrade Dahlem), *InPreCorr*, 15 April 1926.
66. Ibid.
67. The addendum, accidentally published by the British Communist Party, was published in Jane Degras (ed.), *The Communist International, 1919–1943*, Oxford University Press, Oxford and London, 1960, vol. II, 199–200. The existence of this addendum can now be confirmed and its original wording in German found in the archives of the Communist International at RTsKhIDNI, 495-163-243 at pages 215–216. For convenience I have quoted the Degras version.
68. Piatnitsky, 'Achievements and Immediate Tasks in Organisation', 152ff.
69. Ibid., 152–3.
70. 'Conference of representatives from countries with illegal or semi-legal trade unions'. RTsKhIDNI, 534-2-113.
71. Closing speech by Ercoli at the 25th sitting of the 13th Plenum (in French), RTsKhIDNI, 495-171-239.
72. Piatnitsky, 'Party Construction in the Sections of the Communist International'.
73. 'Letter from the Org-Dept of the ECCI Confirmed by the Polit-Secretariat', *InPreCorr*, 31 December 1930.
74. 'Decisions of the Second Org. Conference of Sections of the CI', *InPreCorr*, 5 May 1926.
75. 'Report on the Organisation Conference'.
76. Piatnitsky, 'Achievements and Tasks in Factory and Trade Union Work', 176.
77. Ibid., 174.
78. Ibid.
79. *InPreCorr*, 10 June 1927.
80. *The Communist International: Between the Fifth and Sixth World Congresses, 1924–28*, Dorrit Press, London 1928, 34.
81. 'The Struggle Against Imperialist War and the Tasks of the Communists', *InPreCorr*, 28 November 1928, 1587.

CHAPTER THREE

Comintern's Underground in Western Military Forces

It is obvious that any secret treaties, Government proposals and military orders which by one means or another fall into the hands of Communist Party organisations must be published without delay ...

Communist International[1]

In the early hours of Tuesday 15 September 1931 a large part of the British Atlantic Fleet was riding at anchor in Cromarty Firth, on the east coast of Scotland, near the town of Invergordon.[2] The fleet commander had planned to begin a series of exercises in the open sea that day. At 0600 hours, the normal hour for the naval ratings to 'fall in' and begin the day's work, there was confusion on many ships. At 0630 the battle cruiser *Repulse* sailed but the ships meant to follow her, the *Valiant*, *Nelson*, *Hood* and *Rodney* did not move. On many of the ships, the ratings refused to carry out normal work. A mutiny, or at least an unusual strike, had broken out on board the ships of Her Britannic Majesty.

The previous Sunday morning the ships' officers had posted a notice from the Board of Admiralty announcing that the pay of many naval ratings, the 'proletariat' of the battleships and cruisers, would be cut by up to one-quarter. The notice shocked the ratings, who were proud to serve the empire but who also supported families. On the Sunday and Monday afternoons crowds of ratings held meetings at the shore canteen and a mood of protest grew. The culmination of the protest was a refusal to perform normal duties on the following morning, when the fleet intended to sail. The protest shocked the Admiralty and was quickly reported in the press, which, a fortnight earlier, had reported a mutiny in the Chilean fleet which was violently suppressed. In the case of the 'Invergordon mutiny' the protest lasted 36 hours and eventually the fleet sailed without bloodshed.

The Comintern saw the Invergordon revolt as a 'tremendous indication of the growing threatening clouds of the social thunderstorm which menaces the bourgeoisie of Britain and of the whole world'.[3] The ECCI must surely have also seen it as a tremendous vindication of its strategy of penetration of the military forces of capitalist powers. This strategy had scarcely been examined when the archives of the old Soviet Union were open. It was also linked to some of the first significant charges of espionage in political and diplomatic establishments in the West.

By the time of the Sixth Congress of the Comintern, in the summer of 1928, the leadership of the Russian Communist Party believed that war against the Soviet Union was being planned and could break out in the space of a few years. This was part of a broader political prediction that the tempo of world revolution, which had ebbed since 1923, was now on a rapid up-swing. The belief in the likelihood of war against the Soviet Union caused the Comintern leadership to emphasise what it called 'anti-militarist work'. This meant communist parties world-wide stepping up their propaganda, which argued that the imperialist nations were leading the world's working class to yet another war, bloodier than the last. Less publicly, 'anti-militarist work' meant that communist political work within the armed forces, which had theoretically been a requirement since 1921, was begun in earnest. At the beginning anti-militarist work had two justifications. First was the defence of the Soviet Union through the subversion of the armed forces of likely enemies, while a secondary one was the need for any local revolution to neutralise military forces which might crush an otherwise successful revolution. In order to conduct anti-militarist work, communists all over the world drew on the experiences of underground Bolshevik political work in the Tsarist army and navy.

The Russian Social Democratic Labour Party began its political work within the armed forces in 1902–3, although it was only in the context of the 1905 revolution that an actual organisation could be formed.[4] Lenin attached great significance to the Kronstadt sailors' revolt which had helped spark the 1905 revolution and urged 'special attention to the army' with the aim of bringing soldiers and sailors to the workers' side.[5] In large garrison towns such as Reval, Riga, Batum, Odessa,

Warsaw and Kronstadt as well as Moscow and St Petersburg, party organisations circulated up to 20 illegal news sheets in the period 1905–7. While the illegal nuclei within most garrisons was small, in Kronstadt and Sebastopol the organisation numbered in the hundreds. Nor were the Bolsheviks the only political party to undertake such work. The Social Revolutionaries also conducted 'military work'.[6]

During and after the 1905 revolution over 50 city committees of the Social Democrats created special auxiliary bodies for work within the armed forces.[7] These 'Military Organisations' were 'highly conspiratorial' and usually made up of several propagandists from the committee and three or four Social Democratic soldiers. They published leaflets and held meetings though it is hard to gauge their effect, considering many soldier-peasants could not read.

During 1917 support for the Bolsheviks within the Russian army, largely based on their opposition to the war and support for land distribution, was very significant in the success of the October revolution. This experience led the Russian leadership to insist that communist work within the military forces must be a key condition for admission to the Communist International. Of the 21 conditions designed to differentiate between the revolutionary and reformist wings of social democracy, condition 4 presented by Trotsky at the Comintern's Second Congress in July 1920 read:

> The duty of propagating Communist ideas includes the special obligation of forceful and systematic propaganda in the army. Where this agitation is interrupted by emergency laws it must be continued illegally. Refusal to carry out such work would be tantamount to a betrayal of revolutionary duty and would be incompatible with membership of the Communist International.[8]

One of the early leaders of the Comintern, the Franco-Russian revolutionary Victor Serge, when discussing the falseness and limitations of bourgeois legality noted: '[w]hat is more, legality in the most "advanced" capitalist democracies has limits which the proletariat cannot respect without condemning itself to defeat. Propaganda in the army, a vital necessity is not legally tolerated. Without the defection of at least a part of the army, there is no victorious revolution. This is the law of history.'[9]

The theme of anti-militarist work was revived after the Eighth Plenum of the ECCI in May 1927. This plenum warned of the dangers of a new war against Soviet Russia and repeated Lenin's slogans of 1917 for 'the defeat of one's own bourgeois government' and for the revolutionaries to 'turn the imperialist war into a civil war'.[10] As a consequence, 'the communist parties must work persistently to set up an illegal apparatus for the fight against war' and there had to be 'more intense work in the army and navy'.[11]

By 1928 the ECCI estimated that the tempo of revolution, stabilised since 1923, was reviving. It predicted war against the Soviet Union as well as a major economic crisis in the capitalist world. In such a context, which presaged new revolutionary outbursts, preparing parties for underground political work and for work within military forces became even more pressing.

The Sixth World Congress of the Communist International in 1928 saw the elevation and codification of this position within the 'Program of the Communist International', a major document which argued:

> The Communist International must pay particularly great attention to methodical preparation of the struggle against the danger of imperialist war. Ruthless exposure of social-chauvinism, social imperialism, and pacifist verbiage which merely veil the plans of the bourgeoisie; propaganda for the Communist International's principal slogans; untiring organisational work to accomplish these tasks, for which the combination of legal and illegal methods of work is absolutely essential; systematic work in the army and navy – these must be the communist parties' activities in connection with the war danger.[12]

But this resolution was by no means the complete picture of clandestine political work in the military forces. A separate resolution on anti-militarist work was passed but deliberately never published. In the congress session which discussed the draft of this resolution, the War Commission, its chairman the English communist Tom Bell, said it was unlikely to be published mainly because of its length but also because 'there are sections of the document to be omitted for conspirative reasons'.[13]

Quoting Lenin, Bell also made the point that the onset of war would mean the legal organisations of the workers would disappear and that in order to continue this anti-war struggle it was necessary to have an illegal apparatus.[14] In the same session Manuilsky underlined the need for illegal organisations for anti-war work and praised the French party for having done the best work of all parties inside the army, largely through the Young Communist League.

In the USA work within the armed forces had also been developed before the Sixth Congress. A delegate from the CPUSA, Comrade Harvey, reported:

We have a joint anti-militarist department of the League and the Party whose main work is in the army and the navy. In the past we had the danger that almost all attention was given to work in the reserve forces of the ex-Servicemen. This work is still being continued but we have a subcommittee of the youth which pays attention mainly to work among the students and citizens Military Training camps ... both of these subcommittees are supervised by the central apparatus ... but at the same time the main work of the apparatus deals with the illegal work within the regular army and navy.[15]

Another report on the work of the CPUSA noted that in December 1927 the party had 'contacts' on the USS *New Mexico* and USS *Oklahoma* as well as in army units in New York, New Jersey and Texas. That same month members of the Young Workers (Communist) League joined the army for service in the Panama Canal Zone.[16] Work in the Citizens Military Training Corps (CMTC) was the centre of anti-militarist work by the YCL, but here the young communists found that their initial demands for 'better food and conditions' had little effect since the military food was better than most young workers were used to.[17]

The subsequent work of the communist parties within the armed forces during the 1930s was founded on a key resolution passed at the Sixth Congress.[18] Prepared by the 'Anti-Militarist sub-committee' of the War Commission the resolution, 'The Instruction on work within the armed forces' stated bluntly: '[the] struggle against the imperialist war is impossible without permanently organised and systematic work inside the armed forces of the capitalist countries, with the aim of winning the soldiers and sailors to our slogans and disorganizing and disintegrating the military system of the capitalist countries. Such work is particularly an indispensable premise for the transformation of the imperialist war into a civil war.' Such work, it noted, was part of the 21 conditions for admission of parties to the Communist International but 'must now in the period of the war danger, be strengthened tremendously and with greatest energy. The outcome of a decisive struggle for power depends to a very great extent upon how successful is "the struggle for the army". In order to create the premises for the success of this struggle, there is necessary a constant, systematic work of education and organisation among the armed forces.'

The substance of the resolution, however, concerned not mere revolutionary slogans but practical guidelines on how to build an illegal apparatus within the armed forces that was capable of withstanding savage repression with the minimum of loss, and how to build a similar civilian support apparatus outside. 'All too often this work is looked upon as something mystical and criminal, something that is outside of regular party work, and even called military espionage or conspiracy', it stated. The key to military activity was the construction of a special party apparatus, inside the military and separate from the party.

> Only systematic work gives serious results. This is impossible how-ever without a special apparatus because: first, the specific conditions in this work presuppose a certain specialisation; thirdly [sic] this work even where the Party is legal must be carried on illegally at least to a great extent; it demands a certain organisational isolation from the rest of the Party apparatus; and fourthly, the work necessary for the creation of an illegal organisation inside the army will be greatly facilitated through a special apparatus.[19]

The organisation within the armed forces sometimes simply revolved around a single person but generally should comprise a 'nucleus' of three to five soldiers or sailors at most. Following Lenin's prescriptions for the Bolshevik Party (examined in chapter 1) these nuclei were structured vertically rather than horizontally. 'The individual nuclei have no direct contact with each other. They are connected only with the body standing immediately above them through their leaders. The co-ordination of the work in the army is carried on far more by the auxiliary apparatus outside the army.' As well as the nucleus, the directive also called for a periphery of 'special groups of sympathisers' which should be built around the various nuclei.

This 'civilian apparatus' had to be, from the beginning, 'strictly conspirative'. This involved 'painstaking selection of members' although, interestingly, it could also include 'such non-party soldiers as have proven themselves by their work to be real Communists'. Nor were all party and YCL members in the army necessarily members of the nuclei. Some might be too well known, others might have a drinking problem, for example. Conspiratorial rules meant that all written correspondence had to be kept to an absolute minimum and code used for transmitting addresses. 'In every case where mutually unacquainted comrades are put in touch with each other ... there absolutely must be an inconspicuous Password arranged.'[20]

As with parties operating under strict rules of conspiracy, there was no question of internal democracy in the military apparatus.

> There can be no talk about the eligibility of comrades for election to one kind of work or another inside the army. The only correct method of assigning comrades for any sort of this work is *appointment from above* [original emphasis] on the basis of personal qualifications. The actual members of the nucleus must remain inconspicuous and must carry on oral agitation only under extreme caution. For oral agitation ... there must be other comrades drawn in – *who do not participate in the regular nucleus work.* (original emphasis)

The key to winning support in the military forces was the understanding and articulation of the needs of the rank and file soldiers and sailors. A programme of demands had to be formulated which 'should contain the real demands of the soldiers ... not a single point should be adopted in the programme without an exact investigation of its tenability from the point of view of the actual needs of the soldiers under the given conditions'.[21] The publications of the military cells had to be 'popular and digestible' and not necessarily always be in party's name. These elaborate precautions, the directive stated, were to apply in times of peace, but the ultimate goal after war broke out was to 'turn the imperialist war into the civil war' and to help create a revolutionary situation.

Much of this was repeated in a book, *Armed Insurrection*, published in 1928 in German and in 1931 in French.[22] Commissioned in 1928 by Piatnitsky, the book was a joint product of the Comintern and the Soviet Red Army, particularly its intelligence section, part-written by senior Red Army officer, Joseph Unschlicht.[23] It reinforced the crucial strategic point that military work was primarily political work. 'Upon the degree of disaffection within a bourgeois army depends in great measure the proletariat's chance of overthrowing the bourgeoisie and smashing bourgeois state power.'[24] The history of all revolutions, said *Armed Insurrection*, showed that an army and police force with modern equipment and good commanders were capable of defeating a revolution, even if all other conditions were favourable. The answer was not superior material force but the creation of a political ferment inside the armed forces which neutralised their material superiority. The book used the bloody defeat of the Communist Party of China (CPC) in 1927 as an example. The crucial weakness of the CPC was that it 'never seriously faced up to the fact that its partner was bound, sooner or later, to betray it. Thus it never carried out any agitational work in the army other than what was strictly legal and forebore to organise clandestine cells. This is why the Kuomintang, when it passed over to the camp of counter-revolution, had no difficulty in expelling all communists from the army, and in thereby depriving the Party of all influence of a concrete and organised kind.'[25]

Armed Insurrection recounted the history of Bolshevik work in the Tsarist army and examined the failed revolutions in Estonia (1924) and Germany (1923). For the decade of the 1930s, the book was in fact a manual for Comintern political work within the military forces of Britain, France, the USA, Germany, Japan and other potentially hostile countries.

WORK WITHIN THE BRITISH ARMY AND NAVY

The Communist Party of Great Britain conducted sporadic work directed towards the armed forces throughout the 1920s. This was largely propagandistic in nature, with leaflets and editorials in the *Workers Weekly* urging troops not to fire on fellow workers. In 1925, 12 leaders of the CPGB were jailed for conspiring to publish seditious libels and inciting mutiny in the armed forces.[26] Between 1925 and 1929 several soldiers from army units at Aldershot were removed for 'communistic activities'.[27]

Anti-militarist work in the armies and navies of the West intensified after the Sixth Congress. Of particular concern to the Comintern leadership was the British army and navy, in view of their global role in projecting imperial power. In 1928 the CPGB published a programme for soldiers and in 1929 it began publishing the *Soldiers' Voice*, a newsletter directed at the army.[28] But the initial work was weak and was regularly criticised for its inadequacy by both the ECCI and by the Communist Youth International, KIM (Kommunisticheskii Internatsional Molodezhi). KIM and its sections in individual countries played a significant role in anti-militarist work because of the widespread military recruitment and conscription of teenagers and young men.

In April 1929 KIM reproached the CPGB and its Young Communist League for their neglect of anti-militarist work since the Sixth Congress and urged them to 'resume work among the armed forces' and to produce 'barrack or ship publications written by the soldiers themselves'.[29] To remedy the problem KIM suggested that the British YCL send a cadre to KIM to study anti-militarist work. This formed part of a plan by KIM for special courses in Germany, France, Czechoslovakia, Sweden, Poland and Greece with the aim of producing functionaries and instructors. Among other things, these courses would teach 'the main rules of conspiracy'.[30]

At the Tenth Plenum of the ECCI in July 1929, the work of the British party in the army and navy became a matter of sharp argument. A British delegate, Arthur Horner, reported that 'we have for the first time been really attempting to enter the barracks and the towns where soldiers are concentrated such as Aldershot and towns where sailors from the navy are gathered together such as Chatham'. Leaflets and meetings were received 'very favourably by large numbers of the rank and file' but there was 'strong intervention' by officers and police.[31] However, Comintern expert on anti-militarist work, Boris Vasilyev, regarded the performance of the CPGB as poor. The CPGB General Secretary, Harry Pollitt, replied tartly that 'preparations are in hand for distribution of our literature in the naval ports of Portsmouth, Devonport and Chatham and amongst soldiers in the barracks in Woolwich, Aldershot and other barrack towns … When comrade Vasilyev tells the Plenum that the anti-military work has been closed down, Comrade Vasilyev does not know what he is talking about. That work is going on.'

At the same plenum by contrast, the delegate of the French Communist Party, Pierre Semard, reported that anti-militarist work by the PCF had precipitated a number of incidents including demonstrations in barracks, refusal by soldiers to exercise or to eat and mass reporting on sick parade. Another PCF delegate, Henri Barbe, noted that there had been 57 such demonstrations in the previous two months. Until 1929, Semard said, publications aimed at soldiers and sailors had been legal but they were now banned. The main publication of the PCF, *La Caserne* (The Barracks), was a monthly with a print run of 20–22,000.[32] In 1930, the ECCI was told, the number of demonstrations of French military personnel inspired by the PCF had risen.[33] Sailors from the cruisers *Paris* and *Provence* had demonstrated in Algiers while in

Toulon imprisoned sailors had revolted and had been released after solidarity protests from other sailors and workers. Whereas earlier demonstrations concentrated on demands over food, more recent protests had included slogans hailing the Soviet Union, claimed Barbe at the Eleventh Plenum. Apart from *La Caserne*, some 40 other bulletins based on particular barracks or ships were also produced for short periods.

The criticism by the ECCI and KIM spurred the CPGB into planning anti-militarist work on a larger scale. In May 1930 several British communists were arrested for their work among the military, including two in Wales who were charged under the Incitement to Mutiny Act.[34] They had given out leaflets hidden inside envelopes marked 'Lee's tip for the Derby' and both received long prison terms. At the Aldershot barracks a communist who had spent many years in the army had given out leaflets urging soldiers not to attack Indian workers. He too was arrested and charged with incitement to mutiny. When the CPGB organ, the *Daily Worker*, attacked the verdict its publishers were sentenced to prison terms.[35] In May 1931 one of the future leaders of the CPGB, John Gollan, was charged with incitement to mutiny for handing out copies of the *Soldiers' Voice* during an anti-recruitment campaign and was sentenced to six months' jail.[36]

This determined anti-militarist work preceded the Invergordon naval revolt and shaped the exaggerated estimation of the revolt by the Comintern. Though there was no direct communist involvement in the revolt, communists were involved in agitation about the issue which sparked it.

On 1 August 1931 the report of an inquiry on cost cutting, set up by the British government, was made public.[37] It recommended pay cuts for naval ratings and in the following weeks the cabinet decided to endorse the recommendation. At Chatham during Navy Week the Young Communist League held a public meeting attended by ratings in uniform. Harry Pollitt addressed the rally, which was disrupted when a naval patrol cleared away the uniformed men in the audience. Elsewhere naval ratings discussed among themselves the consequences of such pay cuts on their families.[38]

On the evening of Saturday 12 September the government announced that in response to the report, the pay of ratings would be cut by 25 per cent.[39] At Invergordon where the Atlantic Fleet were moored, the ratings became angry and spontaneous meetings occurred in the Royal Naval Canteen and on a local sports field. By the last meeting, the

1. Staff of the Anglo-American Secretariat of the Comintern at work during the Fourth Congress, 1922. (CPGB Collection, National Museum of Labour History.)

2. Front page of rare manual for underground political work, 'The Rules for Party Conspirational Work', published in 1925. Similar rules were used by the Russian intelligence services. (Comintern Archives.)

3. The opening of the Second Congress of the Communist International, 1920. (National Museum of Labour History.)

4. Earl Browder in China, *c.* 1927, led underground trade union work while posing as a businessman.

5. Jakov Rudnik, posed as M. Hilaire Noulens language teacher, but was the OMS worker for Comintern's Far Eastern Bureau in Shanghai, in 1931. (Shanghai Municipal Police files.)

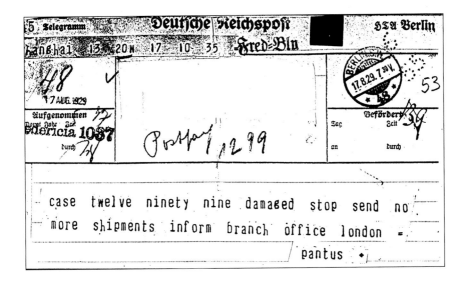

case twelve ninety nine damaged stop send no
more shipments inform branch office london =
pantus

6. Coded cables. The first warns that the authorities know that PO Box 1299 is used by the underground apparatus, the second uses the language of commerce to describe political work. (Comintern Archives.)

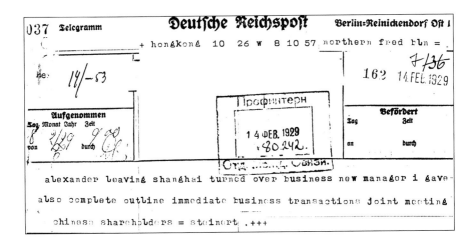

alexander leaving shanghai turned over business new manager i gave
also complete outline immediate business transactions joint meeting
chinese shareholders = steinert .+++

7. Welsh miners' leader Arthur Horner (left) advised Comintern of work in the armed forces in 1929. George Hardy (right) worked illegally in Shanghai with the Chinese Communist Party. (National Museum of Labour History.)

8. Asian and Australian delegates at the Fourth Congress of Comintern in 1922. Later the Pan Pacific Trade Union Secretariat united US, British, Chinese and Australian trade unionists to build underground trade unions.

In Australia, as in Britain, the traditions of Navy discipline are being shattered by technical mutiny, and the hand of the Communist agitator is suspected.

9. Communist work with Western navies began after 1929. A 1931 revolt by Australian sailors prompted this cartoon in *Smith's Weekly*. (Mitchell Library.)

10. Harry Pollitt defended British underground work in the army against Comintern criticism that it was inadequate. Seen here addressing the British Battalion during the Spanish civil war. (National Museum of Labour History.)

11. Underground communists led the biggest section of the Australian Labor
Party in 1939–40. After a split the left-dominated State Labor Party
merged with the Australian Communist Party. (Mitchell Library.)

12. Jack Hughes (right) who was an undercover member of the communist party while
rising to lead the New South Wales branch of the Labor Party. With him is Lance
Sharkey, secretary of the Communist Party of Australia. (Australian Security
Intelligence Organisation.)

13. Osip Piatnitsky, a key figure in the pre-revolutionary Bolshevik illegal apparatus, he headed Comintern underground work until the mid 1930s.

14. One of several false passports carried by OMS worker Jakov Rudnik, who was arrested after a lapse in conspirational rules which also saw Vietnamese communist Ho Chi Minh arrested. (Shanghai Municipal Police files.)

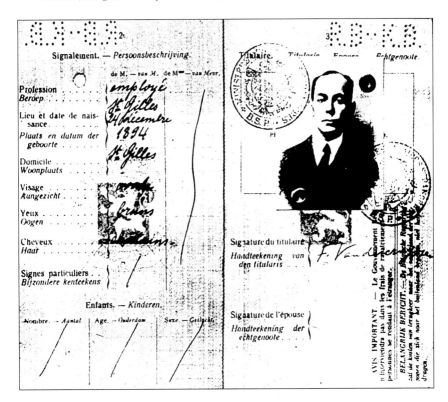

15. American codebreakers unravel a message from Moscow warning KGB resident Semyen Makarov that he is breaching conspirational rules. Such rules were designed to hide the identity of Soviet intelligence workers from their fellow embassy staffers. (US National Security Agency.)

BRIDE
TOP SECRET

USSR   Ref No: S/NBF/T262
                              Issued: '25/11/1952
                              Copy No: 202

        MOSCOW CRITICISES "EFIM" FOR LAX
        OBSERVATION OF SECURITY RULES.

From: MOSCOW

To: CANBERRA   30 May 1946
No.:   121

To EFIM.
            We have received information which shows that
lately you have begun to pay less attention to matters
concerning the observation of security [KONSPIRATsIYa [Sum]
rules in the presence of members of the Soviet [i] collective],
and without considering your position in the line of cover
[LINIYa PRIKRYTIYa] you frequently exceed your rights.
In particular the Soviet [a] collective is struck by
your unpunctuality in coming to work, unwarranted absence
during working hours on journeys to distant towns without
[having][a] as grounds for them such reasons as would be
convincing to the other employees and so on. You make
sharp remarks to colleagues who warn you about this.
It has been stated that you do not always use information
about individual members of the Soviet [i] collective
properly and thereby place people who give you the
information in an awkward position. Within the collective
guesses are made about the reason for your privileged
position .

                              [Continued overleaf]

Distribution

16. A surveillance photo of Wal Clayton, who headed the underground work of the Australian Communist Party and was later recruited to work for Soviet Intelligence in 1945. (National Archives of Australia.)

ratings had, amid some confusion, decided to refuse to work the next morning when the fleet was due to sail. At 0600 hours the following day the ship's company assembled on the cruiser *York* but by 0800 hours most had begun to hold a meeting on the forecastle. On the battleship *Rodney* only 75 men assembled at 0600 while on the *Valiant* hardly any sailors 'fell in' at that hour.[40] The response of the ratings was tentative but by mid-morning most rebels had assembled on the forecastle of their ships and had begun to spur each other on with cheering. On the flagship *Nelson*, sailors sat on the anchor cable and made it impossible to weigh anchor without using force. On the cruiser *Norfolk*, one of the leaders of the revolt, Len Wincott, who later joined the British Communist Party, drew up a letter to the Lords of the Admiralty to 'implore them to amend the drastic cuts in pay'.[41] By Wednesday some assurances had been given by the Admiralty to investigate cases of hardship and by midnight the Invergordon revolt was over and the Atlantic fleet was sailing or preparing to sail to home ports.

For all its drama and historic significance, the Invergordon revolt was largely spontaneous. While acknowledging the efforts of the CPGB, Carew demonstrates that the ratings' own study of the report and the examples of threatened strikes by police and teachers laid the basis of the mutiny, not any agitation by the CPGB.[42] Divine also concludes that there was no outside interference.

The ECCI, however, saw the Invergordon mutiny as immensely significant, partly based on the exaggerated accounts in British newspapers. An article in the *Communist International* described the Invergordon sailors as holding a meeting at which the Red Flag was sung, though this was false.[43] It pointed to previous unrest in the fleet, often due to bad food and brutal discipline. Invergordon was 'an event of world importance' and 'a barometer indicating the storm over England' and the 'social thunderstorm which menaces the bourgeoisie over Britain'. Attempts by the First Lord of the Admiralty, Sir Austen Chamberlain, to downplay the revolt and treat it with lenience should not be believed. 'The English bourgeoisie is always prepared to drown the sailors' movement in blood but it knows that this would start a tremendous explosion in England', it concluded.

The sailors' revolt led to a renewed round of activity within the armed forces which is reflected in CPGB plans for such work now available among the archives of the Comintern. The overall objective was 'the decomposition of the British Imperialist Army and Navy'.[44]

The structure of its 'AM' [anti-militarist] work closely followed Comintern directions:

> The individual cells, the individual members of the local AM apparatus may, under no circumstances be in direct contact with the central apparatus. Connection from step to step and grade to grade must [be] of such character as will prevent the blowing up of the whole apparatus. In Britain especially, we must take into account the existence of a very good Intelligence Service by the Bourgeoisie.[45]

The CPGB's initial plan was to contact sailors and soldiers while they were on their traditional leave period in December–January 1931/2, but this initially failed. Another attempt which began in the first half of 1932 concentrated on strengthening CPGB presence in the ports of Plymouth, Chatham and Southampton and at the military base at Aldershot. A leader of the Invergordon revolt, Len Wincott, who by then had put his name to a pamphlet, *The Spirit of Invergordon*, was one of a number of speakers at meetings held there.

By 1933 the CPGB had some success in AM work. Regular soldiers' newsletters were printed and at Catterick a group of soldiers formed a small cell. 'Certain progress can be recorded in the work among the sailors at Portsmouth and Chatham', the party reported to the Comintern.[46] This was due to an overall strengthening of the CPGB in these areas and, as a result, 'we have been able to draw a few more people into our apparatus and also to get a good deal of work carried out among the sailors' relatives'. While nuclei were formed for a time among soldiers and sailors, the CPGB's AM work largely consisted of identifying the relatives of sailors and soldiers and directing anti-war propaganda to them. The work was made more difficult because of a police spy in the CPGB's south Wales organisation. This led to a police raid on a leading communist at whose home 'they found ... a letter dealing with AM work which he must have had in his possession over nine months. Apparently he omitted to burn it, a piece of carelessness which cost himself and the party dear.' In 1934 the British parliament passed the Incitement to Disaffection Act, aimed at more effectively controlling pacifist and left-wing propaganda directed at the military forces.

The Comintern's determination for its sections to penetrate the military forces of Britain, France and the USA was not limited to those countries alone. Both in Germany and Japan, the local communist parties conducted anti-militarist work. But in the case of Germany after 1933, there was little that the remnants of the German Communist Party could do. So savage and efficient was the terror and so damaging was the split between the Social Democrats and communists that while the Comintern prescribed methods of conspiratorial work, it was to no avail.[47]

The Japanese Communist Party was weak and inexperienced but conducted some work within the Japanese army aimed at demoralising soldiers and undermining Japan's attack on China in 1932–4. Their 'defeatist' slogans were aimed at 'disorganising the rapacious war; [and] should be a call to the soldiers to return home'.[48] In September 1932, the Japanese Communist Party began to publish the *Soldiers' Friend*, an illegal newsletter within the army, and later a similar paper within the navy. These papers attacked the low pay, brutal discipline and other discontents generated within the Japanese army. So determined was the Japanese Communist Party that its method of conducting military work drew criticism from the Comintern over, for instance, its 'troop of death' which distributed illegal leaflets. Such comrades 'exposed themselves to superfluous danger'.[49] Yet this anti-war agitation in the Far East, the Comintern said, 'deserves to be studied and popularised by the fraternal Communist Parties'.[50]

INDUSTRIAL AND POLITICAL ESPIONAGE

From the early 1930s the anti-militarist work of the Comintern began to develop an element of industrial and political espionage.

Specifically, this meant discovering the military–industrial capabilities of capitalist countries but also obtaining defence documents kept under lock and key. Surprisingly, the latter was openly and carefully stated in publications of the Comintern. In 1931 Lozovsky, writing on the role of the trade unions in the war, stated that it was necessary 'to operate in the holy of holies of capitalist society, in the armed forces *and diplomatic service* [emphasis added]. And the class which must do this must be one that is not interested in the preservation of this mystic secrecy and not slavishly inclined before boss-class institutions.'[51]

The Comintern's anti-militarist expert, Boris A. Vasilyev argued that wars are prepared in enormous secrecy and that it was the job of all communist parties to unmask this secrecy. He then asked how can this be done.

It is obvious that any secret treaties, Government proposals and military orders which by one means or another fall into the hands of Communist Party organisations must be published without delay, but the centre of gravity of the work of the exposure of the secrets of the preparation of new imperialist wars and simultaneously the centre of gravity of real anti-militarist work does not lie here: it lies in industries – and in the railway centres, and especially the automobile industry, import and export transport centres – which have military importance.[52]

The reference to secret treaties being published recalled the actions of the new Soviet government in 1918. But the notion of communists obtaining secret documents in their own country is quite a different matter. Industrial espionage which might give warning of war also extended to notionally peacetime industries such as the production of artificial silk. Such factories 'can be converted in the course of a few hours into undertakings for the manufacture of poison gas', claimed Vasilyev. 'This is what it means to penetrate the mysteries of the preparation of fresh imperialist wars and primarily to teach the workers in these undertakings, who have military knowledge to recognise how such undertakings are transformed into munitions works and how it is possible to paralyse this transformation.' To carry out such work needed certain requirements from communist parties.

> The directing organs of the Communist Party can – and must – give special allocations to selected Party members or special groups to carry on concrete work in relation to industries of military importance. But the chief task which the party must undertake is the mobilisation for carrying out these tasks of the initiative of the mass of workers in these industries. To do this very great persever-ance is needed. The ruling class will bring into action the whole repressive apparatus of the Government of the day or summon to its aid the Fascists and Social Fascists. The Communist Parties and the whole working class must make sacrifices in the form of the discharge of known active members, as these members will be involved in every sort of so-called 'trials of espionage' and so on.[53]

By the time of the Twelfth Plenum of the ECCI, in August–September 1932, the expectations of the Comintern were explicit although, as is usual in such resolutions, it was more liberal with criticism than praise.

One of its main resolutions, 'The War in the Far East and the tasks of the communists in the struggle against imperialist war and military intervention against the USSR', drew attention to:

the impermissible weakness of the contacts of the CPs with the principal munition factories, with the chief ports, and with the key points on the railroads, and also to the fact that the anti-war work of the Communist Parties and the YCL in the army, the navy and the special fascist semi-military organisation is in an intolerably neglected condition ... In addition the XIIth Plenum states that the Communist Parties have not succeeded in fulfilling the urgent task of creating legal, semi-legal or illegal control committees and illegal committees of action, based on the masses, in the factories, railroads, ports, and ships ...[54]

A similar theme echoed in the decisions of the Thirteenth (and final) ECCI Plenum in November–December 1933. In attempting to turn the imperialist war into a civil war communists must 'concentrate their forces in each country at the vital parts of the war machine of imperialism'; they must prevent the shipping of arms and troops; organise demon-strations against military manoeuvres and 'intensify political educational work in the army and navy'.[55]

Perhaps the best-known example of the British communist party's industrial espionage work was the 'Woolwich arsenal case'. It centred around a leading member of the CPGB's underground, Percy Glading, who had printed and distributed the *Soldiers' Voice* in the early 1930s.[56] By the second half of the 1930s Glading was working with Arnold Deutsch and Theodor Maly, the agent masters of the Cambridge group of spies.[57] In early 1937 Glading had the misfortune to approach a long-term MI5 agent in the CPGB to help set up a safe house in London. Over the next few months, the safe house was used to photograph documents of a naval gun, among other things. An operation by police later arrested several workers at the Woolwich arsenal who had been passing on the documents. A raid on Glading's home seized cameras and exposed film of pages of documents. Cryptic but decipherable diary notes held by Glading showed a less than thorough conspiratorial practice. However, at least one diary note, a reference to another key agent, Melita Sirnis, was not understood. Sirnis (later Norwood) later passed on information about the British part in the building of the atom bomb, the 'Tube Alloys' project; she was one of the longest-serving Soviet agents in Britain.[58]

In 1935 much of the distilled experience of the Comintern's anti-militarist work was summed up in a document written by Vasilyev, who had become head of the Organisation Department of the Comintern, but was later relieved of his functions. His document, 'Work in the Army', summed up the experience of anti-militarist work from the Sixth to Seventh Congresses.[59] Vasilyev polemicised against the view among unnamed parties 'that work in all other areas should be consolidated and then and only then the army work should come to the forefront'. He described such a view as 'anti-communist'. A case in point was the failure of the Spanish revolution of 1934 because 'no serious work' had been carried out in the army.

Vasilyev's document enlarges upon themes and techniques of Bolshevik underground work which we have already seen. It outlined a number of methods of conducting propaganda within the army. Radical books could be wrapped in the covers of cheap novels or cookbooks, with the first and last few pages dealing with this subject. Young women could be used to carry in messages and literature since police paid less attention to them. A variation on such a technique was used in Manchuria where old people were used since women were banned from barracks. Another method was to set up a laundry near a barracks. Weapons and bullets could be sent along with the dirty clothing and illegal literature could be sent with clean clothing. A similar kind of arrangement could be used if the revolutionaries outside sold food and vegetables to the troops.

Advice of the kind compiled by Vasilyev guided communist work within the armies and navies of western countries for a number of years during the 1930s. Often internal security and intelligence bodies knew broadly about such work and monitored it in the years leading up to World War Two. But both the Comintern and their nemesis, therefore, had an interest in secrecy and little has been written in detail about such work. With the opening of new archival sources both in Russia and countries like Australia, it is now possible to trace underground political work of this kind.

MARXISM AND MUTINY: A CASE STUDY

On the morning of Wednesday 9 November 1932 the Australian Minister for Defence, Senator Sir George Pearce informed parliament of 'a dastardly plot to foment disaffection' in the Royal Australian Navy.[60] The previous evening a group of naval ratings had held a protest meeting in Port Melbourne about their pay and had refused duty on their ship. Pearce attacked a Melbourne newspaper which had reported this and blamed unnamed conspirators who had distributed leaflets to ratings during an inspection of the fleet in Melbourne, urging mutiny to 'force the hand of the government'.

The events leading up to this protest by naval ratings had begun earlier that year. In August, just before the cruiser *Australia* left on a voyage to the Solomon Islands, a petty officer was tried by court martial and demoted for rudeness to a junior officer. During the cruise the crew voiced discontent with discipline, bad food and low pay to the extent that the captain addressed the ratings, heard their complaints and then, as a concession, granted them several half-holidays.[61]

The incidents on the *Australia* led to a debate in federal parliament in October during which a Labor MP suggested that conditions in the Australian navy were similar to those which led to the Invergordon mutiny.[62] The British component of senior officers, he suggested, may have introduced the brutal disciplinary methods of Britain on the Australian navy. Another MP raised the case of the imprisonment and dismissal of a stoker on the *Brisbane*, who in a poem in the ship's paper had complained about poor food during a cruise in the Pacific.

Disaffection also clearly existed because under the Financial Emergency Act which came into force in July 1931, the pay of naval ratings had been reduced by 20 per cent. The parliamentary debate and public comment on naval cuts more generally was a storm warning which the government did not heed.

Three weeks after the parliamentary debate, reports of growing discontent in the navy began to circulate and the *Argus* newspaper reported that naval ratings would soon present a petition to the Minister for Defence.[63] On the night of Tuesday 8 November, 200 naval ratings, many from the *Australia*, walked off their ships to hold a protest meeting about pay cuts on the Port Melbourne dockside. They backed a decision by their welfare committees to demand that at least 10 per cent of the reduction be restored. Officers warned them of the danger of being charged with mutiny and police were called, but after the meetings the sailors returned to their ships peacefully.[64] At a dinner that night for the Lord Mayor of Melbourne, Rear Admiral Hyde complained: 'While the ships have been in port during the last few days they have been flooded with seditious literature from Communist headquarters.[65]

While navy command was digesting the Port Melbourne walk-off, the following morning saw another remarkable act of defiance, this time in Sydney. At 0815 on 9 November ratings from the *Penguin*, a depot ship in Sydney, refused to fall in and instead held a meeting in the mess room to discuss grievances.[66] After being promised time for a meeting the ratings fell in and almost immediately resumed an impromptu discussion led by the chairman of their welfare committee. Work began after the discussion but then stopped again just before noon, when the Captain-Superintendent of Sydney Naval Establishments, Captain Feakes, addressed them, urging patriotism and blaming politicians for pay cuts. The ratings later strenuously denied that any 'red influence was at work'.

It was during the Sydney meeting and under pressure from the widespread reports that a mutiny was in the offing, that Sir George Pearce informed Australia of 'a dastardly plot to foment disaffection' in the navy. The following month Pearce announced a pay increase of five shillings and tenpence a week for every adult rating of the sea-going branch of the navy.[67] In doing so he admitted the main argument of the ratings – that the practical effects of the Financial Emergency Act made disproportionately high cuts to the defence forces compared to the public service.

Australia was one of those countries where Comintern policy on work within the military forces was implemented by the local communist party. By the mid-1930s the influence of the CPA was significant and the civil authorities as well as the navy and army set in motion an elaborate series of security operations to catch them.

But when the notion of political work among soldiers and sailors was first raised at the 1928 annual conference of the CPA it was treated with reserve by the leadership.[68] A proposal from the Townsville (Queensland) branch that the CPA engage in 'systematic propaganda among military forces' was rebuffed because it was both mechanical and impractical. 'This is another attempt to apply certain tasks of the European Parties to Australia where the conditions calling for the action do not exist. We do not have a conscript army in this country nor do we have a standing "volunteer" army such as that of Britain', said one response by the leadership. The leadership did accept that some political work should be aimed at the military forces. In particular, it singled out the Royal Australian Navy, referring to its use in 'keeping order' in China during 1927 and other 'imperialist police purposes in the Pacific'. The main problem was simply the weakness of the party itself, which should concentrate on propaganda among industrial workers and restrict work among the military 'except on special occasions such as the visit of a naval fleet or a military demonstration'. The one partial exception concerned propaganda directed at young men who were military trainees. In this case it would be necessary to point out 'the value of military training which though acquired under the wing of the State may be used to protect the workers on strike and eventually in the workers' challenge to the State power'.

One year later at its 1929 annual conference, the CPA carried a resolution which argued that 'the workers must be prepared, not to boycott war by refusal to render services or by inaction or by pacifist means, but to take advantage of the opportunity to acquire arms and turn them to their account'.[69] When the founder of the Boy Scouts, Lord Baden Powell, visited Australia the *Workers Weekly* accused him of being part of the 'war drive' on the Soviet Union.[70]

When news of the Invergordon mutiny reached Australia, the *Workers Weekly* hailed the event as showing 'the great potentialities of winning the workers of the armed forces to the side of the working class'. In Comintern's eyes, the revolt of the Atlantic Fleet at Invergordon was echoed in Australia. In October 1931, the self-styled 'digger's paper', *Smith's Weekly*, reported that sailors at Westernport, near the city of Melbourne, protested against a wage cut and hoisted a red flag at the base.[71] On the cruiser *Canberra*, when ordered to scrub the decks, sailors had thrown their scrubbing brushes overboard. Reporting the events, Comintern's *International Press Correspondence* noted that the Australian navy 'has long had a reputation for militancy and a number of mutinies broke out in it during the war, mainly directed at the harsh disciplinary code, especially the flogging of boy ratings. This practice they eventually got withdrawn. Today no corporal punishment is permitted in the Australian Navy, although it is still a common practice in the English Navy.'[72] Both the Invergordon and Westernport revolts, *InPreCorr* argued, indicated the 'deep rooted working class resentment against the cuts'.

An inquiry by the Commonwealth Investigation Branch (CIB) reported that the CPA had about 20 contacts on the naval dockyard of Garden Island (NSW), with 'a smaller number' on the *Canberra* and on the sea plane carrier, *Albatross*.[73] Of these contacts, only a section were actually communists, 'but in each case they are definitely there', a CIB officer said. These contacts among the ratings proposed 'a demonstration of some kind' while the fleet stayed in Melbourne.

The contacts on the *Canberra* and *Albatross* were probably the result of activity by the Young Communist League whose Melbourne branch had six members 'in the army or the Navy and [who] are to be activisted [*sic*] in some way in their battalions'.[74] In early May 1931 the *Canberra* began a three-day visit to the industrial city of Newcastle on the east coast of Australia. The local Trades Hall Council fraternally greeted the crew of the *Canberra* and called on them 'to refuse to take up arms against their fellow workers if ordered to do so by the Federal Government'.[75] Later that year the Commonwealth Investigation Branch warned the Royal Australian Navy that the CPA planned to a campaign in the navy.

All of this activity was, of course, dictated by the Comintern's fears of an imminent outbreak of war against the Soviet Union. Much of it, however, missed the mark. Within the navy, by far the more basic source of discontent was pay cuts.

In the normal course of events, minor dissatisfaction by ratings was handled by welfare committees who made representations to the captain. Every two years, a conference of welfare committees was held under the authority of the Naval Board, but the 1931 conference where pay cuts would obviously be an issue was postponed.[76] In 1932 the delayed conference was ordered to be held at three separate locations, on the fleet, at the Flinders Naval Depot in Melbourne and at HMAS Penguin in Sydney. Several days before the protest meetings referred to above, the press reported that a petition would be presented to defence minister, Sir George Pearce. Pearce denounced the reports as 'calculated to create insubordination'.[77]

The extent of Communist Party presence among naval ratings is not clear although it certainly existed. Certainly the CPA knew about the brewing revolt and issued a leaflet which attacked the wage cuts and invited ratings to a meeting at the Capitol Theatre to celebrate the Russian revolution.[78] The CPA's intimate knowledge of ratings' pay was shown in an article published in the *Workers Weekly* shortly after the November protest meetings in Sydney and Melbourne.[79] The article described a series of meetings on board the *Australia*, *Canberra*, *Albatross*, *Penguin* and *Tattoo* which endorsed a 'Programme of Demands' calling for restoration of pay and free train travel. The well-informed and surprisingly moderate article pointed out that as well as pay cuts, a large part of sailors' pay was deducted for shipboard lodging, medical insurance and for deferred pay.

As pay and allowance cuts have been introduced, so has the discipline been stiffened to such an extent that the most frivolous of 'offences' have been met with very severe punishment and forfeiture of pay. It is on the basis of all these injustices that the crew of every ship – the *Australia, Canberra, Albatross, Penguin* and *Tattoo* – have held mass meetings and endorsed the Programme of Demands.

The article, in fact written before the protest meetings though published two days after, prophetically warned that the 'intense dissatisfaction will not long be held in check'.

The November 1932 protests alarmed the Naval Board, which proceeded to abolish the welfare committees and replace them with officer-controlled boards of review, a cause for further discontent among ratings.[80] The 1932 revolt also alarmed the conservative federal government, which suspected the CPA of playing a bigger role than it did. In early February 1933 Dutch sailors mutinied on the ship *Seven Provinces* while it was in the Netherlands East Indies (Indonesia). An alarmed acting prime minister, John Latham, fearing that the CPA would use this example and urge a local mutiny, ordered the Investigation Branch of the Attorney-General's department to watch a Sydney meeting called by the League Against Imperialism.[81] The meeting, which attracted 700 people, expressed solidarity with the Dutch sailors and urged that Australian sailors be allowed to fraternise with the strikers. Naval Intelligence was also worried and detected that 'a number of ratings, particularly those whose homes are situated in the industrial suburbs of Sydney, are becoming somewhat political-minded, largely as the result of associations formed with labour organisations and social clubs.'[82]

While the CPA had contacts in the Royal Australian Navy before 1934, that year marked the beginning of systematic communist anti-militarist work and was part of its contingency plan in the event of banning.[83] A letter from the Central Committee which accompanied the plan urged city committees to 'seriously take up the question of sending party members in to the military forces'.[84] The CC letter closely follows the Comintern's guidelines on work with the army, urging that 'one of the oldest and most reliable members of the District Committee' be placed in charge of the work. 'Those sent into the forces must be very reliable and should not know what other contacts we have unless the committee decides to group 2 or 3 or more comrades together. No two groups should know of the existence of the other.'

One popular issue around which the CPA agitated was harsh naval discipline. In particular many rank-and-file ratings blamed the discipline on English officers who came to the Royal Australian Navy on an exchange system. Many sailors described the attitude of these officers as 'pinpricking' in contrast to local officers who had a 'give and take' attitude. English officers were often present on the *Australia* and *Canberra* where the CPA had a number of contacts and members.[85] In August 1934 the survey sloop *Moresby* was surveying off the coast of north Australia when a rating, Mr Fletcher, hit a petty officer and was disciplined by being placed in irons.[86] This harsh punishment crystallised dissatisfaction with discipline among a wider group of ratings, seven of whom locked themselves in a mess room until the irons were removed. Fletcher was then transferred to a shore jail and the ship ordered to sail to Fremantle, where the seven were dismissed by court martial.[87] The issue of harsh naval discipline was raised on a number of occasions in federal parliament by left-wing Labor MP, Eddie Ward, who took an interest in the conditions of naval ratings, on one occasion calling for an inquiry and the re-establishment of welfare committees.[88] In October 1936 he forced an admission from the Minister for Defence that a steward on the *Australia* had been penalised for 'having negligently performed his duties in laying out an officer's uniform'.[89] Eddie Ward claimed the rating had not placed a collar stud in the shirt of the officer.

At a CPA Central Committee meeting in 1936, CPA leader Richard Dixon argued that a strong campaign was needed 'exposing the abuses being perpetrated within the army at the present time' and to 'explain our conception of democracy in the military forces'.[90] While the voluntary militia was a target for communist work, the CPA should 'above all' try to enter the permanent military forces. 'Efforts should be directed towards obtaining knowledge of military strategy and tactics, the use of arms, the understanding of army organisation to establish broader contacts with elements within the army.' Through this work, the CPA hoped to prepare fertile ground for when large masses of people joined the armed forces when war broke out between the imperialist powers and the Soviet Union.

Both Naval Intelligence and the CIB were aware of the CPA's plans to encourage members to join the militia and navy. Members in the armed forces attended political discussion classes which occurred on a clandestine basis. At one meeting, infiltrated by an agent, none of the participants revealed their name nor their branch of the armed forces.[91] The CPA strategy for members who joined the armed forces was not to carry out propaganda but to 'strive to be 100 per cent efficient as a soldier' and to seek promotion to commissioned rank.[92]

Between 1937 and the outbreak of war in 1939 the CPA played a cat and mouse game with the CIB, Military and Naval Intelligence. The CPA was aware in great detail of the surveillance it was subject to. In one instance in early 1937, the Defence Department issued a circular to all battalion commanders warning them of the CPA's 'Special Department' and of its campaign directed at the armed forces. This information was quickly leaked to the CPA to the chagrin of the Director of the CIB, Colonel Harold Jones, who complained to the Director of Military Intelligence, Major Bertrand Combes.[93] Jones knew that the CPA knew because he had an informer who was a CPA member and who was involved its anti-militarist work. The identity of Jones' agent is not certain but a strong possibility is CPA member Jimmy McPhee who was a petty officer in the Naval Reserve and later shown to be a spy.[94]

THE COLLECTION OF MILITARY INFORMATION BY THE CPA

But there was another side to the CPA's anti-militarist work within the armed forces. Throughout the 1930s the military and security authorities investigated suggestions that part of the CPA's work involved collecting military information. At one point, the CIB believed that Richard Dixon was engaged in espionage and was compiling a report to take to Russia based on military information from CPA cadres.[95] Much of this depended on circumstantial information from informants of varying degrees of reliability; however it fitted with the general approach of ECCI anti-militarist work, as we have seen above.

There is also some evidence from the CPA's own records. A reference to the CPA's collection of military information occurs in a bitter letter to the CPA general secretary, J. B. Miles, from a CPA member associated with the CPA's illegal organisation, Frank Wiggin.[96] Wiggin, who was facing expulsion for sloppy financial practices, referred to a commercial traveller named Garland and argued that because Garland had frequently donated groceries for raffles 'and was the chief party source of naval information, I could not too harshly insist on accounting'. Further, on the basis of public CPA utterances, it was not surprising that the CPA was suspected of espionage. The Movement Against War and Fascism, which the CPA promoted, issued a manifesto which called on members 'to expose everywhere the extensive preparations for war'.[97] This was elaborated in provocative terms in an issue of the movement's journal, *War! What For?* 'The movement,' it argued, 'must develop an efficient intelligence service. We must know what is going on in the way of war preparations and fascist developments. Send along every detail at once … Let every member act as a member of the intelligence service.'[98] Such indications suggest that the CPA may have collected low-level military information but the purpose of this, and whether it was conveyed to Russia, remains an open question. With war looming, the loyalty of the CPA was severely questioned though the party itself had a policy favouring defence of Australia, in line with its opposition to fascism.[99]

The declaration of war in September 1939 radically changed the context of CPA anti-militarist work. While initially welcoming Britain's declaration of war against Germany, the CPA soon changed its stance to total opposition.[100] This meant that the CPA members who were already in the armed forces, and those who rushed to join them before the CPA's line changed in October 1939, had the political task of undermining the war effort from within. In this period, the CPA organised a campaign against conscription and the dispatch of Australian forces overseas.[101] Within army camps its members organised protests about food, discipline and similar issues.

In November 1939 the Military Board issued a document to its commanding officers about the dangers of CPA work within the armed forces and methods of dealing with it. The document warned against the 'tendency to regard subversive propaganda as a subject for amusement rather than serious thought'. It quoted documents from the Sixth World Congress of the Comintern and warned, 'Don't be surprised if the man you are asked to keep an eye on is outwardly a good soldier. The Communist Party does not pick fools or known bad characters for their agents … Don't think that because a soldier laughs at Communism with you he may not think twice about it alone. Today's joke is tomorrow's grievance.'[102]

The document was classified as secret and internally it stressed secrecy in reporting and investigating possible communist activity. Perhaps indicative of the CPA's work within the military forces is the fact that a copy of the document was somehow obtained by the Communist Party of Australia and it survives today in the archives of that party.

NOTES

1. A. Vasilyev, 'The Communist Parties on the Anti-Militarist Front', *Communist International*, vol. 8, no. 14 (15 Aug. 1931), 386–7.
2. This account is based on David Divine, *Mutiny at Invergordon*, Macdonald, London, 1970, 149ff; Len Wincott, *Invergordon Mutineer*, Weidenfeld & Nicolson, London, 1974; and A. Carew, 'The Invergordon Mutiny, 1931: Long-Term Causes, Organisation, and Leadership', *International Review of Social History*, vol. 24 (1979), 157–88.
3. 'The English Atlantic Fleet', *Communist International*, vol. 8, no. 17 (15 Oct. 1931).
4. Speech of Comrade Yaroslavsky at the Sixth Congress of the Comintern, *InPreCorr*, 19 September 1928.
5. Lenin, 'First Victory of the Revolution, *CW*, vol. IX, 432.
6. Speech of Comrade Yaroslavsky.
7. Elwood, *Russian Social Democracy*, 104.
8. *Theses, Resolutions and Manifestos*, trans. Holt and Holland, 93.
9. Serge, *What Everyone Should Know*, 48. Originally published as *Les Coulisses d'une Surete Generale: ce que tous les revolutionaires doit savoir de la repression*, Librairie du Travail, Paris, 1926.
10. Minutes for this plenum (which expelled Trotsky) were never published in the normal way. For extracts of the theses of the plenum see Degras (ed.), *Communist International, 1919–1943*, vol. II, 378–79.
11. Ibid., vol. II, 379, 381.
12. 'Programme of the Communist International Adopted at its Sixth Congress', ibid., 525.
13. Speech by Bell at the opening of the War Commission, RTsKhIDNI, 493-1-531.
14. Third sitting of the War Commission, 10 August 1928, RTsKhIDNI, 493-1-496.
15. Speech by Harvey at the Eighth Sitting of the War Commission, RTsKhIDNI, 493-1-506.
16. 'Report on the Anti Militarist Work of the Young Workers (Communist) League, by Paul Crowch, Anti-Militarist Director', 4 February 1928, RTsKhIDNI, 495-25-1398.
17. Ibid.
18. 'Instruction on Work Within the Armed Forces', RTsKhIDNI, 493-1-531. The final English version dated 20.8.28 is taken from pages 169–89. A later German version in the same file is slightly different even though both versions are stamped 'final'. No version was ever publicly released along with the bulk of the Sixth Congress material. (An almost identical version is found at RTsKhIDNI, 495-20-797.)
19. 'Instruction on Work Within the Armed Forces', 171–2.
20. Ibid., 176, 177.
21. Ibid., 182.
22. A. Neuberg, *Armed Insurrection* (trans. Quintin Hoare), New Left Books, London, 1970, 165–8. This book was originally published in German as *Der Bewaffnete Aufstand* (Zurich, 1928) and in French as *L'Insurrection Armee* in 1931.
23. Unschlicht is described as second-in-command to the People's Commissar for Defence by Erich Wollenberg, an author of *Armed Insurrection*, and as deputy to Dzerzhinsky, the head of Cheka, in Andrew and Gordievsky, *KGB*, 51.
24. Neuberg, *Armed Insurrection*, 151.
25. Ibid., 166–7.
26. Thom Young and Martin Kettle, *Incitement to Disaffection*, Cobden Trust, London, 1976, 45–7.
27. Ibid., 48.
28. Noreen Branson, *History of the Communist Party of Great Britain: 1927–1941*, Lawrence & Wishart, London, 1985, 61; Young and Kettle, *Incitement to Disaffection*, 50.

29. Draft letter to the Secretariat of CPGB and YCL, 1 April 1929, RtsKhIDNI, 533-6-317, 166ff.
30. Untitled, undated document, RtsKhIDNI, 533-6-317.
31. Anti-War Commission of the Tenth Plenum, July 1929, RtsKhIDNI, 495-168-178.
32. Ibid.
33. Speech at the Eleventh Plenum of the ECCI, RtsKhIDNI, 495-169-101.
34. Branson, *History of CPGB*, 61.
35. Ibid., 64–5.
36. Young and Kettle, *Incitement to Disaffection*, 51–2.
37. Anthony Carew, *The Lower Deck of the Royal Navy, 1900–1939*, Manchester University Press, Manchester 1981, 155.
38. Divine, *Mutiny at Invergordon*, 100–5.
39. The sequence of events is based on Divine, Wincott and Carew: see note 2 above.
40. Divine, *Mutiny at Invergordon*, 154–7.
41. Ibid., 158. Wincott later lived for many years in the Soviet Union, where he was arrested and put in a labour camp.
42. Carew, *Lower Deck*, 162.
43. *Communist International*, vol. 8, no. 17 (15 Oct. 1931), 492–4. The story of the Invergordon revolt was greatly embellished by the pamphlet, *The Spirit of Invergordon*, published immediately after by the International Labour Defence (undated). Although it appeared under the name of one of the ratings, Len Wincott, he later admitted to Carew (*Lower Deck*, 249) that he was not the author.
44. Plans and reports of CPGB anti-militarist work are found in RtsKhIDNI, 495-25-1362.
45. Ibid.
46. 'Report on AM work, Jan.–Sept. 1933' signed by 'G', RtsKhIDNI, 495-25-1362, 72–3.
47. 'The German Communist Party in the Struggle Against the Fascist Dictatorship,' *Communist International*, vol. 10, no. 10 (1 June 1933); 'The Lower Functionaries of the Communist Party of Germany', *Communist International*, vol. 11, no. 16 (20 Aug. 1934).
48. 'War and the Immediate Tasks of the Communist Parties', *Communist International*, vol. 11, no. 6 (1 April 1932).
49. 'Examples of the Work of the CP of Japan in the Army', *Communist International*, vol. 11, no. 1 (1 Jan. 1934).
50. 'Some Experiences from the Activity of the CP of Japan in the Army', *Communist International*, vol. 11, no. 14 (July 1934).
51. A. Lozovsky, 'The Trade Unions and the Coming War', *Communist International*, vol. 8, no. 14 (Aug. 1931).
52. A. Vasilyev, 'The Communist Parties on the Anti-Militarist Front', *Communist International*, vol. 8, no. 14 (15 Aug. 1931), 386–7.
53. Ibid.
54. At least one part of this resolution, dealing with Manchuria and Japan had 'Ne pas Publier' (not for publication) in the French version and a similar statement in German. Twelfth Plenum of the ECCI, RtsKhIDNI, 495-170-363, 93–9.
55. 'Fascism, the Danger of War and the Tasks of the Communist Parties', *InPreCorr* (Special Supplement), 5 January 1934.
56. Anthony Masters, *The Man Who Was M: the Life of Maxwell Knight*, Basil Blackwell, Oxford, 1984, 51.
57. Andrew and Gordievsky, *KGB*, 178–79.
58. Christopher Andrew and Vasili Mitrokhin, *The Mitrokhin Archive: the KGB in Europe and the West*, Allen Lane, Penguin Press, London, 1999, 152–3.
59. Details of Vasilyev's career are drawn from informal file notes used by archivists at RtsKhIDNI. His work on the military underground is at RtsKhIDNI, 495-25-1351. A covering note within the file describes the material as 'Comrade Vasilyev's manuscripts on work in the army'.
60. Hansard, Senate, 9 November 1932.

61. *SMH* 11 October 1932. See also the letter read out by Ward during parliamentary debate, Hansard, House of Reps, 9 November 1932.
62. Hansard, House of Reps, 26 October 1932, 1617ff.
63. *Argus*, 5 November 1932.
64. *SMH*, 9 November 1932; *Argus*, 9 November 1932.
65. *SMH*, 10 Nov. 1932.
66. Ibid.
67. *SMH*, 9 December 1932.
68. RTsKhIDNI, 495-94-44.
69. 'Australian workers and the war danger', 1929 CPA annual conference, RTsKhIDNI, 495-94-50.
70. *WW*, 13 Feb. 1931.
71. *Smith's Weekly*, 3 October 1931, 3. No independent confirmation of this specific claim was discovered although at this time two questions were asked in federal parliament about naval discontent (18 Sept. and 17 Nov. 1931.) In answer to the latter question, the government denied that any mutiny had taken place.
72. *InPreCorr*, 19 November 1931.
73. Lloyd to Director, CIB, 19 October 1931, AA (ACT), A6122, item 220, 28.
74. See YCL letters in November 1931 and February 1932, RTsKhIDNI, 533-10-1.
75. *SMH*, 7 May 1932.
76. *SMH*, 1 December 1932.
77. *SMH*, 7 November 1932.
78. 'CPA Interest in Armed Forces, vol. 1', AA (ACT), A6122, item 220, 69. Hereafter referred to as 'Armed Forces, vol. 1'.
79. *WW*, 11 November 1932.
80. Speech of Mr Ward, Hansard, House of Reps, 29 November 1938, 2216–18.
81. 'Armed Forces, vol. 1', 44–7.
82. Letter from Dept of Naval Intelligence to Naval Intelligence, Admiralty, AA A8911/1, item 80.
83. For detail on the 1934 plan, see chapter 5 below.
84. CPA Archives, ML MSS 5021 (add-on 1936), box 5 (76).
85. 'Armed Forces, vol. 1', 93.
86. *Argus*, 4 Sept. 1934, 17 September 1934; SMH 23 August 1934.
87. *Argus*, 17 September 1934.
88. Hansard, House of Reps, 24 September 1936; 1 October 1936; 28–29 June 1937. Ward's call was on 24 September 1936.
89. Hansard, House of Reps, 1 October 1936, 777.
90. Stenographic notes, first session, 20.11.1936, in 'CC Minutes, 1936–40', CPA archives, box 4 (76).
91. 'Armed Forces, vol. 1', 137–9.
92. 'Armed Forces, vol. 1'.
93. A A6122, item 220, 153–61.
94. The exposure of McPhee is detailed in McKnight, *Australia's Spies and their Secrets*, 50, 82.
95. 'Armed Forces, vol. 1', 117, 140–1.
96. Letter dated 5 July 1937 in file, 'F. N. Wiggin 1937', box 85 (159), CPA Archives, ML MSS 5021.
97. AA (NSW) 'Anti-war movement', C320, item CIB 669.
98. AA A6122/40 item 221, part 1, 6.
99. R. Dixon, *Defend Australia?*, Modern Publishers (n.d. but approx. 1936–7). Dixon's pamphlet caused a lively debate in the CPA on defence policy, see *Communist Review* for February, March, April and May 1937.
100. See chapter 6 below.
101. 'CPA Interest in Armed Forces, vol. 2', AA A6122, item 221, part 1, 76–87.
102. CPA Archives, ML MSS 5021, box 85 (159).

CHAPTER FOUR

Underground in Asia

Communist agitation around Shanghai, though underground, is very active. Elsewhere on street walls appears mysteriously defaced slogans such as 'Down with Chiang Kai-shek', 'Down with the Kuomintang'.

The Times, [London] 31 December 1928

[E]ven when the confusion resulting from the Noulens' raid was at its worst, the conspirative system previously established was still effective enough to afford freedom of manoeuvre to the remains of the organisation for the purpose of remodelling its lines and withdrawing its threatened personnel ...

British Special Branch report, 7 March 1932[1]

On 1 May 1929 an unusual meeting of trade unionists took place in Shanghai. The communists who organised the meeting later regarded it as 'perhaps the biggest single feat of illegal organisation' at the time. It was a copy-book version of the kind of illegal activity under conditions of savage repression which was described by the Comintern Commission on Illegal Work:

A guildhall on one of the busiest thoroughfares in the Settlement was booked. Factory workers went to the hall in groups of three or four. Their times of arrival were carefully staggered. They were still arriving when a policeman walked into the hall to ask what was going on. He was politely disarmed and locked in a small room. The meeting was held, 400 people heard a 45 minute May Day address and dispersed into the night. Then the policeman was released.[2]

The description is by a British communist, George Hardy, who worked underground in Shanghai for Profintern, Comintern's trade union wing. Hardy's task was to stimulate the left-wing trade union movement in China and in south-east Asia and he worked closely with historic leaders of the Communist Party of China (CPC) such as Chou En-lai, Deng Hsiao-ping and Liu Shao-chi who were all active in the underground trade union movement, particularly that part centred in Shanghai.

In the period 1928–32 Shanghai was an industrialised city and a busy centre of trade. In the extraterritorial International Settlement and the French concession, British, Japanese, French and German businesses flourished. With its protected status, its relatively modern communications and its European community, Shanghai provided the logical place for building an underground apparatus which would represent the ECCI to the CPC. It was the contact point from which Comintern military experts could be spirited through the lines separating the Nationalists and the Red Army; it was the place where the future leaders of the American Communist Party were blooded. Shanghai drew writer Agnes Smedley to Red China's cause. The Shanghai underground drew German communist, Richard Sorge, who later worked for Soviet intelligence in Tokyo.

Little wonder, then, that when an American military intelligence official investigated 'the Sorge affair' and Soviet intelligence he was led back to the Comintern apparatus in Shanghai, a city he described as 'a veritable witch's cauldron of international intrigue, a focal point of Communist effort'.[3]

China had been at the centre of hopes and fears of a second communist revolution for most of the 1920s, especially after the defeat of the German uprising in 1923. Although the CPC ultimately carried through a revolution based on its strength among peasants, in the period between 1920 and 1933 its strategy included a primary role for the urban working class.

The period between the defeat of the CPC in 1927 and the departure of most CPC leaders from Shanghai to the Soviet areas in 1932–3 has been somewhat neglected by historians, partly because of a certain orthodoxy in scholarship which saw urban events largely in terms of their relationship to rural revolution.[4]

This chapter will study the Comintern's apparatus for underground trade union work in Shanghai in the period 1928–32. This period was one of savage repression directed against the CPC and the trade union movement which it heavily influenced, the All-China Labour Federation (ACLF). The focus of Comintern trade union activity was the Pan Pacific Trade Union Secretariat (PPTUS) which, under its Russian name TOS (Tikho Okeanskii Sekretariat), was the far-eastern wing of the Profintern. The PPTUS in Shanghai was responsible for both supporting the ACLF and developing 'red trade unionism', as it was called, in south-east Asia, Korea, Japan and India. The PPTUS apparatus was in turn, part of a larger network of clandestine organisations in Shanghai, notably the Far Eastern Bureau of the Comintern and Soviet military intelligence.[5]

The underground work of the PPTUS can be schematically divided in the following way. In the initial period between 1927 and 1929 the American communist Earl Browder was the leading PPTUS figure; between 1929 and 1930 the British communist George Hardy was in charge of the work; between 1930 and 1931 when the trade union work was controlled by 'Leon' and 'Kennedy', the code names for two American communists who appear to be James Dolson and Charles Krumbein.[6] In June 1931 the underground apparatus in Shanghai was severely disrupted, though not destroyed, by the arrest of two Russians who were officers of the Comintern's International Liaison Department (OMS). The two OMS officers administered the apparatus which supported the PPTUS and the Far Eastern Bureau of the Comintern. They worked as a language teacher and his wife under the pseudonyms of M. and Mme Hilaire Noulens. Their arrest meant the capture by the Shanghai Municipal Police of a vast quantity of administrative records, which are now held in Washington, DC. Together with newly opened Comintern archives, in Moscow, they allow a valuable insight into the functioning of the Comintern and Profintern underground apparatuses in urban China.

The Communist International through Grigory Voitinsky first made contact with Chinese radicals in 1920. The following year Voitinsky helped found the Communist Party of China, which remained very small until 1925.[7] In this year a national trade union conference formed the All-China Labour Federation (ACLF), whose leaders included many prominent communists and which immediately affiliated to the trade union wing of the Communist International, Profintern or the Red International of Labour Unions (RILU).

The period 1925–7 saw the Chinese labour movement reach its zenith, only to crash to defeat. In large part, the growth of the labour movement depended on the political alliance formed between the CPC (with the full support of the Soviet government) and the nationalist Kuomintang (KMT). In May 1925, shortly after the formation of the ACLF, a strike at a Japanese textile mill in Shanghai was brutally suppressed leading to nation-wide boycotts and strikes against foreign companies and institutions.[8] In June British troops shot Canton students and workers sparking a 16-month strike against the British in Canton-Hong Kong. In Shanghai workers twice rose up against warlord control in late 1926 and early 1927. Finally, in March 1927 an armed workers' revolt took over Shanghai shortly before KMT troops entered and took control. But in April, alarmed by the unrest, Chiang Kai-shek turned on the CPC and its union supporters, bloodily breaking the alliance between them. From that point onwards the KMT government used systematic police and military terror against real and alleged communists and all CPC political and trade union work in cities was conducted in secret.

These epic events in China in 1927 coincided with an idea originated in Australia and taken up vigorously by the Communist International. In 1921, amid rumours of a new war, the Australian trade union movement proposed that a regional organisation of Pacific trade unions be formed.[9] Though raised by Australian delegates at the 1922 Profintern congress the idea languished until 1925 when the general secretary of Profintern, Alexander Lozovsky, informed his executive bureau of the Australian plan to convene a conference of Pacific trade unions in Sydney in 1926.[10] While supporting the initiative, one of the Comintern's far-east specialists argued that Sydney was too far from the 'main lines of communication' and that Australia's racist immigration policy made difficult the entry of delegates from Asia.[11] 'It might therefore be proposed, that although the initial step is being taken by the Australian comrades, the congress should be convened not in Australia but in a real Pacific country in Shanghai or Canton', he said. This is what occurred. Organised at too short notice, the conference attracted few Pacific unions, however a Profintern delegate, 'Comrade Rubanoff' (Rubinstein), ensured that groundwork was laid for a further conference in China in 1927.

The 1927 conference of Pacific unions, planned for Canton, was suddenly moved after a counter-revolutionary coup which destroyed the ACLF and its local leaders. The venue then moved to Hankow which was controlled by a local government of Left KMT and communists.

The Pan Pacific Trade Union Conference opened on 20 May at the People's Club in Hankow after a welcome parade of tens of thousands of workers organised by the local trade unions. In the course of a week the conference heard reports on political and labour movement conditions in Indonesia, Japan, the United States and China.[12] Among the speakers from the ACLF was Lui Shao-chi.[13] Fourteen of the 22 Japanese delegates were arrested on their way to China and the Australian government refused to grant passports to its trade union delegates.[14]

The importance of the gathering and the relatively legal conditions in which it was held was indicated by the presence of the secretary general of Profintern, Alexander Lozovsky. But even while the conference was sitting, the Soviet mission in Peking was sacked.[15] The American communist Earl Browder emerged as a key leader from the conference, which also elected him editor of the *Pan Pacific Worker*, initially published openly in Hankow.[16] Browder forecast a triumphal future for the PPTUS, which would 'help tear down the numerous barriers of language and race prejudice which have kept the mighty armies of workers in the Pacific apart for so many years'.[17] But the CPC–KMT split of 1927, ending with the defeat of the ill-judged Canton uprising in December 1927, forced Browder and the PPTUS to operate in a period of savage repression and deep clandestinity.

Browder had led an American trade union delegation to the founding congress of Profintern in 1921 and in the 1920s, when he spent most of his time in Moscow or China, he was a leading member of the American communist party. From 1930 to 1945 he was secretary of the CPUSA. Working with Browder for the PPTUS was the less well-known figure, Charles Johnson (whose code names were 'Stein', 'Steinberg' or occasionally 'Charlie'), a 46-year-old Latvian who was born Karl Ernestovich Yanson.[18] Already a Bolshevik, in 1908 he migrated to the United States where he later headed the left wing of the American Socialist Party, which split in 1919 and helped form what became the Communist Party of the United States of America.[19] From 1920 to 1922 he represented the American party in Moscow at the Communist International and from 1923 was a member of the Profintern Executive Committee, where he became known to the head of Profintern, Lozovsky, and Pavel Mif (Mikhail Firman) a specialist on China.

From its formation in 1927 the PPTUS was responsible for a number of functions. First, it wrote and printed various publications, initially the *Pan Pacific Worker*, then, after this was moved to the United States, the *Far Eastern Bulletin*, which appeared in both English and Chinese.[20] Second, it provided both advice and money to the ACLF. At this time, before the real beginning of the guerrilla war, this was the strategic core of the Chinese communists and PPTUS officials met weekly with the All-China Federation of Labour leaders.[21] Third, it supported and promoted red trade union work in the Philippines, Japan, Malaya, India, Indonesia and other south-east Asian countries.

The PPTUS was quite open about its own existence within Shanghai. Publications such as the *Far Eastern Bulletin,* defiantly proclaimed on their masthead that they were published in Shanghai. The statutes of the PPTUS stated that the 'seat' of the Secretariat 'is to be situated in the city of Shanghai, China.[22] The Shanghai police and the Kuomintang authorities thus knew that the PPTUS operated under their noses and were constantly alert. And although no Comintern officials were arrested until June 1931, a number of officials and militants of the All-China Labour Federation who worked with the Comintern were arrested, jailed or executed.

In order to conduct such work, a variety of conspiratorial techniques were used to send and receive mail, to hold meetings, to print and distribute documents, to hold larger conferences and to distribute money. For uncoded letters, a system of couriers operated irregularly between Shanghai and the Soviet Union via Harbin, with the dangerous border crossing often assisted by Soviet diplomatic staff and the Soviet security police, OGPU.[23] However most mail was sent using the normal postal system (people such as Browder signing himself 'Russell' or 'Morris') with a variety of cover addresses. A great deal of mail to and from Moscow was addressed initially to cover addresses in Berlin, where the Comintern had an elaborate 'post office' for rerouting mail to its true destination.[24] In case of casual postal inspection, the letters were sometimes couched in a personal tone. For example, those to Profintern's chief, Lozovsky, from the Comintern representative in Australia, Sydor Stoler, usually began 'Cher Papa!' and were signed 'Votre fils qui vous respecte et aime.'[25] Left-wing newspapers and magazines intended for the Far Eastern Bureau of ECCI could be sent openly by addressing them to the 'Universal Clipping Service, GPO Box 1565, Shanghai'.[26]

Yet carelessness and misunderstandings by Moscow and its Berlin 'post office' dogged the communications of the FEB and PPTUS. Bulky envelopes aroused the suspicion of customs authorities, who opened mail and questioned the box holder. An exasperated letter from

Shanghai reported that 'owing to all these acts of carelessness on the part of our comrades, we have now lost three safe addresses within the last six weeks, and they are now keeping a very close watch on all post boxes'.[27] The commercial cable system was used for urgent messages but 'business' language was employed. When Johnson ('Stein') left Shanghai he cabled Alexander: 'leaving Shanghai turned over business new manager I gave also complete outline immediate business transactions joint meeting chinese shareholders – steinert [sic].'[28] (An attempt was made in 1930 to send information from Moscow via radio but this appears to have been an experiment.[29])

The PPTUS illegal apparatus in Shanghai was funded from Profintern headquarters in Moscow. The budget of the PPTUS is unclear but at one point in October 1929, the PPTUS representative George Hardy reported that he had been without funds for two months and asked Moscow to 'cable $10,000 (Gold) and despatch messenger immediately with balance'.[30] The PPTUS, in turn, regularly gave money to the All-China Labour Federation, to the Philippines Congress of Labour and to other red unions in south-east Asia.[31] Profintern paid for the Australian edition of the *Pan Pacific Worker*, for instance, cabling £200 from Germany to the Australian union leader, Jock Garden, in June 1929.[32] Much of the Russian funding for Profintern's activities worldwide was remitted in complex transactions through Swiss and German banks to businesses established by the OMS, typically import–export companies that habitually used cables and exchanged money.

THE BROWDER–JOHNSON PERIOD

The first major task which faced Browder and Johnson in this period was the holding of a full meeting of the Secretariat in February 1928 under conditions of complete illegality.[33] Chaired by the Australian delegate Jack Ryan, who represented the ACTU in Shanghai, the meeting was attended by representatives from the Philippine Workers Congress, the Trade Union Education League (USA), the National Minority Movement (UK), the Japanese red trade union federation, the Hiogikai, the far-eastern section of the Russian unions, an Indonesian union group and the All-China Labour Federation. The meeting discussed the difficult new conditions in China and the collapse of the ACLF. A report noted that in the recent revolutionary upheaval, 'the red unions never had any well planned and detailed organisational system. So at the blow of the political reaction and in the process of transformation (from legal to underground) the organisation has been disintegrated [*sic*].' Another resolution, drafted by Johnson (Stein) urged the ACLF to fight for legalisation and to use 'all existing legal possibilities'. The February meeting decided to hold its next conference in Australia, prior to the 1929 congress of the Australian Council of Trade Unions.

Apart from organising this meeting and arranging delegates for the Fourth Profintern Congress in Moscow in March, the work of the PPTUS had been confined to the production of the *Pan Pacific Worker* which was done under conditions of savage repression. 'Our printing arrangements have broken down entirely', reported Browder in May.

> The trouble came from the Chinese workers in the shop, who resigned in a body rather than continue to print what they thought endangered their necks. The crisis came after another print shop, suspected of having printed a 'red' leaflet had its whole staff of 17 workers taken out and shot. It seems impossible to resume printing at this time, although we may be able to soon, having some encouragement from the proprietor who 'wants the money'.[34]

Although banned, occasional statements by the PPTUS were published in *China Outlook*, an American missionary publication. Largely because of these difficulties an Australian edition of *Pan Pacific Worker* began to appear in April.

While the *Pan Pacific Worker* hailed the red labour movement of China, the actual position was very different. In early 1928 Browder reported to Lozovsky that in Hankow the labour movement had been 'completely wiped out. Of the large cities, only Shanghai and Canton have any open labour movement and in both places it is under the control of the Kuomintang. The illegal trade unions are largely destroyed.'[35] The 'yellow' unions of the Kuomintang, were 'gaining in power and influence'.

But the problem was even worse. When 35,000 silk filature workers went on strike the red union, the ACLF, was taken by surprise. Browder complained that the CCP had effectively fused the ACLF with the party. By allocating the leading ACLF cadres to other political work, it had 'practically abolished' the ACLF. Generally, Browder argued, the Communist Party displayed 'inexcusable confusion about and underestimation of TU work'.

The equivocal position of the CPC on political work in trade unions was a problem which for years dogged the successive Comintern cadres who staffed the PPTUS in Shanghai. Ultimately, the success of the CPC would lie in its work among peasants, but in this period its outlook strongly influenced by the Russian revolution decreed that the working class would transform China. Even so, a resolution from the central committee of the CPC in April 1928 noted that practice did not necessarily fit theory:

> In regard to the situation in all of China, it seems in general the peasants are radical and the workers are backward. The workers are now engaged in no active struggles, and show no development of the illegal trade union organisations. Although the Party organs have committed many military opportunist mistakes in the peasant uprising yet they still lead such actions continuously ... Even where formally a trade union is maintained in fact it is only another name for the Party nucleus, and there are no non-Party members in it (as in Shanghai).[36]

The resolution went on dutifully to urge a 'fight against the tendency of neglecting the labour movement' and urged that the party should 'make the labour movement [the] most important and fundamental work of our Party' so that the workers become the 'advance guard of the peasants and toiling masses'.

In spite of police terror, radical working-class action was not entirely absent. When Japan staged a military incident in Manchuria in 1928 spontaneous anti-Japanese feeling erupted in Shanghai which the yellow (KMT) unions tried to channel. A trade union committee against imperialism was established on which the communists had 7 out of 21 positions but after the local garrison commander took charge of one meeting the seven communists 'were so terrorised that they did not dare to say a word'.[37] On 30 May, National Humiliation Day, six factories in east Shanghai went on strike and an anti-KMT demonstration which Browder estimated at 1,500 took place in the international sector of Shanghai. In the Chinese sector of Shanghai, slogans were milder but industrial action more widespread.[38] The *Times* correspondent reported that 'Communist agitation around Shanghai, though underground, is very active. Elsewhere on the street walls appear mysteriously defaced slogans such as "Down with Chiang Kai-shek", "Down with the Kuomintang" ... The strike in the French concession holding up the tram and electricity and water services obstinately continues and is a purely political affair, the men having no real complaint.'[39]

In the last half of 1928 relations between Browder and Johnson deteriorated, with Browder making official complaints to Lozovsky and during his absence even refusing to leave the key to the PPTUS post office box with Johnson.[40] In December, Browder returned to the United States and from there began to edit an American edition of *Pan Pacific Worker*.[41]

THE HARDY PERIOD

In February 1929 Charles Johnson (Stein) handed over the Profintern work in Shanghai to a new cadre allocated by the Comintern, the British communist, George Hardy.[42] Hardy, whose code name in his reports was 'Mason', had been a member of the Industrial Workers of the World in Canada, the USA and Australia before becoming a member of the Political Bureau of the British Communist Party in 1925–6.[43] In 1923 he participated in the German revolution and in 1928 he became a member of the Profintern Executive Bureau. Before travelling to China posing as a well-to-do businessman, Hardy had experienced underground work in several countries. In Shanghai he became a key figure in Comintern liaison with the CPC. When Profintern tried to withdraw him from Shanghai in late 1929 the Political Bureau of the CPC protested, arguing that he understood conditions in China better than other functionaries with whom they dealt.[44]

One of Hardy's tasks in the first half of 1929 was to organise the attendance of union delegates at the second Pan Pacific Trade Union conference to be held in August. After the 1927 Hankow conference, Australia had been proposed as the venue of the next conference with the support of the new national trade union federation, the ACTU. But in June 1928 the conservative Bruce government, fearful of the threat to the British Empire and white Australia, announced that it would ban the entry of delegates. The PPTUS therefore decided that the second conference would be held on Soviet territory in Vladivostock. The conference was dominated by the recent Soviet–China border clash and the need to 'defend the Soviet Union' and by the prevailing leftist approach which saw reformism as the main danger to the workers' movement. To this extent the conference marked the Soviet domination of a body which originally had a more genuinely internationalist appeal. Alert to the gathering, Japanese, Chinese and British police prevented many delegates from attending Vladivostock and a second, secret conference was held in Shanghai, attended by delegates from Japan, China, the Philippines, Indonesia and Malaya.[45]

Hardy's approach to trade union work in China was, like Browder's, critical of the CPC's labour movement strategy. At one point he reported to Moscow that 'in China the Party as a whole has not even fully grasped the full significance of trade union work' and 'even the PB [Political Bureau of the CPC] is not clear on all [trade union] questions'.[46] Nevertheless, during 1929 there was a mild resurgence of the labour movement. 'Terrorist tactics' were less readily applied by the KMT, reported Hardy.[47] 'This does not mean that there is any evidence that white terror is being discarded as a weapon against the workers for hundreds are still being executed and tortured and it only means more are receiving long prison sentences for such offensices [sic] as distributing literature ... instead of being sent indiscriminately for execution.' In June 1929, according to *The Times*, the Nanking government issued 'drastic regulations' for a weekly search for communist literature in all bookshops. The KMT-influenced Printers Union warned its members that printing such literature 'will be punished mercilessly'.[48]

During this period the ACLF organised its May Day meeting at a guild hall in the centre of Shanghai referred to above. Such tactics were discussed later at a special conference in Moscow of trade unionists who worked illegally or semi-legally where a Chinese union organiser, 'Liu Tsien', described conditions in Shanghai.[49] Meetings were organised within factories in such a way that they could disperse in a few minutes. For example, sometimes two communists would start a fist fight and workers would gather. The 'fight' then stopped and the fighters delivered a short speech to the crowd. At other places, workers' meetings were organised under the cover of a small company shareholders' meeting. 'Liu Tsien' reported that meetings in theatres were held where police were captured to prevent them raising the alarm. But he warned that poorly organised attempts at such meetings had resulted in the loss of many comrades. His report also confirmed Hardy's view that the role of factory nuclei was practically nil and that party committees substituted themselves for workers' nuclei.

While underground techniques had to be rapidly adapted and applied, another key problem which confronted Hardy was how to convince the Chinese communists to take advantage of the extremely small 'legal' possibilities in the situation. After the defeats of 1927 the ACLF had strength only in the seamen's union and the railways union.

A number of red unions had been taken over by KMT forces while the union of postal workers and the Mechanics Union had never been under the ACLF umbrella. The postal workers, for example, were run by 'disciples' of a Shanghai underworld figure who played a considerable role in the 'yellow unions'.[50] Yet the only 'legal' opportunities for trade union work were those created by the existence of 'yellow unions', a designation which covered a range of non-communist unions under the control of the KMT or of employers.

Such legal work was difficult for at least two reasons quite apart from the obvious problems of illegality and terror. First, at the level of the Chinese Communist Party, a 'putschist' approach was strong.[51] This tended to downplay demands based on the basic needs of workers and to emphasise revolutionary calls for uprisings and armed struggle. Second, the Communist International itself, from the Sixth World Congress in 1928, followed a strategy which was similar to the local 'putschism', emphasising the imminence of revolution and damning any co-operation with 'reformist' forces.

In spite of these evident similarities between the CPC and the ECCI, the question of legal work in yellow unions crystallised differences between the two. The CPC leadership tended to dismiss the minority within its ranks who favoured legal work as rightists. The memory of the bloody defeat of 1927 after a period of open, legal co-operation with Kuomintang forces was still very fresh. As well, a number of communists who had recently worked in yellow unions had gone over to the KMT.[52] Yet legal work in reactionary organisations was an established principle of conspiracy. Hardy had the difficult task of resolving this contradiction. At a plenum of the ACLF in February 1929 he criticised the minority within the ACLF who wanted to concentrate on forming red unions within all yellow unions.[53] This amounted to accepting a minority status and relinquishing the possibility of independent red unions. In place of this Hardy urged a flexible strategy. In areas of traditional ACLF strength, red unions would be maintained; but in yellow unions, red fractions would be built to take advantage of legal opportunities, as the minority suggested. Elsewhere, in what he called the 'fascist unions', the ACLF would keep trying to build a small cautious base.

The weakness of the ACLF was due to a number of factors, according to Hardy. Apart from the effects of terror, the CPC often failed to distinguish between itself and the union federation. Thus instead of the unions calling for struggle for better wages and shorter hours, it issued calls for armed revolt.[54] Such calls when expressed by the CPC leader Li Li-san were later to lead to a major split between the CPC and the Comintern. Thus within the party opposite tendencies existed, one wanting to do mainly legal work in yellow unions to avoid repression, the other ignoring any legal possibilities.

At the Tenth Plenum of the ECCI in July 1929, the Comintern's key expert on organisation, Piatnitsky turned to this question and asked: 'But why do the Chinese comrades still waver on the question as to whether to work or not to work in the Kuomintang unions? What is the result? The Red unions are small outfits and the Kuomintang unions are mass organisations.'[55] In response a representative of the Chinese party, 'Tsui Wito' (Chu Chiu-pai) asserted that some work was being done in yellow unions but also linked the desire to conduct legal work with the bogey of 'Right opportunism'.

In September 1929 the ECCI officially endorsed the direction of Hardy and Piatnitsky, criticising the 'remnants of sectarianism which still prevail' in the party.[56] At the same time it argued that the CPC 'must raise the question of resumption of a legal existence by the red trade unions, even if it were under another name and without official sanction, in connection with the revival of the labour movement. The actual leadership of these unions however, must continue to work on a conspirative basis.'

In November 1929 the Fifth Congress of the once mighty ACLF was held under illegal conditions in Shanghai. Hardy gave a report which concluded with the silent 'shouting' of slogans in illegal fashion: 'by one comrade announcing the slogan and each forcibly raising their right hand with a clenched fist'.[57] Although he estimated that 'we can reasonably expect some improvement in the proletarian base of the party', this was to be the last national ACLF conference until 1948.

UNDERGROUND STRUGGLE IN SOUTH-EAST ASIA

While direct contact with the Chinese labour movement was possible in Shanghai, elsewhere in south-east Asia the cultivation of left-wing trade unions by the Comintern took place at several removes.

The most successful activity occurred in the Philippines where an organised trade union movement, the Congresso Obrero de Filipinas (COF) was well established and operated with a degree of legality. While the COF was prevented from attending the 1927 PPTUS conference, it later affiliated and sent a delegate to the February 1928 Secretariat meeting in Shanghai.[58] The PPTUS maintained close contact with both COF leader, Crisanto Evangelista, and the leader of the peasants' federation, Jacinto Manahan, who were undoubtedly among those Browder earlier referred to as 'nucleus of devoted and energetic comrades' in the Philippines.[59]

Both men visited Moscow to attend the Fourth Profintern Congress in early 1928 and in early 1929 there was an upswing in class struggle which George Hardy attributed to 'close contact the PPTUS maintains with our Filipino comrades'. At the same time Hardy had to deal with a personal clash between Manahan and Evangelista after the former withdrew from the COF because Evangelista criticised him for allowing prayers at a peasants' conference.[60] But in May 1929 the COF split, with Evangelista leading a breakaway group. The Far Eastern Bureau of the Comintern accepted the split and Hardy reported that the new COF (Proletariat) soon greatly increased its membership.[61] Hardy issued instructions that the COF (Proletariat) hold a workers' conference to decide on a 'national programme of action and demands' and to discuss Soviet–China tensions and other international trade union questions. McLane's linking of this split to the formation of the Communist Party of the Philippines in August 1930 is borne out by Hardy, who argued that '[o]ur position will always be weak in the Islands until we can form a party group. Evangelista is hesitant ... [and] has given press interviews of a very social democratic character.' To remedy this Hardy urged the dispatch of an American comrade who could work there illegally.[62]

A letter from Hardy to Australian communist Jack Ryan telling him that 'the Philippine comrades are doing extremely well' gives the flavour of the PPTUS work:

> We are contemplating organising a united front conference in the Philippines in order to make a final effort to destroy all the reactionary elements and their organisation. Already their membership has fallen to 8,000 and their main strength is in the tobacco industry ... we are now engaged in a strike which involves unions affiliated to the reactionary organisation as well as our own. If we can win this strike it will give a great impetus to our position in this industry.[63]

Overall, the Comintern archives tend to confirm McLane's analysis which emphasised the significance of the PPTUS and of American communists in shaping the Philippines' political and union situation.[64]

In Singapore and Malaya there was less success. The roots of the communist movement in Malaya lay in the contact between communists such as Sneevliet, Tan Malaka, Alimin and local leftists and trade unionists in the 1920s.[65] By mid-1928 Browder could report that in 'Singapore and the Straits Settlements, an underground trade union movement is very active, which is led principally by Chinese workers who have been trained in the Canton trade union movement'.[66] But the following year, George Hardy reported more coolly that there was 'some evidence of activity in Singapore'. In Malaya, he said, 'most of the members of the Committee of the Chinese Communist Party' had been arrested and some were executed including 'our representative'.[67] But he added that Shanghai was 'completely isolated from Indochina, Indonesia, Siam and Korea'.

Overseas Chinese workers were organised in the Nanyang Federation of Labour, which attended the 1929 conference in Shanghai for delegates barred from the Vladivostock conference. Hardy established that the federation was based in Singapore, had 5,000 members including a small number in Thailand and Indonesia, and used seamen as couriers to communicate with its members.[68]

In February 1930 Hardy sent his 'best confidential translator and a very good comrade' to Singapore to urge local red trade unionists to become delegates for the Fifth Profintern Congress, but this plan collapsed in a wave of arrests in Malaya in April. The arrests occurred immediately after the founding of the Malayan Communist Party at a conference attended by Nguyen Ai Quoc (Ho Chi Minh).[69] Some of those arrested were later executed after deportation to China. Yong, following earlier scholars, interprets the founding of the MCP as a 'brilliant tactical move' by the Russian-based Comintern to weaken CPC influence in south-east Asia but while there was tension between the Comintern representatives such as Hardy and the CPC, there is no evidence in Comintern archives of a rivalry taken to such extreme lengths.

Contact with India was a problem for the PPTUS which was never resolved. In 1927 the All-India Trade Union Congress (AITUC) tried to send delegates to the Hankow conference but they were not permitted to leave India.[70] At the beginning of 1928 a PPTUS representative, probably the British communist T. R. Strudwick, went to India but he was not allowed to enter the country. The Australian communist, Jack Ryan, attended the Ninth All-India Trade Union Congress in December 1928, having departed secretly from Australia with the aim of securing

TUC affiliation to the PPTUS. He reported that 'CID men followed me night and day ever since I reached Bombay' and that an American union delegate was arrested and deported.[71] A vote by the AITUC to affiliate to the PPTUS was narrowly lost. Hardy also tried to make contact with radical forces in British colonies such as India and Malaya through the British Communist Party, but complained: 'They look upon the PPTUS as they look on all colonial work – it is of third rate importance to them.'[72]

Communists and left-wing trade unionists in Indonesia had early contact with those in Malaya but the situation in the Dutch colony was, if anything, more repressive than in Malaya. At the 1927 Hankow conference the delegate from Indonesia, Musso, reported that trade unions could not function legally and that simple conspiratorial techniques were used: 'Javanese workers find other means of coming together and preparing actions against their oppressors. Numerous auxiliary organisations in the form of social and sports clubs have sprung up in spite of the vigilance of the police and the spies.'[73] Browder reported 'no direct connections' with Indonesia while in early 1929 Musso wrote that attempts to reorganise the party 'have been crushed' and the unions dissolved. Sugono, the chairman of the Central Committee, was tortured by the Dutch.[74] In February 1929 Hardy sent a Chinese courier to arrange for delegates to the Vladivostock conference, but this had proved fruitless.[75]

Delegates from Japan's left-wing union federation, Hyogikai, attended the Hankow conference and meetings of the PPTUS in Shanghai in 1928 as well as the 1929 Vladivostock conference. Repression of red trade unions and of the Japanese Communist Party was savage from the late 1920s onwards and this made regular contact with Shanghai very difficult. The necessity to operate illegally made even simple communication very complex. Hardy complained that he was forced to write totally coded letters to safe addresses which changed four times in the space of 12 months.[76] At the June 1929 conference the Japanese delegate did not appear because Hardy received the details of the rendezvous from Japan only half an hour before the appointed time and the delegate left Shanghai without making contact. The methods of maintaining contact included the discreet publishing of certain numbers in the left-wing Japanese press denoting the current codes, a method used by the Bolshevik press.[77] While in 1928 the PPTUS hailed the left-wing Hyogikai, Hardy privately acknowledged that it had lost much of its strength.

THE PPTUS UNDER 'LEON' AND 'EDWARD': 1930–1931

Hardy left Shanghai in mid-1930 and went on to lead the Profintern's maritime work through which it operated an international courier service.[78] His replacement by 'Leon' was accompanied by a sharp deterioration in the security of Comintern activities and a break in contact between Moscow and Shanghai which lasted from June until the end of the year.[79] The security of the conspiratorial work in Shanghai also changed. In September 'Leon' reported to the Profintern in Moscow that the Bureau had issued its first bulletin but this was 'technically almost unthinkable and extremely risky'.[80] However the Bureau continued to work closely with the ACLF and maintained good contacts with the left-wing Filipino trade unions. An organiser was based in Hong Kong with a brief to work with trade unions in Indo-China and Malaya.

In January 1931 after this period of disruption a new plan for work was decided and the leadership of the PPTUS was reconstituted on instructions from the Profintern.[81] New leaders of the PPTUS, 'Leon' and 'Edward', were appointed and their activities can be followed using both the new Soviet archives and the long-standing records of the Shanghai Municipal Police.[82] 'Edward' (or 'Kennedy') was an American, Charles Krumbein, who arrived in Shanghai in early 1931.[83] The previous year he had been jailed in Britain, where police believed he was a Comintern representative. While in jail his partner, Margaret Undjus, visited him. In Shanghai the two lived together under the names Mr and Mrs Albert E. Stewart, with Undjus using the name 'Alice'. The identity of 'Leon' is less certain but a British intelligence analysis suggested that he was probably James Dolson, an American journalist and com-munist who had been associated with Comintern activities in China from 1927 to 1928.[84] Dolson's presence in Shanghai in 1931 is confirmed by other Russian material.[85]

A major preoccupation of the PPTUS was assistance of the ACLF, including the recommencement of the journal *Pan Pacific Worker*. But the ACLF was badly damaged by a major split in the CPC (see below) and much of the first half of 1931 was spent rebuilding small trade union groups within the tram, rail, textile and seamen's unions. A wave of spontaneous strikes in the cotton and silk industries where the workers were mainly women lifted hopes that the tide was turning and 'Alice' made systematic contact with women workers.[86]

Beyond Shanghai, the work of the PPTUS continued. In April–May 1931, 'Leon' visited the Philippines where he found that 'the same handful of 4–5 comrades' were trying to manage the new communist party, the trade union federation and the peasants' federation.[87] The arrests of the Filipino trade union and peasant leaders Manahan and Evangelista for sedition following the founding of the Communist Party of the Philippines in November 1930 led to a PPTUS campaign of solidarity.[88] In early 1931 the PPTUS began to have regular contact with Japanese communists and the trade unions which they led. Around May the Indonesian communist, Tan Malaka, was found living in Shanghai in a debilitated state. After medical treatment and rest, he was due to go south to establish contacts in Indonesia and India. Their continual frustration with colonies like Indonesia, Malaya and India led the PPTUS to write an 'open letter' criticising American, Dutch and French CPs for neglecting colonial work and demanding that the Executive Bureau of Profintern discuss this.[89]

This frustration also resulted in determination to develop work based in Singapore and Malaya, evidently because it offered access to India and Indonesia, as well as having a growing left-wing movement. This decision to work in the British colony was later to become crucial to the fate of the PPTUS. In early 1931 the PPTUS decided to send two cadres on visits of six to eight weeks, 'during which time they are to find out and establish permanent connections with Indonesian and Hindoo comrades in Singapore and through them with these respective countries'.[90]

At the beginning of 1931 the underground trade union movement in China received a serious blow. This came not from the KMT government but from within the CPC. Over the previous two years criticism by the ECCI had been growing of the adventurist political strategy proposed by a key member of the CPC Politbureau, Li Li-san. This had culminated in a letter from the Comintern in November 1930 and the arrival at this time of a Comintern representative, Pavel Mif, who helped unseat Li Li-san at the Fourth Plenum of the CPC in January 1931.[91] The plenum also isolated the 'Right' faction (creating a three-way split), one of whose key leaders was a leading trade unionist, Lo Chang-lung.

The ACLF, perhaps closer to the day-to-day concerns of workers, was a base of opposition to Li Li-san's strategy which called for immediate armed uprisings and political strikes. In February 1931 'Leon' reported disturbing information about the state of underground communist work among trade unions in Shanghai.[92] At a faction meeting of ACLF cadres, 18 out of 19 had voted against the line of the fourth plenum, that is, against the clear wishes of the Comintern and the CPC majority. This split in the party resulted in most of the union activists in the ACLF breaking away and this left the CPC and the PPTUS with very few forces, reported 'Leon'. He railed against the treachery of the 'Right' faction. 'This faction used our people, our apparatus, our printing press, our money – for their own fractional purposes. The Treasurer of the ACLF (Ou-Yu-Min) absconded with over 3,000 Mex, probably under Lochanlun's orders.'

Worse than this, all earlier assumptions about the strength of the underground union movement were discovered to be false. Before the split, he explained, 'Leon' had believed the membership of the red trade unions in Shanghai to be between 700 and 800. 'It is now clear that what really existed was – an apparatus, self-contained and almost completely isolated from the mass and their daily struggles (with but very few exceptions).' When he asked about previous claims, the Chinese comrades 'smile and shrug their shoulders and say they were never true!' To help retrieve this drastic situation, 'Leon' also passed on to Moscow the request of the Chinese party that Lui Shao Chi be sent back to help lead the trade union work.

The situation worsened in April and June 1931 when two events badly damaged the Comintern apparatus in Shanghai and severely tested the effectiveness of its conspiratorial practices.

The first occurred in April 1931, when a member of the Political Bureau of the CPC, Ku Shun-chang, was arrested by the KMT in Hankow and revealed details of CPC organisation leading to the arrest of a large number of communist cadre in Shanghai. Key CPC leaders who escaped arrest disappeared but in spite of such precautions the general secretary of the CPC, Hsiang Chung-fa, was arrested and executed in June 1931.[93]

The arrest of Ku Shun-chang and his co-operation with the KMT meant that the Far Eastern Bureau of Comintern and PPTUS apparatuses also had to take rapid precautions and a 'wild state of disorganisation' followed as they struggled to preserve their lives and their organisation.[94] Just before his arrest, Ku had organised an unsuccessful attempt to smuggle two Soviet military advisers to the Red Army and so they had to leave immediately.[95]

The PPTUS leader, 'Leon', was on the point of returning from the Philippines to rejoin his colleagues Krumbein ('Kennedy') and Margaret

Undjus ('Alice'). On June 9 Krumbein reported to Moscow that most of the members of the Far Eastern Bureau had left and that the arrests since April had 'to a very large degree shattered our apparatus'. He closed his letter with the following: 'we feel certain that if we once can get our comrades on the correct track that things will take a rapid turn'.[96]

A rapid turn began on 1 June, when a courier for the Comintern's OMS, Joseph Ducroux, was arrested in Singapore. Ducroux had travelled from Shanghai to Hong Kong where he had met the Vietnamese communist, Ho Chi Minh. Shortly afterwards, British police intercepted an 'invisible ink' letter from Ho Chi Minh to a leading Malayan communist which set up a meeting with Ducroux.[97] This plus some unusual behaviour by Ducroux led to his arrest along with that of several members of the Malayan Communist Party immediately after the meeting.

Ducroux had been on a mission for the OMS to India and when passing through Shanghai had been given a Shanghai postal address used by the OMS.[98] When he was arrested, the police found both the Shanghai address as well as some reference to Ho Chi Minh. This breach of conspiratorial practice which broke down the compartmentalised structure of two other fields of work led to the arrest of Ho Chi Minh and to the arrest in Shanghai of two key Comintern cadres, Jakov Rudnik and Tatiana Moiseenko.[99] The latter worked under the pseudonyms of M. Hilaire Noulens and Mme Noulens.

In fact, Rudnik and Moiseenko stood at the conspiratorial heart of the Comintern's Shanghai apparatus. Both had worked for Soviet intelligence in the 1920s and then for Comintern's OMS.[100] As OMS officers, they were responsible for the entire technical and administrative support of the Far Eastern Bureau of Comintern and for the PPTUS. On top of this, following the crisis engendered by the April arrest of Ku, a large number of the PPTUS and FEB documents were given to Rudnik and Moiseenko for safekeeping since it was accurately assumed that Ku was unaware of the identities of the OMS officers.

Shortly after the British police arrested M. Noulens (of whose activities they had no inkling at first) they began to discover a treasure trove of letters, cables, finance records, addresses, ciphers and bank books, all related to the Comintern. These in turn allowed them to establish the movements of Comintern officials as well as their code names. In an analysis of the 'Noulens case' one year later, British intelligence declared that it 'afforded a unique opportunity of seeing from the inside, and on unimpeachable documentary evidence, the working of a highly developed Communist organisation of the 'illegal' order ... one moreover which ... is still in operation in spite of the set-back'.[101] Of particular interest was a large number of letters from 'the notorious Annamite communist, Nguyen Ai Quac' (Ho Chi Minh). The 'most outstanding document' was a report from the CPC on the revenge killings of members of the family of Ku, carried out under the direction of Chou En-lai.[102]

With their identities still unknown, the two OMS officers were tried, sentenced to death, then jailed instead and survived to return to Russia in 1939, a date which, ironically, ensured that they survived the worst Stalinist repression. On their return, they wrote a detailed report which is now available.[103] Combined with other Soviet archives and the British analysis, we can now grasp the underground structure in Shanghai and get a picture of its operation. The Far Eastern Bureau, staffed by eight or nine Europeans, was oriented to China and was the source of an annual subsidy to the CPC of £95,000. It was also responsible for the selection of students to attend the Communist University of the Peoples of the Far East. The PPTUS had a staff of three Europeans and directed a subsidy of about $25,000 per year to the ACLF. It liaised with red trade unions in south-east Asia and Japan.

The conditions in Shanghai required a high degree of skill in conspiratorial work. The OMS judged that meetings between Comintern officers and the CPC in public places such as cinemas, cafés and parks were far too dangerous and so private apartments had to be used.[104] Rudnik ('Marin') noted that before he began work in Shanghai, he was told that a number of professional people would be able to make their apartments and offices available for conspiratorial purposes. But nothing like this occurred. Renting multiple apartments, he discovered, was complicated because most of them were leased by four large companies. This meant that a large number of passports and pseudonyms had to be used by Rudnik and Moiseenko to avoid obvious questions regarding one man's apparent need for so many apartments and offices. To add to this, the two most senior figures in the FEB, Pavel Mif and Ry'llski ('Austen') spoke only Russian, making translation and interpreting a major task. Mif could not walk around Shanghai in daylight hours because it was judged that, as the former director of the Communist University for the Peoples of the Far East, he might meet former students who now supported the KMT.

120

Both the FEB and PPTUS used the normal postal service but all letters between Shanghai and Russia were sent to Berlin to the address of 'some petty communist' who transmitted them to an intermediary from whom they were sent to Moscow. Long cables were broken into coded portions, 'each portion being sent to a different address and out of its proper sequence in the composite message'.[105] Similarly, a system of couriers operated between Russia and most of the major centres in east and south-east Asia.

Rudnik was meticulous in his conspiratorial technique, but not perfect. An American report into the Noulens Affair, prompted by the discovery that Richard Sorge had spent 1930–2 in Shanghai, noted that while under arrest, Rudnik asked to change into a grey suit. Examination of the suit by the Shanghai Municipal Police revealed that 'the three tabs bearing the tailor's name had either been deliberately cut out or frayed, so that they were illegible. Most of the buttons had been changed too. The trouser buttons, however, were untouched.'[106] Tailors' marks on the buttons led to the identification of Rudnik with another person, 'Mr Alison', adding another small piece to the jigsaw puzzle of Comintern presence in Shanghai.

How effective was the system of conspiracy which was used by the Far Eastern Bureau, the PPTUS and the two OMS officials? On first glance it would seem to have failed dramatically. The arrests of Rudnik, Moiseenko, Ducroux, the Malayan communists and Ho Chi Minh were severe blows; the apparatus and connections from Shanghai to Singapore were unusable; the mass of documents offered British and American intelligence an insight into Comintern which was unparalleled since the Arcos raid in Britain in 1926.

Yet the damage was limited. In spite of being able to identify a number of Comintern officials by code name, residence, dates of arrival and travel and personal habits, the British were unable to arrest any of these individuals. Except in the case of 'Edward' and 'Alice' (Krumbein and Undjus) no independent identification was established, which meant that figures such as Pavel Mif and Gerhart Eisler (later a top official in East Germany) slipped through the net. As well, there is no evidence of damage to the officials and apparatus of the CPC. We can conclude therefore first, that the system of establishing false identities and the use of pseudonyms largely worked well. Second, in spite of the collapse of compartmentalisation between the FEB and the PPTUS (Rudnik held the records of both), the more significant 'compartment', between the CPC and the Comintern, remained solid. Third, the raid did not affect Soviet military intelligence based in the city and one of its principal officers, Richard Sorge, followed the progress of the trial and did not leave Shanghai until late 1932.[107]

This was also the conclusion of the British police and intelligence who thought it 'unwise to take too optimistic a view' of the raid and arrests. It was 'to be regretted that Austin, Schneider, Stewart (Kennedy) and Margaret Undjus (Alice) should have been able to cover their tracks and slip away unscathed. And it is a tribute to the efficacy of the system of concealment employed by these people that, except in the case of Stewart and Margaret Undjus, so few of their personal details have been betrayed by the papers as to render their reappearance in the same area, or elsewhere, free of any grave risk to themselves.'[108]

Moreover, the British discovered that the Rudnik–Moiseenko arrests did not stop the continued functioning of the Comintern apparatus. While the trial of those two OMS officers was proceeding during the latter half of 1931, they had reason to believe that the remnants of Comintern were reporting it to Moscow:

> [E]ven when the confusion resulting from the Noulens' raid was at its worst, the conspirative system previously established was still effective enough to afford freedom of manoeuvre to the remains of the organisation for the purpose of remodelling its lines and withdrawing its threatened personnel, that the organising centres at Moscow and Berlin never really lost their grip on the situation and that gradually and furtively the Comintern's Far Eastern staff are re-establishing themselves.[109]

We can be less certain about the consequences for the CPC's underground trade union work, but it is clear that the practice of the CPC underground was much less successful. This was not only because of severe repression but also because of a major strategic mistake. The fundamental problem lay in the CPC's unwillingness or inability to work in a 'mass' way in the manner prescribed by Lenin's reinvention of the Russian conspiratorial tradition. The only way to break out of conspiratorial isolation was to look to the 'yellow' trade unions and to conduct 'legal work' within them. This was made impossible by a combination of the ECCI's Third Period policies, which discouraged this, and by the CPC's own putschist orientation and its memory of the 1927 disaster, which was preceded by co-operation with KMT forces.

The consequence was that, as more recent Chinese scholarship points out, 'the [CPC] underground had no strategy to join hands with the neutral elements in the labor movement … and attacked all organisations other than the red unions.'[110]

NOTES

1. 'Communist Activities in China, Federated Malay States etc. (The "Noulens Case")'. This is a thorough account, probably from the British Security Service (MI5), of the meaning of the documents uncovered during the Noulens' arrests. Referred to hereafter as 'Communist Activities in China, etc.', Shanghai Municipal Police files, RG 263, D2527/45, NARA.
2. George Hardy, *Those Stormy Years: Memories of the Fight for Freedom on Five Continents*, Lawrence & Wishart, London, 1956, 208.
3. Charles A. Willoughby, *Shanghai Conspiracy: The Sorge Spy Ring*, E. P. Dutton & Company, New York, 1952, 274.
4. A useful summary of the CPC organisation in Shanghai from 1920 to 1949 can be found in Patricia Stranahan, 'Editor's Introduction' to a special issue of *Chinese Studies in History*, winter 1994/5 on the theme of 'The Communist Party in Shanghai'.
5. Information from Soviet military intelligence (GRU) based in Shanghai is found in files of the PPTUS, RTsKhIDNI, 534-8-120.
6. Their identities are discussed below.
7. V. I. Glunin, 'The Comintern and the Rise of the Communist Movement in China', in R. A. Ulyanovsky, *The Comintern and the East*, Progress Publishers, Moscow, 1979.
8. Ming K. Chan, *Historiography of the Chinese Labor Movement, 1895–1949: A Critical Survey and Bibliography*, Hoover Institution Press, Stanford, 1981, 87–8.
9. Frank Farrell, *International Socialism and Australian Labour*, Hale & Iremonger, Sydney, 1981, 126–8.
10. Lozovsky's report, 23 October 1925, RTsKhIDNI, 534-2-29.
11. Bulletin no. 5 of the Fourth Session of the RILU Central Council, 13 March 1926, RTsKhIDNI, 534-2-36.
12. RTsKhIDNI, 534-4-182, 183.
13. Chan, *Historiography*, 102.
14. A. Lozovsky, *The Pan Pacific Trade Union Conference*, RILU, Moscow, 1927, 8.
15. Ibid., 23.
16. *Pan Pacific Worker*, vol. 1, no. 1, 1 July 1927.
17. Ibid.
18. RTsKhIDNI, 495–65a. This is a collection of several *ankheta*, or credential documents, showing his political biography for various conferences and official positions.
19. Johnson's role in the formation of the united party is recounted in Theodore Draper, *The Roots of American Communism*, Viking Press, New York, 1957, 269–70.
20. The *Pan Pacific Worker* was the name of at least three different publications. The first was published from 1 July 1927 and based in Hankow. The only copies of it which I have found are held in the International Institute for Social History in Amsterdam. The second was an Australian edition, produced by the Pan Pacific Relations Committee of the Australian Council of Trade Unions which first published on 2 April 1928. The third was an American edition, published from San Francisco after Earl Browder left Shanghai in December 1928.
21. Letter, 19 November 1929, RTsKhIDNI, 534-4-283.
22. 'Statutes of the Pan-Pacific Trade Union Secretariat', *Pan Pacific Worker*, 2 April 1928 (Australian edition).

23. A letter from an unidentified Comintern cadre from Shanghai to the Foreign Department, OGPU about one such crossing in February 1928 can be found in RTsKhIDNI, 534-8-97.
24. See references in Browder's letters of 22 May 1928 and 1 June 1928, RTsKhIDNI, 534-4-216. The references to 'Max' are numerous and 'Max Zeise' is mentioned in RTsKhIDNI, 534-4-250.
25. Letters from Sydor Stoler in Australia to Profintern Executive Bureau, RTsKhIDNI, 534-4-224.
26. Examples in RTsKhIDNI, 534-4-293.
27. Letters in English and German dated 27 June 1929, RTsKhIDNI, 534-4-250.
28. Cable stamped 14 February 1929, RTsKhIDNI, 534-4-283.
29. Letter from Leon, dated 8 October 1930, RTsKhIDNI, 534-4-319.
30. Letter from Mason, RTsKhIDNI, 534-4-283.
31. Numerous Profintern remissions to France, Spain, Denmark, Portugal, Britain and to the Profintern courier apparatus operated through seamen and seamen's clubs and are recorded in RTsKhIDNI, 534-4-242. An unsigned letter dated 22 February 1930 from a PPTUS functionary (almost certainly George Hardy) notes financial assistance to 'our Chinese organisation' and to unions in Singapore and the Philippines, RTsKhIDNI, 534-4-316.
32. See note dated 20/6/29, RTsKhIDNI, 534-4-242.
33. 'The Pan Pacific Secretariat Meeting', five-page report by Browder, RTsKhIDNI, 534-4-216.
34. Letter to Comrade Alexander from Charles and Russell, Shanghai, 22 May 1928, RTsKhIDNI, 534-4-216.
35. Browder to Secretariat, RILU, 8 May 1929, RTsKhIDNI, 534-4-216.
36. 'Resolution on the Trade Union Movement', dated April 1928, RTsKhIDNI, 534-4-216.
37. Letter from Charles and Russell, 22 May 1928, RTsKhIDNI, 534-4-216.
38. Letter from Charles Sexi and Earl Russell, 1 June 1928, RTsKhIDNI, 534-4-216.
39. The Times, 31 December, 1928.
40. Letter from Charlie to Sydor Stolar, undated, approximately November 1928, RTsKhIDNI, 534-4-224; Stolar blamed the fight on 'fractionalisme Americain' in a letter of February 1929 (534-4-293).
41. Among Comintern workers there was a controversy over whether Browder's departure was the result of a bitter quarrel with Stein (Johnson) or whether he became aware that he was being watched by the Shanghai police. Quarrels certainly took place but increased surveillance also seems highly likely, see letter from 'Crosby' and 'Marion' to Alexander, 30 January 1929, RTsKhIDNI, 534-4-283.
42. Cable from Steinert to Alexander, 14 February 1929, RTsKhIDNI, 534-4-283.
43. Many of Mason's letters are signed with a 'G' and Hardy's autobiography, Those Stormy Years, also relates his experience in Shanghai. The following is based on selections of a Comintern 'autobiography' by George Hardy in his personal file at RTsKhIDNI, 495-198-1120.
44. Handwritten letter addressed 'Profintern c/– Comintern, Nov. 25th', RTsKhIDNI, 534-4-283.
45. Pan Pacific Monthly, [San Francisco] no. 33 (Dec.–Jan. 1930).
46. Mason to Alexander, 19 November 1929, RTsKhIDNI, 534-4-283.
47. Mason to Alexander, 3 May 1929, RTsKhIDNI, 534-4-283.
48. The Times, 24 June 1929.
49. 'Conference of countries with illegal or semi-legal unions', RTsKhIDNI, 534-2-113.
50. Chan, Historiography, 107.
51. A. M. Grigoriev, 'The Comintern and the Revolutionary Movement in China Under the Slogan of the Soviets (1927–1931)', in Ulyanovsky, Comintern and the East, 362.
52. Mason to Alexander, 19 November 1929, RTsKhIDNI, 534-4-283.
53. Mason to Alexander, 23 February 1929, RTsKhIDNI, 534-4-283.
54. Mason to Alexander, 3 May 1929, RTsKhIDNI, 534-4-283.

55. *InPreCorr*, 30 August, 1929.
56. 'Resolution of the ECCI on Communist Work in the Trade Unions of China', *InPreCorr*, 20 September 1929.
57. Mason to Alexander, 19 November 1929, RTsKhIDNI, 534-4-283.
58. *Pan Pacific Worker* (Australian edition), 15 April 1928.
59. 'Report in the Activities of the PPTUS', RTsKhIDNI, 534-4-216.
60. Mason to Alexander, 23 February 1929, RTsKhIDNI, 534-4-283.
61. Letter of 20 September 1929, RTsKhIDNI 534-4-283.
62. Ibid.
63. 'Geee to Jack', 14 October 1929, RTsKhIDNI, 534-4-294.
64. Charles B. McLane, *Soviet Strategies in Southeast Asia: an Exploration of Eastern Policy Under Lenin and Stalin*, Princeton University Press, Princeton, 1966, esp. 128–31.
65. Cheah Boon Kheng, *From PKI to the Comintern, 1924–1941: The Apprenticeship of the Malayan Communist Party*, Southeast Asia Program, Cornell University Press, Ithaca, NY, 1992, 6–7.
66. 'Report on the activities of the PPTUS since the February Plenum', RTsKhIDNI, 534-4-216.
67. Hardy is apparently basing this on press reports which I cannot confirm. He attributes the report of the execution to a member of the Politburo of the CPC. Letter, 3 May 1929, RTsKhIDNI, 534-4-283.
68. Letter of 20 September 1929, RTsKhIDNI, 534-4-283.
69. Yong cites a contemporary British report: C. F. Yong, *Chinese Leadership and Power in Colonial Singapore*, Times Academic Press, Singapore, 1992, ch. 11.
70. *InPreCorr*, 19 July 1929.
71. *Pan Pacific Worker*, 15 January and 1 April 1929.
72. Mason to Alexander, 19 November 1929, RTsKhIDNI, 534-4-283.
73. *Pan Pacific Worker*, vol. 1, no. 1, 1 July 1927, 11.
74. Musso, 'The White Terror in Indonesia', *InPreCorr*, 8 March 1929.
75. Mason to Alexander, 23 February 1929, RTsKhIDNI, 534-4-283.
76. Mason to Alexander, 19 November 1929, RTsKhIDNI, 534-4-283.
77. Mason (Hardy) complained that 'The code letters published in the Japanese press are not PPTUS code', letter dated 19 November 1929, RTsKhIDNI 534-4-283.
78. As with many dates and events, it is difficult to establish the departure of Hardy and the arrival of Leon from the archival documents because of their conspiratorial and incomplete nature. The last letter from Hardy to 'Alexander' is dated 22 February 1930 (file 312). Leon's first letter is dated 19 August 1930 (file 319). On Hardy's position in the maritime union see Nollau, *International Communism*, 149.
79. See letters from 'Leon' dated 19 August and 8 October 1930 in RTsKhIDNI, 534-4-319.
80. Undated letter, probably September 1930, headed 'Dear friend', RTsKhIDNI, 534-4-319.
81. Two copies of instructions worded slightly differently are found in RTsKhIDNI, 534-4-360. The Plan of Work, dated 4 March 1931, is found in RTsKhIDNI, 534-4-369.
82. 'Shanghai Municipal Police, formerly classified Investigation Files, 1916–47', NARA, Record Group 263. See Jo Ann Williamson, *Records of the Shanghai Municipal Police, 1894–1949*, National Archives and Records Administration, Washington, DC, 1993.
83. Details of Krumbein's work as 'Kennedy' is in Frederick S. Litten, 'The Noulens Affair', *China Quarterly*, no. 138 (June 1994), 492–512. This is a detailed account of the FEB's operations which identified the Noulens couple by their Russian names for the first time. Krumbein was national treasurer of the CPUSA from 1938 until his death in 1947. Bernard K. Johnpoll and Harvey Klehr, *Biographical Dictionary of the American Left*, Greenwood Press, Westport, CT, 1986, 233–4.
84. 'Communist Activities in China, etc.'
85. This is a September 1939 report by Yakov Rudnik ('Hilaire Noulens') which is found at RTsKhIDNI, 579-1-151. This document (referred to hereafter as the 'Rudnik Report') is not publicly available, being part of a Comintern personal file, however, Dimitri Moiseenko,

the son of Yakov Rudnik and Tatiana Moiseenko, kindly made available a summary of it. This identifies Dolson as the MOPR representative on the Far Eastern Bureau in 1928–9 and refers to him leaving Shanghai in the first half of 1931 following the betrayal of the CPC leader Ku. It does not however identify him as 'Leon'.

86. Alice to Alexander, 8 June 1931, RTsKhIDNI, 534-4-370.
87. Letter of 24 February 1931, RTsKhIDNI, 534-4-370.
88. McLane, *Soviet Strategies*, 165–7.
89. 'To the Executive Buro of the RILU', 17 March, 1931, RTsKhIDNI, 534-4-370.
90. Plan of Work, 4 March 1931, RTsKhIDNI, 534-4-369.
91. Richard C. Thornton, *The Comintern and the Chinese Communists 1928–1931*, University of Washington Press, Seattle, 1969, esp. ch. 9.
92. Leon to Alex, 24 February 1931, RTsKhIDNI, 534-4-370.
93. 'Communist Activities in China, etc.', 32.
94. Ibid., 32.
95. Rudnik Report.
96. Edward to Alex, 9 June 1931, RTsKhIDNI, 534-4-370.
97. 'Communist Activities in China, etc.', index, 6. The reference to Ducroux's behaviour is this document at 18.
98. Ducroux's role is based on his personal memoir dated 8 October 1969 provided to me by Dimitri Moiseenko, the son of the two OMS officers, Rudnik and Moiseenko. A number of articles have been written about Ducroux, often contradictory in their details: Laurent Metzger, 'Joseph Ducroux, a French Agent of the Comintern in Singapore (1931–1932)', *Journal of the Malayan Branch of the Royal Asiatic Society*, vol. 69, part 1 (1996); Dennis J. Duncanson, 'Ho Chi Minh in Hong Kong, 1931–32', *China Quarterly*, no. 57 (Jan.–Mar. 1974); Yong, *Chinese Leadership*, chs. 11, 12. Because of the damage done as a result of Ducroux's arrest, his own account cannot be assumed to be absolutely reliable.
99. Litten, 'Noulens Affair', 492–512.
100. Personal interview, Dimitri Moiseenko, 21 December 1996.
101. 'Communist Activities in China, etc.' 1.
102. Ibid., 33.
103. That is, the Rudnik Report.
104. All this is based on chapter 7, 'The work of OMS', in the Rudnik Report.
105. 'Communist Activities in China, etc.', 16–17.
106. 'The Noulens Case', File 2527/44-92, RG 263, NARA, 27. See also appendices, file 2527/41, RG 263, NARA.
107. Personal interview, Dimitri Moiseenko, 21 December 1996; F. W. Deakin and G. R. Storry, *The Case of Richard Sorge*, Chatto & Windus, London, 1966, 65–81. The role of Soviet military intelligence in Shanghai in protecting the work of the Comintern is confirmed in 1929 cables to Lozovsky, RTsKhIDNI, 534-8-120.
108. 'Communist Activities in China, etc.'. Austin was Ry'llski from the FEB and Schneider was an OMS officer, according to the Rudnik Report.
109. Ibid., 39.
110. Rao Jingying, 'The Shanghai Postal Workers' Union: Sample of a Yellow Union', in E. J. Perry and J. N. Wasserstrom (eds.), *Chinese Studies in History: Shanghai Social Movements 1919–1949* (fall–winter 1993/94), 151.

CHAPTER FIVE

The 1930s: from the Underground to Espionage

> For conspiracy itself is dull work. Its mysteries quickly become a bore, its secrecy a burden and its involved way of doing things a nuisance. Its object is never to provide excitement, but to avoid it. Thrills means that something has gone wrong ... I have never known a good conspirator who enjoyed conspiracy.
>
> Whittaker Chambers[1]

> The first duty of an underground worker is to perfect not only his cover story but also his cover personality ... I was baptised the hard way, in Nazi Germany and Fascist Spain, where a slip might have had consequences which can only be described as dire.
>
> Kim Philby[2]

In the 1920s the repression faced by newly created communist parties demonstrated the need for the clandestine techniques developed in Russia before the revolution. In the following period, which began when the ultra-leftist Third Period coincided with the 1929 Wall Street crisis, another expression of *konspiratsya* made itself felt in the West. Soviet intelligence began to recruit middle-class American, German and British communists.

The vehicle for the recruitment was frequently the Communist International and a number of recruits believed, initially, that they were working for Comintern rather than for Soviet intelligence. This period also saw the Comintern intensify its call for legal communist parties to construct an illegal apparatus. Specifically, Comintern also issued instructions for parties to select a group of members who would cease to be open about their membership.[3] These two interconnected tracks, one covert and the other overt, one involving espionage and the other underground political work, form the subject of this chapter.

THE AMERICAN COMMUNIST UNDERGROUND

The central European and Russian tradition of underground work was brought to the Communist Party of the United States not only by Comintern doctrine but also by the many immigrant workers who for a long period made up the majority of that party's membership. This tradition was so strong that in the early stages of the formation of the CPUSA Comintern ordered the party to cease operating as underground cells and to have a public presence.[4]

During the 1930s however, Soviet intelligence agencies co-operated closely with the political underground of the CPUSA. The details of this co-operation and of the functioning of the CPUSA's underground figured prominently in one of the Cold War's most controversial episodes, in which an ex-CPUSA member, Whittaker Chambers, testified that a leading civil servant, Alger Hiss, was a secret party member and had collected information to give to the Russians. The broad sweep of Chambers' allegations are now beyond doubt.[5] Recent searches of the Comintern archives have revealed a number of documents that not only tend to confirm Chambers' claims but also give some insight into the methods of *konspiratsya*. These documents show the close and witting connection between leaders of the CPUSA, such as Browder, and Soviet intelligence, and also the close co-operation between the NKVD and Comintern, the former often using the files of the latter to vet candidates for espionage tasks.[6]

Chambers had been a CPUSA member since 1925, had worked as a journalist on the *Daily Worker* and in 1932 was briefly appointed editor of *New Masses*, a party literary journal.[7] In 1932 he was asked by the CPUSA to work in its underground organisation. The underground in the period of the early 1930s closely and elaborately followed the practices of *konspiratsya*. In his account of his work in the CPUSA underground, Chambers devoted a section to outlining techniques which are very similar to those in the Comintern's Rules for Party Conspiratorial Work.[8]

All meetings were by pre-arrangement. For example when I met Don [John Sherman] we would agree before we parted when and

128

where we would meet next. Telephones were always assumed to be tapped ... For unscheduled or emergency meetings there was a 'reserve meeting place' ... Before any meeting, at least half an hour and preferably one or two hours, should be spent wandering around town, changing conveyances and direction to make sure there was no surveillance.[9]

Meetings were arranged in busy public places like diners or movie houses, with punctuality always vital. If members of the apparatus were arrested they had to assert their innocence at all times and divulge nothing. 'Decades of underground experience had shown that any suspect who admits to one fact, however trifling he may believe it to be, will end by telling all', declared Chambers.[10] During Chambers' first period in the underground a New York dentist, Dr Phillip Rosenbliett, was an important link. His surgery and waiting-room acted as a liaison point, with 'patients' who were given messages or material when they saw the dentist. In the slang of the Russian underground, Rosenbliett's surgery was a *yafka*.

But while the New York underground group knew the theory, they did not always practise it. In this first period, as Allen Weinstein notes, the underground apparatus was 'crude and haphazard'. Chambers was very indiscreet, maintaining non-party friendships and ostentatiously hinting to some party members that he was doing 'secret work' (behaviour which brings to mind the behaviour of Guy Burgess, see below). Some members of his underground group knew each other socially and met collectively at a safe house on 51st Street, a practice which later changed to prevent members of the same group knowing the identity of others, Chambers recalled. Chambers' underground group based in New York was responsible for maintaining a communications system (using micro-film and 'secret writing') which used German seamen as couriers between Germany and the Soviet Union and the United States.[11] Its other role was to gather industrial and military information on behalf of the Soviet Union. In this period, Chambers' group acted in liaison with a succession of Soviet illegals who were their bosses. Chambers' personal role was a courier between the Soviet illegals and Max Bedacht, the head of the CPUSA's various underground groups.

The illegals represented the GRU, the intelligence wing of the Soviet Red Army which, at that time, was the main Soviet intelligence organisation. The most significant of the illegals was 'Ulrich' (Alexander Petrovich

Ulanovski), who had been a revolutionary under Tsarism and had worked in the 1920s for the GRU in China. In the period 1932–4 the New York group had little success in industrial espionage and, in one instance, when they contacted CP members working at a submarine building company and were able to photograph blueprints, one worker soon confessed to the FBI. The compartmental structure of the underground organisation preserved it from exposure.

In 1934 the GRU agent Ulrich disbanded the group and began transferring agents like Whittaker Chambers to the-then leader of the CPUSA underground, Joseph Peters. Peters' experience with underground work began in Czechoslovakia and Hungary. After being transfered to the CPUSA in 1924, Peters became responsible for organising its underground group in New York in 1930. In 1931–32, he was in Moscow, attached to the Anglo-American Secretariat of Comintern, as a trainee in organisational matters.[12]

In 1934, Peters introduced Whittaker Chambers to the next phase of his work for the underground. He was to be a courier and liaison worker for a CPUSA party branch of government officials in Washington. The branch, known in accounts of this period as 'the Ware group', after its key member, Harold Ware, met as a group in an apartment. Members knew each other by their real names, paid dues and discussed how to operate in the 'New Deal' government agencies for which they worked. In this period, although members of the group copied government documents for the CPUSA, the group was not primarily an espionage group. Later though, some members engaged in espionage.[13]

Many of these CPUSA members worked for the Agricultural Adjustment Administration (AAA) and a number lost their jobs when it was purged of left-wing influence in 1935. By this stage, a key player in the events, lawyer Alger Hiss, had moved from the AAA to a Senate committee investigating the armaments industry and, according to Chambers, copied a number of State Department documents which were then photographed and given to Russian contacts. Hiss's transfer to the Senate committee prompted Peters to separate Hiss and another communist, Harry Dexter White, from the Ware group to form the basis of a more secret group.[14] Both were clearly 'going places' and conspiratorial safeguards were stepped up.

In one odd episode in 1936, Peters proposed that the purloining of government documents become more systematic and that they be sold to their Russian contact, 'Bill' to raise money for the CPUSA.[15] Apparently

'Bill' saw one set of documents obtained from a senior Treasury officer, Harry Dexter White, and rejected them as uninteresting. But shortly afterwards his attitude changed and the 'second apparatus' began to pass secret material to the Russians. In part this was because Hiss had moved once more, to the office of the Assistant Secretary of State, Francis Sayre, and because a new Russian contact, Boris Bykov, had begun to urge Peters and Chambers to begin systematically to collect government documents. This they did, using a number of covert CPUSA members.

The techniques of *konspiratsya* followed by Chambers, Peters and their Soviet contacts in this period generally accorded with that of the Rules for Party Conspiratorial Work, although there were differences. Chambers' adherence to conspiratorial methods in this period became more discreet than it had been in New York. However, as he noted himself, he broke at least one rule of underground work and became a personal friend of Alger Hiss. This action did exactly what the designers of the conspiratorial techniques feared: it endangered Hiss's security. Years later Hiss had to explain to the House UnAmerican Activities Committee how it was that he had known Chambers so closely, including lending him money.

Another breach of the practice of compartmentalising underground work occurred when, according to Chambers, Bykov also arranged to meet Hiss face to face to discuss how the latter could obtain State Department material. While such a meeting was a breach of conspiratorial method, in other instances Bykov rigidly (and absurdly) followed his tradecraft training. He evaded non-existent surveillance by violent and rapid movements, jumping on subway trains as they were about to leave, entering large stores and leaving by a second exit, suspecting all window-shoppers of being *geheimpolizei* (secret police). Bykov also insisted, for example, that Chambers give money to four of his Communist Party sources, a proposal that Chambers rightly rejected as crude and dangerous. After negotiation, Chambers agreed to give each an expensive oriental rug, along with words of thanks from Soviet authorities. This too featured in establishing a case against Hiss and other recipients. But another side of Bykov's behaviour, Chambers argued, damaged some of the unwritten rules of underground work:

> by almost every word he uttered, and the tone he uttered it in, he gave me pointedly to understand that he did not trust me. Underground work cannot exist without mutual trust. For a man not to

be trusted in the underground is the next step to being charged with disloyalty to it. And the fact that a man is suspect destroys in advance practically any chance that he might have to establish his innocence. The walls simply cave in and the ground drops from under his feet.[16]

By 1938, extensive espionage was under way in Washington but Chambers' feelings of disillusionment were growing, partly because of the great purges in the USSR, partly because of Bykov's outlandish behaviour. Worried that his defection could bring reprisals, Chambers preserved some government documents and microfilm as 'insurance'. Years later they were produced as evidence to establish his credibility and to damn Hiss. These documents show that Soviet intelligence had a significant window into secret American diplomacy. They included a large number of copies or summaries of State Department documents and cables dealing with military and foreign affairs matters between January and April 1938. Other material was in Hiss' handwriting and some copied cables and documents appeared to be typed on Hiss' typewriter. Clearly far more than this was given to the Russians and Hiss's espionage and that of others continued during World War Two.[17]

THE CAMBRIDGE GROUP

In Britain in the early 1930s the overlap between Comintern and Soviet espionage was less pronounced than in the United States, as far as we know. The best-known group of spies, Kim Philby, Guy Burgess, Donald Maclean and Anthony Blunt, all studied at Cambridge University, where they developed into communists. Unlike the Washington-based apparatus of the CPUSA, they did not operate as part of any underground political apparatus but worked directly with Soviet intelligence officers. Even though Philby placed himself in the tradition of underground workers, there was no history of underground work in Britain, nor any real need for it, as compared, say, with Russia.

The actions of this group during the 1930s, as they moved from university leftism towards espionage, form a case study both in the links between Comintern and Russian intelligence and in the practical appli-cation of the rules of conspiracy. While the stories of the Cambridge group have been told and retold, it has to be remembered that this trajectory of recruiting young enthusiasts on the basis of politics in an advanced, democratic society and transforming them into intelligence agents, was, at the time, a step into uncharted territory. Cold War accounts by journalists promoting the myth of Philby's 'icy calculation and ruthless dedication' have been dented by accounts based on Soviet archives which show instead his psychological dependence and vulnerability.[18] Similarly, the following reinterpretation, based on several studies which use KGB files, emphasises the compromises with the rules of conspiracy, rather than the imagined well-oiled machine of Soviet espionage.

The recruitment of the key figure, Kim Philby, shows the seamless nature of the distinction between the Comintern underground and Soviet intelligence. In 1933 the conclusion of Kim Philby's studies at Cambridge coincided with his decision to become an active Marxist.[19] In doing so he asked the advice of a Cambridge academic and CPGB member, Maurice Dobb, 'how I should go about it'.[20] As others have remarked, instead of simply recruiting him to party membership, Dobb advised him to contact the Paris-based World Committee for the Relief of Victims of German Fascism.

Though the founder of the committee, Willi Munzenberg, was a talent spotter for the KGB, there is no evidence to suggest that he saw the potential of Philby.[21] Members of his committee in turn advised Philby that he could best help the anti-fascist cause in Vienna by working for the Comintern-based group which went under various names, International Organisation for the Assistance of Revolutionaries, Red Aid, or MOPR, its Russian acronym. Years later Philby explained clearly his transition. The Munzenberg group was 'a perfectly legal and open group'. This group then 'passed me on to a communist underground organisation in Vienna'.[22] The work of MOPR became crucial in the period 1933–4, which saw a bloody attack on the Austrian Left with the shelling of workers' apartments and the lynching of a number of its leaders. Thousands of Austrian communists and socialists were on the run, joining thousands more fleeing the first waves of Hitler's repression in Germany.

Philby's work for MOPR began his underground career. Working first as a courier, then as an activist smuggling refugees out of Austria, he came into contact with the tradition of *konspiratsya*.[23] It is clear that this was a purely political activity and Philby had not yet been recruited to Soviet intelligence because at this stage he made little attempt to hide his leftist beliefs from other Britishers whose assistance he sought.[24] As well, we now know from a personal memoir in the KGB archives to which limited access has been given, that Philby initially tried to join the CPGB on his return from Austria.[25] A number of accounts have credited KGB illegal Teodor Maly with the spotting and recruitment of Philby in Austria.[26] But in his KGB memoir Philby indicates that it was the left-wing Austrian photographer Edith Tudor Hart who met him through his wife and passed his name to an KGB illegal worker in Britain, Arnold Deutsch. Deutsch recruited Philby and instructed him at great length in the art of *konspiratsya*, to the extent that sometimes Philby expressed frustration with his teaching:

> Otto and I met regularly. And he taught me the rules of conspiracy. He hammered them into my head: how to call the necessary person on the phone, how to check, how to recognise a tail in a crowd, and other basics. I got sick of it once and asked politely: 'Otto you are telling me this for the tenth time. In the same words. I have memorised it. Like poetry.' 'The tenth time?' he asked, 'Well that's only the beginning.'[27]

From 1934 onwards, Philby constructed an identity to hide his real beliefs and behaviour, joining the Anglo-German Friendship Society and running a pro-German newsletter. He successfully angled for a position as journalist on *The Times*, covered the Franco side of the Spanish Civil War and systematically cut off connections with left-wing Cambridge friends. By mid-1940, with Burgess' assistance, he had secured a low-level job in the Secret Intelligence Service (SIS or MI6). There he taught something similar to underground technique to agents who were to be dropped into occupied Europe to conduct sabotage and propaganda. As he later noted, he was uniquely qualified for this. 'The first fact to distinguish me from my colleagues was that I was alone in having had personal experience of life underground. Not one of the others had ever dreamt of lowering his voice when passing a policeman in the street.'[28]

Philby's conspiratorial practice was more thorough and careful than that of Burgess and Blunt. Yet like all of his colleagues he was several times betrayed by his sloppiness, only to be rescued by the incompetence of others. His memoirs, *My Silent War*, opens with a dramatic incident in which he was picked up by the Francoist Civil Guards while he was a *Times* journalist in Spain. He was questioned about his reason for not carrying a trifling local permit and his luggage thoroughly searched. Unknown to the police, he was still carrying rice-paper instructions on enciphering messages which he had received from his Russian contact in England in his pocket. As a search of his body was about to begin he emptied his pockets, throwing his wallet in such a way that his captors turned to make a grab for it, allowing him a second for 'a crunch and a swallow' to destroy the dangerous rice-paper. As Philby later concluded, 'the really risky operation is not usually the one which brings most danger, since real risks can be assessed in advance and precautions taken to obviate them. It is the almost meaningless incident ... that often puts one to mortal hazard.'[29] A better justification for the 'rules of conspiracy' could hardly be found.

Throughout all this time, Philby was in regular contact with his Soviet case officer, meeting regularly in Narbonne, a French town just over the border from Spain.[30] Another, more dangerous, incident in Spain was to surface in 1951 when he was interrogated while under suspicion from SIS. Asked how he had supported himself in Spain while not on the *Times* staff, Philby faltered. The whole exercise had been in fact financed by the Russians, who had even used Burgess as a conduit for funds. His interrogator, MI5's Dick White, took this stumble as 'absolutely significant' and Philby was sacked from the SIS shortly afterwards.[31]

Donald Maclean was the first of the Cambridge group to enter the heart of the British government when he successfully applied to join the Foreign Office in 1935. Recruited personally by Philby the previous year, he was probably the most productive agent of the group, sending thousands of cables and reports from London, Paris and Washington over the next 16 years.[32]

One of the most striking episodes throwing light on Maclean's conspiratorial practice occurred in 1938 when he began an affair with his Soviet case officer, known only by her code name 'Norma'. The choice of a female case officer was due to the KGB's estimation that their late night contacts would be less likely to arouse suspicion, according to Costello and Tsarev.[33] The affair resulted in exactly the kind of security problem which the Russians feared: 'Norma' revealed to Maclean the code name by which he was known ('Lyric') as well as her own. The Russians came to know this because of another elementary error when Maclean hand-wrote a letter, signed 'Lyric', to the KGB, welcoming the resumption of contact which had been broken for six months because of the Stalin purges of the intelligence services. Later that year Maclean was assigned to the Paris embassy and 'Norma' although reprimanded, was also reassigned to Paris. The problems with their relationship did not end there. Maclean then fell in love with an American woman, Melinda Marling, in Paris and a stormy confrontation broke out between himself and 'Norma' in January 1940. On top of all this Maclean compounded the problem by revealing to Marling his actual role as diplomat/spy. With some difficulty, the matter was resolved by physical separation of 'Norma' from Maclean, largely due to the German invasion of France.

The most indiscreet of the Cambridge group was Guy Burgess, as many have repeatedly pointed out. We now know that his recruitment to Soviet intelligence was forced on his recruiter, Alexander Orlov.[34] As Maclean began cutting his ties with overt communist politics and building up a right-wing front, Burgess refused to accept this and eventually forced Maclean to admit his real reasons. The incorporation of Burgess into the group introduced a continuing unstable element, which in 1951 finally proved disastrous when he defected on the spur of the moment with Maclean. Burgess thereby drew attention to Philby, his close friend.

Another reason for reluctance to recruit Burgess must have been his trip to Russia in 1934, on which according to his own fanciful account he said he met Piatnitsky and Bukharin.[35] The separate visits to Russia by both Burgess (1934) and Blunt (1935) are also a testimony to the contingent and almost haphazard process of recruitment, in contrast to the portrayal in popular accounts of a well-oiled plan run by an all-knowing Soviet mastermind. According to the rules of conspiracy, such a wanton show of political preference was absolutely ruled out if one was being recruited to the intelligence service. Burgess later joined the staff of an extreme right-wing parliamentarian and became a member of the Anglo-German Friendship Society. Yet as a BBC talks producer and in private, his left-wing beliefs continued to bubble to the surface.[36] In 1936 Guy Burgess told a friend, Goronwy Rees, whom he was trying to recruit: 'I want to tell you that I am a Comintern agent and have been ever since I came down from Cambridge.'[37] Whether Burgess believed his work was for Comintern or whether it was merely a convenient way of initiating the recruitment, it indicates that on some level there was a seamless connection between working for the Comintern underground and working for Soviet intelligence. Despite his erratic conversion to the right, Burgess joined SIS in 1938 though he was later terminated in 1940, only to join the Foreign Office some years later.

Anthony Blunt, who was by the early 1930s a Cambridge don, was formally recruited to Soviet intelligence in 1937, according to recently released KGB documents, much later than earlier accounts.[38] This explains the seemingly cavalier act (for an intelligence agent) of openly writing left-wing art criticism such as his 1937 essay 'Art Under Capitalism and Socialism'.[39] Blunt's initial role was largely as a talent spotter and he recruited the son of a wealthy American family, Michael Straight. Straight later recalled a briefing on conspiratorial technique by a Russian who 'said a few trivial things about telephoning from public booths to avoid detection. Then he departed. He was more like the agent of a small time smuggling operation than the representative of a new international order.'[40] After this Straight was given half of a torn piece of paper as a recognition symbol for a later meeting in the US and worked with Soviet intelligence until the Nazi–Soviet pact.

Blunt's left-wing articles, and his 1935 trip to the USSR, subsequently almost blew his cover. In 1939, as he took tentative steps towards his goal of penetrating British intelligence by joining in the Field Security Police, he was questioned about them. Again, wartime laxness saved the day. In any case Blunt was accepted into MI5 in 1940 where he soon transferred to his preferred section – counter-espionage – enabling him to report on measures against Soviet and German intelligence.

There is another element which should be mentioned in any discussion of *konspiratsya* and the tradecraft of espionage. Burgess and Blunt, while they were surely instructed in the methods of *konspiratsya*, must also have already learned a great deal about clandestine meetings, messages and the habits of secrecy from their experience as homosexuals in a deeply repressive British society. In this sense they were prime candidates for intelligence. Similarly, Whittaker Chambers was a repressed homosexual, having a number of casual lovers during his period in the CPUSA underground.[41] In this context the comment of one of Guy Burgess' lovers, Jack Hewit, about the milieu in which they moved, is telling. 'There was a sort of gay intellectual freemasonry which you know nothing about. It was like the five concentric circles in the Olympic emblem. One person in one circle knew one in another and that's how people met.'[42] Though they are not concentric, the analogy of the Olympic rings is an apt representation of the compartmentalised structure of a conspiratorial organisation, which was sometimes know as the 'chain' system. In addition, Burgess' charm and his ability to make contact with homosexuals in high places was one of his most useful qualities for the Russians, even though they scorned his sexuality as a perversion and detested his bohemian and libertine character.[43]

The KGB defector, Alexander Orlov, who was personally aware of the recruitment of Burgess, singled out the targeting of homosexual western diplomats for special mention. Writing in the mid-1950s, he observed that his strategy had been 'remarkably successful'.[44] Orlov goes on to make a point remarkably similar to Jack Hewit's comment about 'gay freemasonry': 'The Soviet intelligence officers were amazed at the sense of mutual consideration and true loyalty among homosexuals.' He was almost certainly referring to Burgess and his recruiting attempts within his circle.

The most significant lesson that can be learned from the history of the Cambridge group is that while the 'rules of conspiracy' are easy to formulate, concrete circumstances temper or occasionally sweep them aside. The elementary principle of compartmentalising different underground workers was breached from the start when Philby personally recruited Maclean.[45] The recruitment of Burgess, initiated independently of Moscow by Orlov, compounded this breach of *konspiratsya* much to the anger of Moscow, as Costello and Tsarev note. The three even referred to each other, jokingly, as the Three Musketeers. In 1936 Moscow Centre complained at length about this breach of security but little could be done.[46]

Later, in 1941 Moscow became increasingly alarmed at continuing contact between Philby, Blunt and Burgess. It demanded that its case officer stop this practice but he replied that it was 'impossible' and this breach of conspiratorial practice became an added element in the Moscow Centre's growing suspicion that Philby might have been a double agent.[47]

The original handlers of the group, Maly, Deutsch and Orlov, were men who originally learned the rules in political circumstances and then applied them to intelligence. Unlike later professional KGB officers, they tempered the rules to fit the situation and this probably explains both the daring success of the Cambridge group as well as its flaws. Yet they also drummed the lessons of *konspiratsya* into the group. It is interesting to note Deutsch's reasons for the need to imbue the Cambridge group with awareness of conspiratorial practice:

WAISE [Maclean], SYNOK [Philby] and our other agents in England have grown up in a climate in which the legality of our Party is upheld in an atmosphere of democratic illusions. That is why they are sometimes careless and our security measures seem exaggerated to them. If any relaxation of security was permitted on our part, they would become even more undisciplined. That is why, when running them we should stick strictly to the essential security measures even at the risk of cutting faintly ridiculous figures.[48]

The breaches of conspiratorial practice were not all on the side of the 'relaxed' agent-handlers like Maly, Deutsch and Orlov. Philby's secret reports from the Franco side in Spain were mailed by him to an address in Paris which he later found out was the Soviet embassy.[49] Though coded, in invisible ink and signed by pseudonyms it would not have taken long to identify him, had the reports been copied by the French police and passed on to the Franco side.

The eventual exposure of the Cambridge group, however, was not due to such breaches but to the breaking of coded Soviet cables which pointed to Maclean as a source of information when he was stationed in the US. That they were not identified until relatively late was partly due to the success of conspiratorial technique (and also to the inefficiency of British intelligence and the tumult of the Second World War).

COMINTERN'S UNDERGROUND: COMBINING LEGAL AND ILLEGAL MEANS

From the earliest days of the Great Depression, the Comintern had strongly promoted the construction of underground organisations in affiliated parties, arguing that depression would quickly lead to war with consequent savage repression. In the democratic West, this did not occur but the triumph of Nazism in Germany was sufficient to sustain this strategy throughout the 1930s. In 1933 the Comintern issued its most definitive public statement of 'conspirative' principles. Much of the statement drew on the 'Rules for Party Conspiratorial Work' already discussed. In the concrete circumstances of the early 1930s, namely the brutal attacks aimed at communists in central Europe, this statement argued that illegality provided the best defence. Slowness in accepting this, it said, was due to 'legalist superstitions'. In the place of Leninist doctrine calling for the combination of legal and illegal work, the Comintern tipped the balance towards illegal work. Its cardinal point echoed the experience of the Russian underground.

The basic principle of illegal work of the Communist Parties – worked out through decades of Bolshevik underground activity –

is the ability to preserve the mass character of the party in its underground activity during the most savage terror. The essence of illegality does not lie in hiding a small group of people from the enemy; it lies in carrying on uninterrupted mass work.[50]

Compartmentalisation was one key. Important sections of the party, such as the leadership and the printing and distribution apparatus, had to be isolated from each other. It was 'impermissible to use the same address or quarters for different organisations. Tying them up in one big knot aggravates the dangers of a raid', it argued. Another hazard of underground work, based on the Russian experience, was the tendency to concentrate too many secrets in the technical (printing and adminis-trative) apparatus and then to neglect this apparatus. Codes, address lists and safe houses had to be frequently changed. An illegal party had to be surrounded by 'a large cadre of sympathisers and revolutionary, non-party activists'. The German experience meant that centralisation of party work, so long a feature of Bolshevism, had to be tempered so that central organs were at least physically separate. An independent local leadership was also needed 'which will be able to react immediately to events, without waiting for directives from the centre'.

This and other calls by the Comintern for conspiratorial organisation took root in individual communist parties not only because of their loyalty to the Comintern but also because it responded to local conditions. The upsurge in communist militancy in the West, as a result of the Depression, and the Third Period leftism led to an accompanying tightening of legal and extra-legal repression aimed at that militancy. In turn this provided the conditions in which the practical application of the principles of *konspiratsya* became a realistic option. In the section that follows, I examine an aspect of the political underground which was downplayed by the Comintern in the early 1930s – the struggle to combine legal methods with more usual illegal methods.

LEGAL AND ILLEGAL METHODS IN AUSTRALIA

The struggle by the Australian Communist Party against its banning, which set important legal precedents in Australian common law, began in an almost shame-faced manner. The leadership of the party was clearly wary of appearing to believe in 'legalist superstitions'. The circumstances for its struggle was the long reign of a conservative federal government which held office from December 1931 until 1941. In this period it passed a series of laws aimed at banning the CPA and repressing militant unionism.

At the beginning of this period, the Communist Party of Australia was in the throes of internal upheaval. In December 1929 the annual CPA conference had dismissed most of its existing leadership for 'right wing deviationism'. This internal upheaval was followed by the intervention of a Comintern 'instructor', Herbert Moore Wicks, who 'Bolshevised' the CPA.[51] Wicks (who used the name Herbert Moore in Australia) was a member of the CPUSA and encouraged a dogmatic approach, brooked no opposition and expelled several leading communists.

The election of 19 December 1931 saw the sweeping defeat of a brief, ineffectual Labor government which had been overtaken by the events of the Depression. Its replacement was a government led by the United Australia Party under Joseph Lyons and his deputy John Latham. It took office amid popular fears of communism and a campaign promise to outlaw it.

One week before the triumphant win by conservatism, the CPA leadership realised that it was not prepared to face outlawry and that there was an '[a]lmost complete absence of satisfactory underground contacts' and this put the party into 'a very weak position to meet the situation of illegality'.[52] The Political Bureau decided on an elementary plan of action that sketched out a pattern which would become familiar for the next 30 years. '[An] Apparatus must be prepared so that we can function in the event of being declared illegal' and a 'second line of leadership' had to be developed to replace arrested leaders.[53]

At the end of December 1931 a report to Central Committee spelt out precautionary measures in more detail.

> Where mail is used for confidential letters, addresses unknown to our enemies must be used. In the localities, a system of couriers must be organised to establish personal contact with the various Party organs when delivering instructions and literature ... In the event of arrest, members must not answer any questions either at the preliminary hearings or in the Courts. The Party will wage a strenuous struggle for a legal existence ...[54]

To meet the threat the CPA responded in two ways. First, it was determined to continue its activity under conditions of illegality. It urged its supporters to learn from the negative example of the Industrial

141

Workers of the World (IWW) which collapsed after being banned in World War One.

> The IWW made no definite preparations to meet the capitalist attack, nor did they take any steps to protect their organisation. They helped the capitalists to suppress them with their romantic talk of 'filling the capitalist gaols' and in many cases seeking voluntary martyrdom.[55]

Second, it placed a high priority on remaining legal. 'Opportunist ideas that the Party "will grow under illegal conditions" must be exposed as tending towards the liquidation of activity.' Mass activity against war and fascism was the answer to the proposed ban.[56] But while it hailed 'legal methods' in principle, its practice was less than whole-hearted.

The new conservative government's Attorney-General was John Latham, a man who 'vehemently despised' communism.[57] In May 1932 he placed before parliament a series of tough amendments to the Crimes Act, similar but more far-reaching than previous amendments introduced in 1926–8. Both were aimed at militant unionism and the CPA. The 1926–8 amendments included one year's jail for members of unlawful associations; jail or deportation for those who 'by speech or writing' advocated revolution or the destruction of property; six months' jail for selling literature of an unlawful association and the confiscation of all property held by an unlawful association.

The new amendments would give power to the High Court or state supreme courts to 'declare' a body of people to be 'an unlawful association', thus remedying a defect in the 1926 law. Under its provisions averments presented by the Attorney-General to the court constituted a *prima facie* case and the onus of proof lay on the body of people to establish it was not an unlawful association.[58]

Introducing the bill, assistant treasurer, Stanley Bruce argued that it would 'help the Government excise a social cancer'.[59] 'In these restless times when subversive doctrines are being preached, and the loyalty of the community and the stability of our institutions are being undermined, the widest power to deal with unlawful associations is essential in the interests of society', he said.[60]

On 1 September the federal government summonsed the publisher of the *Workers Weekly* , Harold Devanny, charging him under Section 30D of the Crimes Act with soliciting funds for an unlawful association. To fight Devanny's prosecution and thereby defend the legality of the party, the CPA had engaged solicitor Christian Jollie-Smith, who had been a founding member of the CPA and a non-party barrister, Clive Evatt. Evatt's view was that the CPA could retain its legality through making a case on purely legal grounds. In a magistrate's court he argued that the section of the Crimes Act under which Devanny was charged was unconstitutional. As well, he argued '[t]here is nothing unlawful about being opposed to war'.[61] The pleadings were to no avail and Devanny was convicted and sentenced to six months' hard labour. Evatt announced an immediate appeal to the High Court.

With outlawry a real possibility and little faith in the High Court, the CPA dramatically foreshadowed its imagined future:

> We must ... utilise the remaining breathing space to make sound preparations to ward off the blows of the bourgeoisie, to prove ourselves worthy comrades in arms of our heroic brothers in the Communist Parties of the White terror countries – China, Italy, Hungary and others – who have not only maintained but successfully built Bolshevik parties and conducted revolutionary struggles under conditions of pitiless terror.[62]

Far from being pitiless terror, the government's legal offensive was pitifully incompetent. As the CPA's lawyers probed the government case, they found it fraught with legal blunders to the extent that the original summonses were withdrawn and reissued. But the crucial weakness was that simple facts could not be established. The government's document conflated the work of the CPA with a number of closely affiliated front organisations such as the Militant Minority Movement (MMM), the Unemployed Workers' Movement, the International Labour Defence and the League Against Imperialism. In this case, there can be no doubt that the *ad hoc* committee planning the anti-war demonstration was effectively in the hands of the CPA, but the government's case assumed rather than proved this.[63]

Behind the scenes the CPA had its own wrangles. Clive Evatt's advice provoked a torrid debate within the CPA leadership about defence tactics. From the start of the case the Political Bureau was concerned to guard 'against creating legalistic illusions'.[64] Advice from Jollie-Smith and Evatt was firmly that the case could be won on legal grounds without the need for a leader of the CPA to enter the witness box. The Political Bureau rejected this and insisted that the president, Lance Sharkey, appear as a witness to 'put the party position – that they attack the party as the spearhead of the working-class movement, to vindicate the party and show it as the champion of the workers' struggles'.[65] In the event, Evatt's advice prevailed over Sharkey and no revolutionary statement from the dock was forthcoming. This was later condemned by the Political Bureau, but excused as 'due to inexperience'.[66]

The High Court case before six judges revealed grave weaknesses in the case against Devanny. On 8 December 1932 the court upheld Devanny's appeal, quashed the conviction and a majority of five judges criticised the crown's case. It was a stinging slap in the face for the federal government.

Yet the significance of this legal and political victory in the High Court was hardly understood by the CPA, which took great pains to minimise it. The reasons for this are bound up in the CPA's view that democracy in capitalist society was a sham. To hail the decision would be to give credit to a conservative institution of capitalist society. It would also mean acknowledging that power in capitalist society was dispersed in a number of institutions which sometimes clashed on major issues. Thus the *Workers Weekly* headlined the article on the Devanny judgement with the words 'Prelude to new attacks' and 'We must have no legalist illusions'. The article warned that 'the High Court is not in any way a defender of the right of workers to organise and collect funds for their struggle against capitalism; it has only decided that Latham must try again'.[67]

The taste of outlawry in 1932 impelled the communists to redouble their efforts in constructing an underground for the rest of the decade. Shortly after the High Court decision the Central Committee emphasised that the threat of illegality was still present and that the party still had to prepare a strong underground organisation. In part this was due to their sheer disbelief that the handling of the federal government case could have simply been incompetent. Party secretary J. B. Miles confessed he was 'suspicious about the stupidity in the Devanny case. It was so awfully stupid that it looks as though it was real.'[68]

The Central Committee man charged with reporting on illegality, Sam Aarons, emphasised that further attacks were expected. He signalled two key themes that were to become central to the handling of illegality by the CPA over the next two decades. The first concerned the paradox of defending the legality of the party under capitalism. On the one hand communists were deeply cynical about the law and viewed liberal democracy as a sham, as their response to the High Court judgement demonstrated. On the other, Aarons argued that 'We have to contest every position, fight to the last ditch on every small point, where the democratic rights and freedoms of the workers are concerned.'[69] He contrasted this determination to defend democratic rights with 'a tendency to get underground at the first approach of the threat of illegality'.

Aarons' second point also appeared contradictory or paradoxical. He argued against those who separated mass work from the question of illegality.

> The question of whether the party shall have a continued legal existence will only be determined in so far as we have penetrated the ranks and taken up the immediate questions of the working class ... The factories are our basis, in the question of the fight against illegality. If we have strong nuclei in the important factories no action can drive the party out of existence.[70]

The Central Committee meeting of December 1932 had before it a clear directive from the Communist International regarding preparations for illegality.[71] This letter was prefaced by a statement that 'increased persecution of communists requires the strict fulfilment of the directives of the ECCI'. It described elaborate conspiratorial methods to be used in factories, but linked mass work to underground work:

> The names of the members of the nucleus must be kept secret, the meetings of the nucleus must be held in private houses, only the members of the nucleus must know the place and time of the meetings and the place of the meeting should be changed as often as possible. In the cases when the members of the Party in the factories, e.g. among the miners, are already known to the management ... the names of the newly accepted members must be kept secret. *The illegal work of the nucleus must in no case lead to a restriction of the mass work of the nucleus, to its separation from the workers.* (emphasis added)[72]

This last point, as we have seen, was a key strategic concept derived from Lenin's reworking of the Russian conspiratorial tradition. It was crucial to political survival and contains the rationale for going underground in the first place. It was both the method and the goal.

The Comintern directive laid down strict guidelines for the reconstruction of the CPA in the event of the federal government successfully banning it:

There must be such a reconstruction of the party committees that will allow for the greatest flexibility in their work, the closest contact with the lower organisations and the ability to display great initiative and self reliance. In particular, it is advisable in the future to set up Party committees with a small membership (7–11 members), changing the existing practice in which the District Committees have 25 or more members.[73]

The issue of going underground was openly discussed in the CPA newspaper which reprinted an article by Comintern leader Osip Piatnitsky:

A great number of examples from the history of the Parties of the Comintern show that when Parties and revolutionary trade unions without any organisations in the factories are driven underground, they immediately lose contact not only with the masses but in many cases even with their own members. There is absolutely no guarantee that the Communist Parties in the most important capitalist countries will not be driven underground.[74]

Piatnitsky's latter prediction soon came true. In January 1933 Adolf Hitler became chancellor of Germany and later that year the German Communist Party was outlawed.

The brush with illegality in the second half of 1932 combined with the advent of Hitler meant that the CPA began to employ more seriously conspiratorial methods which emerged from the experience of European and Russian socialists. The result was a plan drawn up in 1934 for an illegal apparatus.[75]

The 1934 plan is posited on the possibility of an attack on the CPA with little warning, including a rounding up of members of the Political Bureau by the police. It therefore proposed that two members of the eight-person Political Bureau 'go into illegality' immediately and work from private homes rather than party offices. The other six would follow them into 'complete illegality' at signs of 'approaching critical events or anticipation of attack'. The plan recognised that this raised the problem that the Political Bureau would effectively be isolated from the membership and from the district leadership of the party. The answer was to create an alternative leadership, described as a 'working leadership'. These leaders would be a small group of three to five whose main qualification, apart from some organisational and political ability, was that they were not known to the police or public as CPA members. This construction of a second, illegal 'working leadership' was to be followed at the lower levels of the party and in the CPA's street units (local branches).

The key determinant in the success of the plan was the successful functioning of a communications system. In the city of Sydney, where the national leadership worked, the preferred method was personal contact and the use of couriers between Political Bureau members and the district leadership. Another method was material 'deposited in a certain place (house, office, etc.) to be collected by comrades receiving the instructions, or by specially appointed comrades'. This was clearly the method that later became known in espionage training as 'the dead letter drop', a method which did not use the official postal system and which created a 'cut-out' between the sender and the receiver of the message.

In other major cities the use of the normal postal system was necessary. In order to do this successfully two things were needed: first, a system of what is usually known as cover addresses or accommodation addresses, second, 'a cipher system for all important Party directives'.

The plan also took account of the need for reserves and sympathisers. These were to be drawn from 'fraternals' – closely allied bodies such as the Friends of the Soviet Union, the Militant Minority Movement, the League Against Imperialism and the International Labor Defence.

The 1934 plan concluded:

> Only the PB [Political Bureau] and the Secretariats of the various DCs [District Committees] would know of the existence of the illegal apparatus and only the PB in Sydney and the Secretaries of the DCs would know the actual composition of the central groups. Outside of these comrades and the members of the illegal apparatus, not one party member would know of the existence or personnel of such an organisation ...[76]

The attack on the CPA did not come in the form that its plan expected. However, some elements of the plan did have an immediate application in the CPA's drive to build party groups in factories. In many factories such groups had to operate as underground cells and in this way party members received an elementary training in secrecy. An article in the *Communist Review* talked about the process following the recruitment of a small number of workers in a factory:

> The first procedure is for the comrade who did the recruiting to visit each member *personally* [original emphasis] and make arrangements

147

for a meeting. Each comrade should be given a pseudonym and should be known by it within the party. It is well to remember that in all capitalist countries the factory unit is illegal. Bearing this in mind every meeting should be organised on a conspirative basis.[77]

These points were not lost on the nemesis of the CPA, the Commonwealth Investigation Branch which watched the CPA closely and was aware of its underground activities both in political life and in military circles (ch 3). It also grasped the connection between these techniques and the Russian underground tradition, arguing that

> There is a distinct failure to appreciate the secrecy with which the Communist Party works. The local party is trained by men, in turned trained in technique in Russia, by people who were hounded for years by the police of Europe and perforce had to learn every trick of secrecy and evasion of authority.[78]

Yet as events would show, the defence of the party's legality depended once more on courts rather than on conspiracy.

While the CPA felt more comfortable in agitational political activity than in the conservative world of the courts, it was to win another legal victory in the latter half of the 1930s. The High Court's rejection of Devanny's conviction allowed the CPA and its fraternal organisations to continue to function legally but with a major disadvantage: they could not openly use the postal system to distribute copies of their publications. The postal ban was part of the Crimes Act they had not challenged.

These bans were quite effective in disrupting the political work of the CPA and its fraternals. The circulation within Australia of newspapers like the Militant Minority Movement's *Red Leader* dropped and in order to send copies of it to the RILU in Moscow, seamen were enrolled as couriers when they travelled to Vladivostock, Hamburg and San Francisco. Between 1932 and 1937 the CPA found it very difficult to receive copies of Comintern publications like *International Press Correspondence.*[79]

In 1933 the CPA began publicly protesting against the postal bans. *Workers Weekly* revealed to its readers that '[w]ithout any publicity scores of working class publications are being seized and condemned. And the veil of silence with which the authorities cover their work makes it more effective.' The *Weekly* noted that '[w]hen Norman Lindsay's pornographic novel "Red Heap" was banned then the liberal Press protested loudly against this unnecessary interference with the "liberty of the subject".'[80] With some reluctance it appealed to liberal intellectuals to join it in campaigning to overturn the ban while insisting that in any case, the ban was an inevitable consequence of capitalism.

In May 1935 the Friends of the Soviet Union (FOSU) demanded to know the reasons for the ban on their magazine *Soviets Today* and threatened the government with legal action to overturn it. The positive acceptance of legal means by FOSU shows just how far the CPA had come since its reluctance to use 'bourgeois legality' three years earlier. When the issue came before the federal cabinet it appeared that the ban would be overturned. Acting Attorney-General Thomas Brennan advised that the ban on *Soviets Today* 'had not proved effective to prevent the distribution of that publication' and that it should be lifted 'rather than become involved in litigation in which the Commonwealth may not be in a position to produce evidence satisfactory to a Court'.[81] The change in policy, he suggested, could be explained by the improved relations between Britain and Russia and on Russia's admission to the League of Nations.

But Brennan's advice was rejected at a cabinet meeting in May 1935 and in June the CPA demonstrated its new-found acceptance of the weapons offered by bourgeois legality. A member of the CPA and FOSU, W. Thomas, sought an injunction to restrain the Commonwealth from destroying copies of publications and from preventing their transmission by post. He also boldly claimed £5,000 damages because of the ban. This time, the CPA clearly overcame its fears of 'legalist superstitions'. The Commonwealth responded by raising the stakes and commencing legal action to have the High Court declare both FOSU and the CPA as illegal associations. This galvanised the CPA and in an article in the Comintern's *InPreCorr,* Sharkey vowed that the CPA and the workers 'will fight this latest attack of the ruling class to the last ditch'.[82]

In November, the CPA and FOSU began a strategy of using their legal standing in the case to demand detailed information from the Commonwealth on which it had based its case. This would effectively place the onus of proof on the Commonwealth, thus reversing the roles of the parties and giving the CPA and FOSU an advantage. At one court hearing the Commonwealth noted that the legal action by the CPA might force the revelation of information held by the 'Intelligence section' of the Commonwealth government.[83] The second attempt to ban the CPA dragged on until 1937. The case was settled by an out of court agreement which saw the government lift the postal bans in exchange for dropping the case.

The CPA's successful defeat of the second attempt to ban it was an expression of the classic Leninist formula of combining legal as well as illegal methods of struggle. In this case 'legal' methods literally involved struggle in the legal arena, although the vast bulk of the CPA's political work in trade unions and elsewhere was public and 'legal' in the Leninist sense.

NOTES

1. Chambers, *Witness*, 233.
2. Philby, *My Silent War*, 1980, 180.
3. B. Vasilyev, 'Organisational Problems in Underground Revolutionary Work', *Communist International*, vol. 8, no. 15, 1 September 1931.
4. Klehr, Haynes and Firsov, *Secret World of American Communism*, 22 note.
5. Allen Weinstein, *Perjury: the Hiss-Chambers Case*, 2nd edn, Random House, New York, 1997. Klehr *et al.*, *Secret World of American Communism*. Weinstein's sources include corroboration of Chambers' testimony by a former Soviet agent who worked with him, Nadya Ulanovskaya (107–8), recently released Soviet documents (325–7, 508–13), and papers from the Hiss legal defence team. This is quite apart from long-standing evidence such as the microfilm and documents in Hiss' hand, tendered by Chambers in the defamation proceedings launched by Hiss.
6. Klehr *et al.*, *Secret World of American Communism*, ch. 6, 'The American Communist Party, the Secret Apparatus and the NKVD' and ch. 3, 'The Secret Apparatus of the CPUSA: the Early Years'.
7. Chambers, *Witness*, ch. 5. Weinstein, *Perjury*, ch 3.
8. Chambers, *Witness*, 205–10. Also, see ch. 2 above.
9. Chambers, *Witness*, 205.
10. Ibid., 208.
11. Weinstein, *Perjury*, 106.
12. Klehr *et al.*, *Secret World of American Communism*, 73–83.
13. Chambers, *Witness*, 246; Weinstein, *Perjury*, 120–4, 171.
14. Chambers, *Witness*, 243.
15. Weinstein, *Perjury*, 137; Chambers, *Witness*, 265–6.
16. Chambers, *Witness*, 291.
17. Klehr *et al.*, *Secret World of American Communism*, chs. 7, 8.
18. John Costello and Oleg Tsarev, *Deadly Illusions*, Century, London, 1993, 169.
19. Philby, *My Silent War*, 15.
20. Phillip Knightley, *Philby: the Life and View of the KGB Masterspy*, André Deutsch, London, 1988, 36.
21. Yuri Modin, with Jean-Charles Deniau and Agnieszka Ziarek, *My Five Cambridge Friends*, Farrar, Straus & Giroux, New York, 1994, 49.
22. Knightley, *Philby*, 36
23. Genrikh Borovik, *The Philby Files*, Warner Books, London, 1995, 17.
24. Knightley, *Philby*, 42–3.
25. Costello and Tsarev, *Deadly Illusions*, 130–1; also confirmed by Borovik, *Philby Files*, 25.
26. Andrew and Gordievsky, *KGB*, 158–9.
27. Borovik, *Philby Files*, 33.
28. Philby, *My Secret War*, 43–44.
29. Ibid., 21.
30. Costello and Tsarev, *Deadly Illusions*, 171.

31. Penrose and Freeman, *Conspiracy of Silence*, 395.
32. Costello and Tsarev, *Deadly Illusions*, ch. 8, esp. 218–19.
33. Ibid., 209–17.
    New research has emerged on the identity of 'Norma'. She was in fact an American Communist, Kitty Harris, who worked with Earl Browder in China from 1927 to 1929, then in Europe and in the UK with Arnold Deutsch and later Grigory Grafpen. She became Maclean's handler in London in 1938. Igor Damskin and Geoffrey Elliott, *Kitty Harris: The Spy with Seventeen Names*, St Ermin's Press, London 2001.
34. Ibid., 225.
35. Andrew and Gordievsky, *KGB*, 169.
36. Penrose and Freeman, *Conspiracy of Silence*, 200–15.
37. Ibid., 211–12.
38. Costello and Tsarev, *Deadly Illusions*, 245–6.
39. Penrose and Freeman, *Conspiracy of Silence*, 167.
40. Michael Straight, *After Long Silence*, W.W. Norton, New York, 1983, 121.
41. Weinstein, *Perjury*, 103–4.
42. Penrose and Freeman, *Conspiracy of Silence*, 219.
43. Costello and Tsarev, *Deadly Illusions*, 226–7.
44. Orlov, *Handbook of Intelligence*, 16.
45. Philby claimed publicly not to have known that Maclean had been recruited until years later, but this is shown to be false by his KGB memoir, Costello and Tsarev, *Deadly Illusions*, 148.
46. Borovik, *Philby Files*, 85.
47. Ibid., 200.
48. Costello and Tsarev, *Deadly Illusions*, 194.
49. Ibid., 167.
50. 'On the Question of Illegal Work', *Communist International*, vol. 10, no. 23 (1 December 1933).
51. Barbara Curthoys, 'The Comintern, the CPA and the Impact of Harry Wicks', *Australian Journal of Politics and History*, vol. 39, no. 1 (1993), 23–36. Johnpoll and Klehr (*Biographical Dictionary of the American Left*, 414–15) say he was a police informer for most of his radical career. Wicks later wrote an account of the revolutionary movement and his part in it (*Eclipse of October*, Holborn Publishing Co., London, 1958), but there is little reference to Australian events.
52. 'Minutes of PB meeting held 12/12/31', RTsKhIDNI, 495-94-70.
53. Ibid.
54. 'Political Report to the CC, 31/12/31', RTsKhIDNI, 495-94-68.
55. *WW*, 11 March 1932.
56. Ibid.
57. Clem Lloyd, 'Evatt, Menzies, Latham and the Anti-Communist Crusade', in *Seeing Red: the Communist Party Dissolution Act and Referendum, 1951: Lessons for Constitutional Reform*, Evatt Foundation, Sydney, 1991, 104.
58. See parliamentary debate on the amendments in Hansard, House of Reps, 20 May 1932, 1141ff; 23 and 24 May 1932, 1185ff.
59. Hansard, House of Reps, 20 May 1932, 1141.
60. Hansard, House of Reps, 20 May 1932, 1142.
61. *SMH*, 26 October 1932.
62. *WW*, 2 December 1932.
63. (1932) 48 Commonwealth Law Reports, *The King v Hush*, ex-parte Devanny, 499.
64. PB minutes, 2 September 1932, RTsKhIDNI, 95-94-95. (Note that this *fond* is marked as 95 rather than the normal *fond* number, 495.)
65. PB minutes, 30 September 1932, RTsKhIDNI, 95-94-95.
66. PB minutes 29 October 1932, ibid.
67. *WW*, 16 December 1932.
68. CC Minutes, 1932, box 3 (76), CPA Archives, ML MSS 5021, add on 1936, 21.

69. Ibid., 40.
70. Ibid., 40.
71. The letter is stamped with the number 2861 and found in CC Plenum, 25–7 December 1932, 163 in RTsKhIDNI 495-94-92. It is not immediately obvious that it is from the Comintern. However the 'Resolution on the situation in Australia and the immediate tasks of the party', which accompanies it, is clearly from the Anglo-American Secretariat of Comintern. It briefly discusses illegal work and then states 'see directives in the Org. letter'. The letter begins at hand-numbered p. 161 and concludes on p. 168 in this file. (A copy of 'Resolution on the situation etc.' is also found in box 8(76) of the CPA Archives.)
72. Letter 2861, 163.
73. Ibid., 165. This directive reflects the discussion at the Anglo-American Secretariat meeting in August 1932. See statement by (Sergei Ivanovich) Gusev, RTsKhIDNI, 495-72-155, 55.
74. WW, 12 August 1932.
75. 'Immediate Steps in Preparation for Illegality', (1934 is written by hand on document), CPA Archives, ML MSS 5021, add-on 1936, box 5 (76).
76. Ibid.
77. R. Cramm, 'Organisational Questions', in Communist Review, vol. 1, no. 8 (November 1934), 22–3.
78. Letter 21 April 1938, AA (ACT) A6122/40, item 221, part 1.
79. Soon after the imposition of the ban, Frederick Bateman, the secretary of the International Labor Defence, noted the 'inability to obtain InPreCorr,' letter, 30 May 1933, RTsKhIDNI, 539-3-234. In a letter to the ECCI dated 8 August 1935, Sharkey complained that 'not one copy of the CI magazine has reached Australia for several years': RTsKhIDNI, 495-94-121.
80. WW, 15 December 1933.
81. Cabinet submission, 'The Soviets Today – Transmission through the Post', Agenda 1429, in AA (ACT) A467 item Bundle 89/Part 1/SF 42. This is entirely misconstrued in The Origins of Political Surveillance in Australia (Angus & Robertson, Sydney, 1983) where Frank Cain states (251) that Brennan recommended the declaration of FOSU as an unlawful association.
82. L. Sharkey, 'New Attack on the Legality of the Communist Party of Australia', InPreCorr, vol. 15, no. 50, December 1935.
83. 'CPA and FOSU: re. action of the Commonwealth under Crimes Act Part 2', AA (ACT) A432, item 35/779/Part 2.

CHAPTER SIX

A Trojan Horse within Social Democracy

It cannot be expected that those Social Democratic workers who are under the influence of the ideology of class collaboration with the bourgeoisie ... will break with this ideology of their own accord, by the actions of objective causes alone. No. It is our business, the business of Communists, to help them free themselves from reformist ideology ... there is no more effective way for overcoming the doubts and hesitations of Social Democratic workers than by their participation in the proletarian united front.

Georgii Dimitrov at the 33rd Sitting of the Seventh World Congress of the Communist International

In 1935 the Communist International made a sharp turn in its political outlook opening a period designated as the 'popular front against fascism'.[1] Previously it had described even social-democratic and labour parties as 'social fascist', arguing that they were little different from fascist parties because they supported capitalism. This line proved disastrous especially for the German Communist Party (KPD) but also for Europe as a whole. As the strength of Hitler's National Socialists grew, the communists and Social Democrats fought each other, rather than uniting. The shock of Hitler's appointment in January 1933 as Chancellor of Germany and the defeat of the German communists led to the calling of the Seventh World Congress of Comintern.

At the congress the new Secretary of the Communist International, Georgii Dimitrov, outlined the dramatic shift.[2] The choice of Dimitrov as Secretary was significant. Dimitrov had recently been accused by Hitler's government of trying to burn the Reichstag. 'During the trial, in several exchanges between Dimitrov and Hermann Goering the Nazi leader lost his temper and shouted threats of what his men would do to Dimitrov once they had him outside the court. Dimitrov's replies were quiet, reasonable and courageous. He presented the Communist movement as the defender of the values of Western civilisation – especially of rationality and the rule of law.'[3] At the congress Dimitrov acknowledged certain mistakes by communists including an 'impermissable underestimation of the fascist danger' and a 'narrow sectarian attitude'. To defeat fascism it was necessary to form a united front of all workers, regardless of their political party stance.

> The Communist International puts no conditions for unity of action except one, and that an elementary condition acceptable to all workers, viz., that the unity of action be directed against fascism, against the offensive of capital, against the threat of war, against the class enemy. That is our condition.[4]

There was also a new liberality in the application of the line which would take 'various forms in various countries, depending upon the condition and character of the workers' organisations and their political level, upon the situation in the particular country'. Even within fascist Germany it was necessary to organise, said Dimitrov, invoking the capture of Troy: 'the attacking army ... was unable to achieve victory until, with the aid of the famous Trojan Horse it managed to penetrate to the very heart of the enemy's camp'.[5] Instead of denunciations of 'social fascists', Dimitrov referred to 'the ... camp of Left Social Democrats (without quotation marks)'.

The strategy of the popular front has been widely examined by historians of the communist movement and is now being rediscussed in the light of new archival sources. In France and Spain, where a communist party was relatively strong, it sought a formal alliance with the social democratic and anti-fascist parties, usually in the form of a people's front. In the English-speaking world, where it was usually smaller, as in Australia or the United States, it appears to have used a different strategy. This involved the creation of an underground group within the main labour or social democratic party. In the United States, the CPUSA inititally tried to create a left-wing, third party as an alternative to the Democratic and Republican parties. To this end they were active in Minnesota's Farmer–Labor Party, Wisconsin's Progressive Party, the campaign to 'End Poverty in California' (EPIC), the American

Labor Party in New York and radical groups in Washington and Oregon.[6] In the context of the Depression, a number of these groups garnered significant voter support, particularly the Farmer–Labor Party. Whether these groups would have united and run candidates against Democrats, especially Roosevelt, is doubtful. But the CPUSA's putative strategy was abandoned after the Comintern advised that support for Roosevelt was more important, largely because of the needs of Soviet foreign policy. These hitherto unknown strategies of covert penetration were closely watched by the Anglo-American Secretariat of the Comintern, which hoped to influence national governments formed by social democratic parties in the direction of collective security with the USSR.[7]

COMMUNISTS IN THE AUSTRALIAN LABOR PARTY

The newly released archives of the Communist International and the records of the now-disbanded Communist Party of Australia (CPA) provide evidence for such a political strategy in Australia. After the change in political direction represented by the Seventh Congress in 1935 the CPA began to recruit members of the Australian Labor Party (ALP). Rather than urging them to leave the ALP, these new communists were asked to remain inside the Labor Party and became undercover members. By 1939, dual members, allied with the indigenous, non-communist left wing, had ousted the leadership and taken control of the largest and most politically powerful of the six state branches of the ALP, that of New South Wales (NSW). Two covert CPA members became senior officers of Labor in NSW, one of them the General Secretary. In the state of Western Australia, where a similar strategy was followed, a secret member of the CPA became a member of federal parliament.[8] The growing success of this strategy in Australia was halted after the Soviet–German Non-Aggression Pact. The pact provoked a series of events in which the undercover communist wing split the NSW branch of the ALP and formed the 'State Labor Party'. While this split helped deny Labor office in the national elections of September 1940, the communist presence also deflected plans for a wartime government of national unity of Labor and conservatives.

Historians' knowledge of this significant aspect of the Seventh Congress's policies is scanty. When a communist presence in the Labor Party is acknowledged, it is invariably minimised. No historian of Australian Labor has understood either the depth of CPA penetration or its origins. Most assume that some kind of communist presence must have existed because the communist-led State Labor Party ultimately amalgamated with the CPA in January 1944.[9]

The evolution of the CPA's strategy towards the Labor Party began with a 1935 proposal discussed by the Political Bureau of the CPA which stated that it was advisable 'to organise Left-wing movements in the Labor Party in order to fight for the united front proposals' and to urge 'members of the Labor Party who join the Communist Party [to] retain their membership in the Labor Party and carefully work for united front proposals'.[10] In a report to the CPA congress in 1935, CPA leader Lance Sharkey argued that in addition to joint trade union activity '[i]t is also possible that certain of the Party members go into the Labor Party to work in such a way that all leftward elements in the Labor Party are brought to the leadership in order to ensure the acceptance of the proposals of the united front.'[11]

The change towards Popular Front policies coincided with, and perhaps contributed to, a series of union successes for the CPA which were reported in detail to the Comintern.[12] In 1935–6, communists won the leadership of railway, mining, maritime and metal industry unions. More than this, the CPA itself was growing. A report to the Comintern noted: 'The outstanding feature of our latest recruits is the number who have previously been leading activists of the ALP and are at present leading trade union activists.' Further, 'our successes in the trade unions, to a large degree are due to these comrades who have great authority and were already minor trade union officials prior to joining our party.'[13]

Within the labour movement both CPA and ALP members shared a common culture. They spoke the same language, worked alongside each other and both held socialism to be the goal, albeit to be achieved by different roads. This had always been so but with the more liberal policies of the Seventh Congress this shared culture meant a steady stream of recruits as well as union election successes for the CPA. These communist victories in trade unions had a direct impact on the power balance within the Australian Labor Party, because unions were affiliated to the party and directly represented in Labor congresses.

A KEY RECRUIT

The CPA success in trade union elections and in recruitment of ALP members hooked something of a prize catch in the shape of one talented union official, Jack Hughes.[14] At the time of his recruitment in 1935, Hughes was an assistant secretary of the Federated Clerks' Union. In 1936 he won an official position on the Labor Council of New South Wales, the umbrella group for all unions and an organisation which played a key role within the Labor Party machine.

Yet on the surface, 1936 was a year in which Labor splits healed. Since 1931 two Labor parties had existed in New South Wales (NSW); one supported the NSW-based Jack Lang, the other allied itself to the federal Labor Party. Jack Lang was a former NSW state premier who commanded a mass following in Sydney and other parts of New South Wales. A demogogue and fiery speech-maker, he had clashed with the banks at the height of the Depression, then been dismissed as state premier by the Governor, a relic of Australia's colonial past.

The early 1930s saw Lang establish political supremacy within Labor, defeating the weaker 'Federal Labor Party'. By 1936 a tenuous remarriage was concluded between the two parties. This prompted Lang to try to increase his dominance. His first target was the radio station owned by the trade union council, the NSW Labor Council.

The Sydney-based Radio station 2KY had been set up in 1925 as the 'first labour radio station in the western world'.[15] Lang urged the council to integrate it with the *Labor Daily* newspaper which he controlled, a move designed to entrench his own political power. The Sydney newspaper *Truth* summed up Lang's move:

> Two great assets of the NSW Labor Party – the 2KY wireless station and the *Labor Daily* – are plums for which many people have hungrily licked their lips. Some have been able to take a bite, but nobody – yet – has been able to snatch them for their own, their very own. Mr Lang is now trying to pluck these golden plums.[16]

Truth's description of the 'chilly, alert atmosphere' of the Labor Council when Lang addressed it on 2KY was an indication of the storm which would gather strength over the next three years. The communists, both overt and covert, and the non-communist left wing opposed Lang's move to integrate the radio station with the newspaper and, to widespread surprise, his plan was defeated.

In August 1936 the unions in the Labor Council called what would be the first of many meetings to oppose Lang's control of the party machine. Lang immediately expelled four members of parliament, 17 union officials and a number of others. 'This lit the fire', recalled Hughes many years later.[17]

In December 1936 another major conference of anti-Lang unions and ALP branches was held. By this time it was clear that Lang was also trying to entrench his total control of the *Labor Daily*. In the preceding months the militant unions had begun to organise the union shareholders to vote against Lang directors on the newspaper's board. But after the ballot opened it became clear that Lang's men had systematically tried to rig the vote. Ballot papers disappeared, others never arrived at union offices. On Christmas Eve 1936 the result of the ballot for directors was due to be announced but before that could be done the Miners' Federation began a legal challenge to the conduct of the ballot.

In the following year, 1937, a pending federal election led to an uneasy peace in the factional warfare. In June the four expelled MPs were readmitted to the NSW branch after demands from the federal ALP executive. The anti-Lang dissidents continued to mobilise, although Lang remained firmly in control of the state party machine. In October the factional warfare revived. Labor had lost the federal election and in the *Labor Daily* case the equity court largely accepted the claim of the anti-Lang unions that their board candidates each gained an average of 19,000 votes to the Lang unions' 14,000. On appeal the full court partially reversed this result but it was clear, as anti-Lang unionists pointed out, that 'future ballots will result in Mr Lang's influence being completely destroyed'.[18]

In 1937 the anti-Lang forces had formalised their opposition to Lang by creating a nameless seven-person committee to direct their struggle. Later that year it appointed a full-time organiser, Walter Evans. Evans had been a member of the ALP state executive in 1932 and also a member of the left wing of the Labor Party.[19] By 1937 Evans had become an undercover member of the CPA. As dual members of the CPA and ALP, Hughes and Evans would lead the growing anti-Lang struggle within the NSW branch of the Labor Party for the next two years.

Throughout the period Hughes remained in contact with the CPA largely through Ernest Knight, the CPA official who was responsible for party work among the trade unions in Sydney. Knight had a nondescript office unadorned by any sign near the dockside in Sydney. Hughes, as a Clerks' Union official, excited no attention by visiting Knight's office as he did hundreds of other city offices to collect membership dues. As an increasingly significant Labor Council official, he could also regularly visit all left-wing unions and thereby keep in touch with leading CPA trade union officials. On one level there was no secrecy at all about the growing alliance between CPA members and the anti-Lang Labor forces. At the weekly meetings of the NSW Labor Council this co-operation occurred in public. As well, there appears to have been at least two types of dual membership of the ALP and CPA. While Hughes' membership was 'deep cover', other communists' allegiances were not so hidden. The editor of the miners' union newspaper, Edgar Ross, who was a member of the Botany ALP branch, recalled that his CPA membership was known to non-communist anti-Lang ALP members.[20]

In the following years the organisation of the communist underground in the ALP became more systematic and was directed by the CPA Political Bureau which met every six weeks. Both Hughes and Edgar Ross (the most senior surviving dual members) state that they did not know the identity of all the dual members in the ALP, but their identities must have been known to the CPA Political Bureau. Both Hughes and Ross later minimised the degree of organised CPA activity within the ALP and claimed that there was never a fraction meeting of this group or any other defined organisational expression. Yet minutes of the Political Bureau clearly record such a meeting.[21]

In February 1938 the anti-Lang forces tasted victory when they took possession of the offices of the *Labor Daily*. Behind the scenes the Political Bureau of the CPA discussed the situation and devised 'a plan covering the taking over of the *Labor Daily* and replacement of various members of the staff'.[22] The price of victory was the repayment of a loan which Lang had earlier made to the newspaper. The Labor Council decided to make a clean break and to change the format and name of the newspaper. What emerged in late 1938 was the *Daily News*. To bankroll this undertaking Hughes called on a rather unusual source. For some time he had been cultivated by the general manager of the Bank of New South Wales, Sir Alfred Davidson, a forward-looking banker who made a habit of selecting and promoting talented young people.[23] Davidson had been appalled by Lang's hostility to the banks while premier and made overtures to Lang's enemies on both the right and left. For example, Davidson paid for an organised tour by Hughes of interstate trade union centres when the anti-Lang forces were trying to influence the ALP federal executive. Davidson apparently looked on

Hughes as a possible national Labor leader with whom he could garner some influence. In establishing the *Daily News*, Hughes used his influence with Davidson to get a substantial bank loan.[24] A version of the Hughes–Davidson relationship appeared in Lang's autobiography, in which Lang said that in 1938 Davidson invited the visiting British labour figure, Ernest Bevin, to a dinner with Hughes, Evans, Lloyd Ross and F. O'Neill, all labour dissidents.[25] At the time, however, Hughes' contact with Sir Alfred Davidson was by no means public. The unusual alliance between a communist and a top banker was one of the odd consequences of the CPA's underground work in the Labor Party.

COMINTERN'S WATCHFUL EYE

The growing CPA influence within the Labor Party was of great interest to the Communist International largely because of its wider campaign against isolationism and in favour of collective security. From July to November 1937 the Anglo-American secretariat of Comintern held a series of discussions on 'the Australian Question' and spent considerable time on the closely intertwined issues of foreign policy and the position of the Labor Party.[26] Among those present were French Comintern leader André Marty and British representative Robin Page Arnot, as well as CPA Political Bureau members Richard Dixon and Jack Blake.[27]

To achieve a collective security pact linking the Soviet Union to Britain, the election of Labor administrations in countries of the British Empire was crucial. To achieve this the CPA worked to strengthen anti-fascist feeling in the society generally but in particular to use its secret members in the Labor Party to change its isolationist policy. In early July, Dixon addressed the Anglo-American secretariat arguing that Australia's main responsibility was to work for a change in British policy which was then both warlike and opposed to collective security involving the Soviet Union.[28] Change was possible because 'the British Government is sensitive to Dominion pressure'. To 'bring about such a rupture with this Empire front on foreign policy, it is essential to defeat the Lyons government and elect a Labor government'. Dixon noted that Lang's group was dominated 'by the Catholic element' and that this was the reason that the Labor Party had made no declaration on Spain, although the trade unions on the NSW Labor Council had. Dixon summed up as follows:

Just a few words about our views on the question of influencing the Labor Government should it be elected. Our first line is that we expect to bring pressure to bear on the Labor Government through the trade union movement. Secondly, our line is to bring about a plan of getting as many Communists as possible within the LP. The Party in New South Wales has one or two Communists in the LP Executive. In Victoria out of 46 organisations, we have about 34 in which we have Communist organisation. At the same time we are trying to get direct union representation at the LP conference. This would mean we would probably control in the future the LP conference.[29]

In spite of the CPA's growing successes with this tactic, Marty made a number of wrong-headed criticisms.[30] He began by criticising the strong trade union roots of the CPA, even though this was the very thing that had given it such strength in the Labor Party. Marty argued that this meant the CPA was tainted with anarcho-syndicalism. '[T]he whole leadership is composed of trade union functionaries', he complained. Anarcho-syndicalism led to a neglect of political work, as opposed to union work, and was one explanation for the lack of growth of the CPA, he said. Marty reiterated Dixon's point on peace and collective security. Australia had the potential to affect global politics through the election of a Labor government which would in turn affect British foreign policy. 'The power of the Dominions – Canada, Australia, New Zealand – is very high. They must speak and [then?] they can change the policy of the British Government with the help of the British working class.' In the Pacific, peace through collective security was necessary as a defence against Japanese aggression.

A similar point was argued by another member of the Anglo-American secretariat, Franz Mehring, who argued that in order to defeat Labor neutralism, the CPA should 'show that Australia is being threatened by the aggression of Japan'. The CPA's later targeting of the export of Australian scrap iron to Japan was to crystallise much of the debate over foreign policy both within Labor and Australia more generally. Bans on Japanese ships culminated in a major confrontation in December 1938 when CPA-influenced waterside workers refused to load iron bound for Japan. Though the iron was eventually loaded, the bitter dispute threw into sharp relief the communists' policy of sanctions versus the neutralism of federal Labor.

CLOSER TO VICTORY

In 1938 the CPA's dual-track strategy of working within and outside the Labor Party began to pay dividends. In spite of the loss of the *Labor Daily*, Lang remained in control of the NSW Labor Party but had led the ALP to another defeat in the March 1938 elections. The federal executive of the ALP began to sniff the wind as the power base of the mighty Lang slowly ebbed away. In early 1939 the federal executive finally acted decisively. It decided that a 'Unity Conference' of Lang and anti-Lang groups would resolve the split. The February meeting of the Central Committee of the CPA was addressed by Hughes and Evans, at that stage nominally prominent Labor figures.[31] In May the CPA executive held a meeting with its Labor Party fraction which discussed the coming Unity Conference at length. The meeting concluded that the emergence of a parliamentary-based 'centre party' was crucial to the outcome of the conference and resolved to 'strive to the utmost' to work with them. It also decided to fight to alter the basis of representation of unions and branches. Both aims would be achieved and both proved crucial to the outcome of the conference.[32]

The Unity Conference inspired by the federal executive finally took place on 26–27 August 1939. While Lang glowered from the public gallery, the result on the conference floor soon showed the anti-Lang forces were in control. Hughes moved the key resolution structuring the future organisation of the party which won 221 to 153. Shortly afterwards fist fights broke out in the gallery and order had to be restored.[33] The conference put undercover CPA members in key roles on the executive. Jack Hughes became Vice-President (an office he held simultaneously with the powerful presidency of the New South Wales Labor Council) and Walter Evans became General Secretary of the NSW branch of the ALP. A week later Hughes conducted a ballot for parliamentary leader and a rebel from the Lang camp, William McKell, finally toppled Lang.

It is one of the ironies of politics and history, that a moment of triumph is often followed by an inexorable plunge into disaster. During the Unity Conference there had occurred what seemed at the time merely a minor disruption. A delegate unsuccessfully proposed the suspension of standing orders to discuss the international position. But the chance for a debate was brutally cut short by uproar when he explained his motive. He wished to move a resolution 'expressing abhorrence with the onward march of fascism' and viewing with disgust the signing of the German–Russian Non-Aggression Pact. Criticism of Russia was guaranteed to provoke loud opposition from the anti-Lang left. However, defence of this pact became the seed of destruction which would destroy both the CPA's influence and the strength of the broader left within the NSW branch of the Labor Party for decades to come.

The Non-Aggression Pact was quickly followed by a German invasion of Poland, which was then divided between the USSR and Germany. On 3 September, Britain, which had undertaken to assist Poland, declared war on Germany. Initially however, due to poor communication with the USSR and following the logic of the united front the CPA and its undercover Labor fraction boldly declared their *support* for Britain's war against fascism.[34] In a radio broadcast for a federal by-election in the seat of Hunter, Jack Hughes echoed these sentiments.[35] But as the line of the Communist International became clearer the CPA's attitude to the war soon began to change toward one of opposition to Britain's war on Germany. This had two consequences for CPA dual members who had fought for three years to unseat Lang and had won at the Unity Conference just a month earlier. First, instead of remaining in the broad stream of militant unionism, they now had to swim against the tide of incomprehension of their own sympathisers, whom they had won by their opposition to fascism and isolationism over the previous three years. The second consequence flowed from this very public shift in the line: communist dual members in the Labor Party rapidly became identifiable as dogmatic adherents of the CPA.

The resulting situation was the undoing of the CPA's new-found influence in the Labor Party, but this was of no consequence to the Anglo-American secretariat of the Comintern. A Comintern report noted that the Australian government of R. G. Menzies was 'the weakest government in the British Empire'.[36] It anticipated that the Menzies government would be replaced by a Labor Party whose leadership 'is being increasingly put under pressure by the growing anti-war movement'. It noted with satisfaction that the CPA had rectified its line on the war with a statement on 8 December 1939, admitting that the party had 'misunderstood the importance of the Soviet–German Non-Aggression Pact'.[37]

After the CPA's political somersault on the war, the issue of communism in the Labor Party sharpened. With the Easter 1940 annual conference approaching, John Hughes received a call from the state

Labor leader, William McKell, whom he had helped to install. McKell wanted to meet him. Hughes later recalled:

> When I got to his office, he not only closed door but he locked it. He said: 'I'm glad you could come. I've got the security records of all the communists in the Labor Party. I think we ought to go over it together. With the conference coming up, we want to make sure we don't have any of these birds on [the next executive].'
>
> I said: 'That's a very good idea, Bill.' And I'm thinking, 'I guess my name will feature prominently here.' Then I thought, 'Well if that's so, that's so, I'll handle it.' Anyhow, it wasn't. That was surprise number one. And I wasn't sure of that until we had really finished.[38]

The result of the meeting was that while at least one undercover member (Herbert Chandler) lost his place on the proposed ticket for the 1940 executive, he was replaced by others: Ted Walsham, a railway shop steward, and James Starling, a teacher. Over 50 years later it is difficult to identify with certainty all the dual members who reached the executive level of the ALP in this period. On one level it was of secondary importance to the fact that the political line of the CPA was clearly accepted by a broad group of non-communist anti-Lang forces on the executive. However, it is essential in understanding the strength and strategy of the CPA to identify as accurately as possible its actual members in the leadership of the ALP.

The 1939 Unity Conference elected a 32-member executive which contained at least five. They included Hughes, Evans, the union officials Barker and Glasson, and the mayor of a mining town, H. B. Chandler. At the 1940 conference the 32-person executive included Hughes, Evans, Barker and Glasson, plus Walsham, Starling and Sloss, who became a city councillor with left-wing support and later a member of parliament.[39] A group of five or seven communists from an executive of 32 could exercise considerable weight, given that they were held in high regard, acted *en bloc* and held the vital full time position of General Secretary.

As the annual Easter 1940 conference drew closer, the CPA forces, in line with Comintern, became alarmed about the possibility that Britain and France would conclude an agreement with Hitler who would then turn the war to the East. This issue came to a head on the second day of the conference on Saturday 23 March.[40] A subcommittee of three, Jack Hughes, Bill Gollan and Lloyd Ross, all undercover CPA members, drafted a tough resolution. It read, in part:

> The Labor Party has always been opposed to imperialist wars and today in the present war situation we demand that every energy be utilised to bring about a cessation of hostilities and the establishment of peace at the earliest opportunity on a just and equitable basis in order to avoid the slaughter of millions. We declare that the Australian people have nothing to gain from the continuance of the war.

The resolution effectively declared that Australia should refuse to assist Britain, which had declared war on fascist Germany. In place of loyalty to empire it substituted loyalty to the anti-war traditions of the labour movement. The parliamentary Labor leader, William McKell, who was a co-opted member of the committee, took no issue with its general tenor but insisted that one sentence be deleted. This was agreed to but it was then restored on the conference floor. The sentence read:

> The conference makes it clear that, while being opposed to Australian participation in overseas conflicts, it is also opposed to any effort of the anti-Labor government to change the direction of the present war by an aggressive act against any other country with which we are not at war, including the Soviet Union.

The resolution and its rider created uproar from the Langite minority. Hughes told the conference that the war 'is just a war of adventure and plunder in which we should have no concern'. In a phrase that would come to symbolise the stance of the new leadership of the ALP he said: '"Hands off Russia" is the policy of the labour movement today as it has been in the past.' Amid interjections suggesting he was a not a Labor man, but a communist, Lloyd Ross predicted 'within a few months we will be asked to stand side by side with Imperialist Britain in a war against the only real Social[ist] State in the world. We won't be there.' Ross was cheered for this comment and the 'Hands off Russia' resolution passed by 195 to 88.

For conservative prime minister Menzies, the Easter conference opened a vital chink in Labor's armour in the coming federal election in that it allowed the conservatives to link federal Labor with the taint of unpatriotic and anti-British feeling. Menzies argued that the resolution was treason and marked a stage in the disintegration of federal Labor's war policy and challenged its leaders to rebut it. Yet the 'Hands off Russia' resolution – or the assumptions on which it drew its support – was not so extreme or absurd as it might appear today. The labour movement and the ALP had not forgotten the bloody cost of the 'war to end wars' in 1914–18, and prior to September 1939 a significant strand of Labor opinion, including the parliamentary leader at the federal level, John Curtin, was passionately isolationist.

In Moscow the spirit of the resolution was in tune with the Comintern. In March 1940, André Marty dictated directives for Australia and New Zealand. In discussing work in the unions and the labour parties, Marty urged:

> We must not forget for one moment, that the British Empire must disappear and that in this fight the social democratic parties also shall disappear. The question is how can we convince the honest members of the Labor Party and the trade unions to unify with the Communist Party, the revolutionary party and create in this manner the organisational foundation of the working class. Here is the way to destroy the rule of the reformists in the workers' movement.[41]

But it was the communists, not the reformists, whose influence was to be destroyed. In 1994 Hughes concluded: 'We followed the party's line with the war when it was so off beam and a denial of everything we had been fighting and struggling for, the defeat of fascism and all the rest of it. [Because of this] in one minute, virtually ... it went down the drain.'

As the war in Europe intensified the Hughes–Evans position became increasingly untenable. In April Germany invaded Norway and Denmark. In May the phoney war ended with the German *blitzkreig* invasion of The Netherlands and Belgium followed by the attack on France. The public desire to assist Britain with Australian troops overwhelmed the earlier reservations and hopes for peace on which the 'Hands off Russia' resolution was built. Within Australia forces grew calling for a government of national unity with the conservative United Australia Party. But the NSW executive of the Labor Party strongly opposed this and attacked other Labor forces who supported it.

A special federal ALP conference in June 1940 opted for a more pro-war stance, agreeing to conditional participation in the European war.[42] Shortly after this another split developed between the left-controlled

NSW branch and the federal leadership. The conservative federal government, with support from the Labor opposition, had proposed to amend the National Security Act to give extra powers to require individuals to place 'themselves, their services and their property at the disposal of the Commonwealth'.[43] This was bitterly opposed by the Hughes–Evans forces, who publicly supported five Labor federal MPs who opposed the amendments.

On 2 August the federal executive of the ALP moved decisively and suspended the left-dominated NSW executive.[44] It denounced the 'inspired and unwarranted propaganda circulated in NSW about a proposed National Government' and reaffirmed its own rejection of a national government. Trying to avert a split, the executive offered a secret deal to Hughes. In exchange for his support to drop Evans, Hughes would become a junior minister in the next national Labor government. After consulting with the CPA leadership, the offer was rejected and with it died the intriguing possibility of a communist minister of the crown.

On 17 August the suspended Hughes–Evans leadership reconvened their forces with eighteen members of the old executive. They decided to create a new party – the 'Australian Labor Party, State of NSW'. This body became the vehicle of what remained of the alliance between the undercover CPA members and the non-CPA Labor left. It failed to win significant electoral support and in January 1944 it amalgamated with the Communist Party, with five of its leaders becoming members of the Central Committee of the CPA: J. Hughes, W. Gollan, H. Chandler, E. Ross and A. Wilson. At least four and possibly all five were already secret members of the CPA. So ended one of the most intriguing but little-known episodes in underground communist political work in an advanced democratic country.

What were the long-term results of the CPA's penetration of the Australian Labor Party? The most significant result was their opposition to the creation of a national government, that is, a non-party government of national unity. From the outbreak of war until August 1940 pressure grew to form a national government which, for the communists, was an absolute anathema because it meant class collaboration. In April the former leader of the rural-based Country Party, Sir Earle Page, publicly called for a national government, but was rebuffed by federal Labor opposition leader, John Curtin. A government armed with sweeping defence powers and lacking an opposition would be too powerful, Curtin argued.[45]

Powerful forces within Labor urged for a national government. In early June Curtin called a federal conference to discuss Labor's war policy and the *Sydney Morning Herald* noted: 'It is believed that an influential section of the conference will advocate the formation of a National Government on the lines approved by the British Labour Party.'[46] A special federal conference in June 1940 revealed the key supporter of national government – Queensland premier Forgan Smith whose proposal for a national government the conference rejected.[47] The conference opted for a more supportive, war-fighting role than previously, agreeing to reinforcement of the AIF and conditional participation in the European war. But the strength of the left and of Labor tradition was also shown in declarations of an 'excess war profits tax of 100 per cent'. Instead of national government, it plumped for the establishment of a cross-party Advisory War Council. Almost immediately Forgan Smith recommenced agitation for a national government, calling for a 'a new pack, a new shuffle, a new deal'.[48] A month later Menzies offered just such a 'new deal', promising Labor five or six cabinet posts and finally even offering to stand down as Prime Minister, if necessary.[49]

In the federal election campaign of 21 September 1940, Menzies campaigned on the policy of a national government, among other things. The election saw an equally divided federal House of Representatives with the fate of Menzies' government depending on two Independent MPs. Labor continued to resist any move towards a national government and Menzies finally agreed to form an Advisory War Council (which included Labor appointees), a position he had previously rejected. In August 1941 he again appealed to Labor to form a national government, was rejected and resigned as Prime Minister. His party held office until the two Independents finally withdrew their support on 3 October 1941. A period of eight years of Labor government then commenced. It was the first significant period of Labor control of federal government and saw many social reforms.

The significance of Labor's rejection of a national government can be seen in comparison with the British Labour Party. Labor in Australia governed a country at war in its own right from October 1941 until August 1945. This period saw state regulation of manpower, commodities and industrial development. Unions were consulted widely, federal powers were permanently centralised and postwar planning began in 1943 with Labor ideals firmly in mind. By comparison, British Labour was the junior partner in Churchill's war cabinet and only began its reforming drive when it began to govern in its own right after the 1945 elections.

The influence of CPA–ALP dual members played a significant although not decisive role in avoiding the conservative path of a national government. Throughout the period in which Menzies enticed Labor to join him, Labor's leader John Curtin never wavered in his opposition to national government. While in modern times such a stance by a leader would carry enormous weight, in this period this was less so. Curtin's opposition to national government may have also been a response to the opposition to it within the party, a tone set by the NSW branch, which warned early and often about such a proposal.

Another influence on Labor's policy and hence government policy from 1941 to 1949 was the CPA's unwavering socialist commitment. This was translated to the ALP through the NSW branch and later by its influence in the trade union movement. Combined with the indigenous (but weaker) socialist tradition, this led to a commitment in postwar reconstruction to a strong public sector, a welfare programme and an unparalleled degree of regulation of private enterprise which lasted long after the postwar reconstruction period and after Labor's loss of federal government in 1949.

Against these factors consideration must be given to the counter-productive actions of CPA dual members for most of the period of the Hitler–Stalin pact, from October 1939 to June 1941. Most significantly, the CPA's strategy led to a period of electorally damaging public conflict. It began with the 'Hands off Russia' resolution, which led to a renewed split by Lang, then to defiance of the federal party on the National Security Bill, then to expulsion of the CPA-led Labor faction. Labor went to the September 1940 poll split into three groups. Predictably, it lost.

Historians have previously found it difficult to describe what actually occurred within Labor between 1936 (the beginning of the revolt which unseated Lang) and 1940 (the split) because of the secrecy of the CPA's undertaking. This has led to a lack of understanding of the internal dynamics of the NSW ALP's confrontation with the rest of the ALP which began with the Easter conference in March 1940. Superficially, the 1940 split resembled previous Labor splits, but the crucial element was in fact a highly ideological grouping of undercover members of the Communist Party who came to lead a mass reformist party following the strategy of the Communist International.

NOTES

1. A version of this chapter originally appeared in the *Journal of Contemporary History*, vol. 32, no. 3 (July 1997), 395–407.
2. Dimitrov's speech can be found in *VII Congress of the Communist International, Abridged Stenographic Report of Proceedings*, Modern Publishers, Sydney, n.d., 124ff.
3. Alistair Davidson, *The Communist Party of Australia*, Hoover Institution Press, Stanford, 1969, 74.
4. *VII Congress*, 143.
5. Ibid., 160.
6. Klehr *et al.*, *Secret World of American Communism*, 9, 10.
7. A key delete of the 'Australian Question' took place in late 1937. Minutes of these meetings of the Anglo-American Secretariat are held in the Comintern files on the Communist Party of Australia. These are held by the Russian Centre for the Preservation and Study of Documents of Recent History, Moscow (RTsKhIDNI). The 1937 discussions are found at RTsKhIDNI 495-14-19 (July); 495-18-1212 (July); 495-14-19 (Sept.-Nov.).
8. Donald Mountjoy was the member for Swan from 1943 to 1946. His status as a secret member of the CPA was revealed by another dual member of the CPA and ALP, William Gollan. Oral history transcript of Gollan (tape 2, page 3) in Laurie Aarons collection, Mitchell Library, Sydney.
9. The principal study of J .T. Lang and Langism, *The Big Fella*, Melbourne University Press, Carlton South, 1986) by Bede Nairn argues that the displacement of Lang 'was complicated by the new, bold infiltration of Labor by the Stalinists, which played into the hands of Lang'. As we will see, communist infiltration did not complicate the anti-Lang struggle, it led it. Graham Freudenberg's *Cause for Power: the Official History of the NSW Branch of the Australian Labor Party* (Pluto Press, Sydney 1991) is cautious about the extent of their influence. The historian who comes closest to identifying the CPA role is Don Rawson in his essay 'McKell and Labor Unity', in Michael Easson (ed.) *McKell. The Achievements of Sir William McKell* (Allen & Unwin, Sydney, 1988). Rawson notes that 'the Communist Party of Australia strongly supported the industrialists', but adds, 'some members of the CPA by concealing their membership of the party became influential members of the ALP. The ALP has often been accused of containing "secret communists" and "fellow travellers" but during 1939–40 in New South Wales there was more substance to this charge than at any other time.'
10. 'United front policy for Australia' in 'CC Circulars and Statements 1933–41', Box 5 (76) CPA Archives, Mitchell Library, Sydney.
11. Ibid.
12. 'Report of Australian Party from August 1st to March 1936'. RTsKhIDNI, 495-20-7.
13. Ibid., 11.
14. Much of the personal material about Hughes is based on a series of four taped interviews conducted by the author with Jack Hughes at his home in Bateau Bay, NSW in 1994–5. A letter from Jack Hughes, dated 20 March 1996, is also used.
15. Raymond Markey, *In Case of Oppression*, Pluto Press, Sydney, 1994, 266.
16. *Truth*, 26 April 1936.
17. Hughes interview with author, 5 May 1994.
18. *SMH*, 11 December 1937.
19. Robert Cooksey, *Lang and Socialism*, Australian National University Press, 1976, 19; Evans' position on the executive is referred to in 'PB Minutes, 1933-38' in box 15 (76), CPA Archives.
20. Letter from Edgar Ross to author, 17 November 1995.
21. The minutes of the Political Bureau for 10 May 1939 show a meeting 'with L. P. fraction'. PB Minutes 1939 in box 16 (76) in CPA Archives.
22. Minutes of Political Bureau, 10 February 1938 in CA Roll 10419, 495-14-305.
23. C. B. Schedvin, 'Sir Alfred Davidson', in R. T. Appleyard and C. B. Schedvin (eds.) *Australian Financiers: Biographical Essays*, Macmillan, Melbourne, 1988.

24. Davidson's largess to the *Labor Daily* was a source of trouble for him later with the bank's board. See Schedvin, 'Sir Alfred Davidson', 360.
25. J. T. Lang, *The Turbulent Years*, Alpha Books, Sydney, 1970, 184–5.
26. RTsKhIDNI, 495-14-19 (July); 495-18-1212 (July); 495-14-19 (Sept.–Nov.).
27. As was often the case, foreign communists adopted aliases. Dixon appears as 'Emery' in the minutes and Blake as 'London'.
28. Secretariat meeting, 9.7.37, speaker: Emery. RTsKhIDNI, 495-14-19.
29. Ibid.
30. 'Meeting of the Secretariat on the Australian Question, 11.7.37', speaker: Marty. RTsKhIDNI, 495-14-19.
31. A list of invitees to the meeting includes a number of named people (e.g. Ross, Nelson) with the exception of 'J. H., W. E.', which I take to refer to Jack Hughes and Walter Evans.
32. See 'PB Minutes – 1939' in box 16 (76), CPA Archives for list of invitees and for 'Meeting of Central Exec. with LP fraction', 10.5.39'.
33. A sober account of the conference is found in the *Sydney Morning Herald*, 28 August 1939.
34. *Tribune*, 5 September 1939.
35. '10 Minute Record – Speech for Hunter By-election', in John Hughes Papers, Mitchell Library, Sydney.
36. 'Die K.P. Australiens zum Kriege', in RTsKhIDNI, 495-20-4. I am grateful to Hans-Dieter Senff for a translation of this document, from which this quotation is taken.
37. Ibid.
38. Hughes interview with author, 9 May 1994.
39. According to Edgar Ross (letter 17.11.95), Glasson, Starling and Walsham were definitely members of the CPA, while Barker, Kilburn Erwin and Sloss were 'close'. Jack Hughes identified Barker, Glasson, Walsham as members and said that Sloss was 'very close' (interview 16.11.95). Another interviewee, Eric Aarons, is 'almost certain' that Sloss was a dual member for part of this time.
40. This account is drawn from the *Sydney Morning Herald*, 25 March 1940.
41. 'Allgemeine Direktiven fuer Neuseeland und Australien' (Common directives for New Zealand and Australia). The document is dated 7 May 1940 but was dictated by Marty on 11 March. In RTsKhIDNI, 495-20-4. I am grateful to Hans-Dieter Senff for this translation.
42. *Daily News*, 20 June 1940.
43. Hansard, House of Representatives, 20 June 1940.
44. *Sydney Morning Herald*, 3 August 1940.
45. *Daily News*, 9 April 1940.
46. *SMH*, 7 June 1940.
47. *Daily News*, 20 June 1940.
48. *SMH*, 21 June 1940.
49. *SMH*, 20 July 1940.

CHAPTER SEVEN

Fighting Fascism through Espionage

Myths about espionage die hard. People imagine that a secret agent takes courses in some school where he is initiated into the arcana of the occult science of intelligence ... I have never taken a course in espionage ... My school was my life as a militant. Nothing could have better prepared me to lead a network like the Red Orchestra than the twenty tumultuous years of activity – often clandestine – before I entered Soviet intelligence.

Leopold Trepper[1]

The year 1939 saw events in Europe moving swiftly to recast the fortunes of nations and political movements. It saw the defeat of the Spanish republic beginning with the fall of Barcelona on 26 January. In March, Hitler entered Prague and annexed Czechoslovakia, thus ending the illusion of the Munich agreement which British prime minister Neville Chamberlain had claimed would bring 'peace in our time'. Several days later the Soviet government issued one of many similar proposals for talks between France, Britain and the USSR to limit German expansion. Chamberlain rejected the proposal as 'premature' and a similar diplomatic dance continued until August. On the 23rd of that month to the surprise of all sides, Germany's foreign minister, Ribbentrop, and Soviet foreign minister Molotov signed the Non-Aggression Pact in Moscow.

Nine days after the German–Soviet Non-Aggression Pact, Germany invaded Poland and under secret protocols of the pact, Poland was divided between the USSR and Germany. On 3 September Britain, which had undertaken to assist Poland, declared war on Germany. The period that followed saw the might of German forces turned against France and Britain while the Non-Aggression Pact between Germany and Russia held until June 1941.

The Russians, however, had been planning on fighting a war in Europe since at least 1937. As part of these preparations, they made increasing use of their supporters in the local communist parties. Nearly all these parties had at one stage developed underground apparatuses for political purposes. In the 1930s, Soviet intelligence had used this advantage to obtain industrial and scientific information to assist its industry. By the late 1930s the political underground in the United States and Europe had begun to be mobilised for the direct defence of the Soviet Union. Throughout this period and the war that followed, many western communists saw nothing wrong with passing information from their own governments to the Soviet Union. Particularly after 1941, Russia was allied with Britain and the US and a great deal of technical and material support was being given to the USSR through official channels. This partly explains the position of scientists such as Ted Hall, who worked on the Manhattan Project which built the first atomic bomb and who passed on a great deal of valuable information. Other scientists such as Klaus Fuchs passed atomic secrets to the Soviet Union out of a loyalty which stemmed from a deeper political commitment.

Such supporters saw espionage as a natural continuation of their political commitment. They included, for example, the group which began with Kim Philby and the European communists who formed the core of the Russians' Red Orchestra networks working in Nazi-occupied Europe. The latter were joined by non-communist sympathisers, notably anti-Nazi Germans, some with aristocratic connections, who co-operated with the USSR as a way of fighting fascism, which they judged the greater enemy.

These actions were later to nurture the seeds of the Cold War which followed World War Two. The wave of domestic anti-communism during the Cold War, particularly in the US, had at its heart a series of spy cases. For American anti-communists the issue which most symbolised the treachery of the left was the Soviet penetration of the project to build the atomic bomb. The mode of its penetration is a classic example of the tradition of *konspiratsya*.

THE MANHATTAN PROJECT

The Anglo-American project to build an atom bomb was officially revealed to Stalin in July 1945 by US President Harry Truman. But Stalin's KGB had for almost two years been collecting information about the project which they code-named 'Enormaz' and which the West called the Manhattan Project. The Russians used several sources to keep track of the complex process, the heart of which was a highly secret laboratory at Los Alamos in New Mexico. Their key sources were two left-wing scientists, the young American nuclear physicist Ted Hall and the German scientist Klaus Fuchs. Almost certainly there were other significant sources who have not been identified.[2] Playing a crucial role in servicing these sources were two very different couriers, Harry Gold and Lona Cohen, both of whom were skilled in the tradecraft of *konspiratsya*.

As a student in Germany, Klaus Fuchs had first joined the Social Democratic Party and then the Communist Party just as it was making its fatal encounter with triumphant Nazism in 1933. In the six months before he left Germany he was, in his own words 'in the underground', leaving secretly to attend an anti-fascist conference in France, then settling in England.[3] He studied physics at Bristol University, later developing his scientific work at the University of Edinburgh. During this period he was a member of a growing group of German communist exiles in Britain who had organised covert party branches in a number of British cities.[4] Fuchs took part in anti-Nazi and left-wing activities, a fact later downplayed lest it cause embarrassment to lax security forces when his role as a Soviet source was revealed.

From May to December 1940 Fuchs was interned as an enemy alien. But by mid-1941 he had been recruited to the British atomic effort, the Tube Alloys project, and shortly afterwards he was in contact with Soviet intelligence. In August 1941 the GRU in London reported contact with Fuchs, who gave the first indication of work which would lead to the construction of the atomic bomb.[5] Before he left for the United States in 1943, Fuchs regularly met his contact, Sonia Beurton, and passed information to her. Earlier Beurton had been active in China in the 1930s for the GRU and before she met Fuchs had worked for the Swiss part of the Red Orchestra (see below.)[6] Thus by the time Fuchs had transferred to Los Alamos and had met his US contact, 'Raymond', he was familiar with the basic protocol of *konspiratsya*. In their dealings with him, the KGB code-named him 'Charl'z' and 'Rest'.

The courier for the information from Fuchs was Harry Gold, the son of a Russian Jew who was attracted to socialism as a result of hardship and racism.[7] His work for the Russians began with industrial espionage in the mid-1930s, collecting scientific information which was routed through an American contact to the Russian trade organisation Amtorg. The arrangement for this was relatively loose and in 1943 when Gold met his new controller, Anatoli Yakovlev, things were tightened up. Under Yakovlev '[t]here were more explicit instructions on meetings and fallbacks, strange recognition signals and coded conversations'.[8] Gold was dubbed 'Goose' for the purposes of coded cables between New York and Moscow.

In early 1944 his controller 'Sam' (Semyon Semyonov) warned that he would be given a new and important task.[9] Using the cover name 'Raymond', Gold found it was to meet the scientist Klaus Fuchs, who would provide valuable information on the research into building an atomic bomb. To recognise each other at their first meeting, Gold carried a pair of gloves in one hand and a green book in the other while Fuchs carried a tennis ball. At this meeting Gold established that Fuchs 'was aware of whom he was working with'.[10]

During six more meetings Fuchs handed over information which proved very valuable for Soviet efforts to build an atomic bomb. At the eighth scheduled meeting, Fuchs did not appear, nor at the fall back meeting. With difficulty Yakovlev found Fuch's sister's address and thereby discovered where Fuchs had gone.[11] It was to a high mesa in New Mexico, Los Alamos, the most secret part of the Manhattan Project. Two more meetings were arranged in the town of Santa Fe, close to the bomb-building site. Another of Gold's tasks was to meet a soldier-technician, David Greenglass, who would give technical information about the detonation process.

Gold was a most peculiar underground worker. He had never joined the communist party and in the 1930s seemed to mix mainly with small-time communists who, like him, were sending industrial formulae to Russia. He later spoke only vaguely about socialist beliefs and mainly felt an attachment Russia on the basis of its alleged protection of Jews and support for workers. As well, he was something of a fantasist.[12] Yet Gold seemed extremely devoted, paying for many of his expenses himself and going through the complicated and frustrating contortions which *konspiratsya* involves.

But while knowledgeable about some of the rules of conspiracy, in other aspects he was extremely careless. 'On returning from a journey, he simply stuffed armfuls of unsubmitted blueprints, drafts of reports, note cards, street maps and the like into a spare closet in the cellar of his Philadelphia home.'[13] Reflecting on the secret and time-consuming contact work involved, Gold said later that it 'was a drudgery and I hated it'. Finally, when placed under minimal pressure by the FBI he made a full confession, implicating many of his contacts, some of whom he regarded as friends.

The Russians' judgement that he was to be entrusted with courier duty to service Fuchs is hard to understand, though presumably it was partly because Gold had some scientific knowledge. Gold's confession to the FBI led to David Greenglass, whose confession led to his brother-in-law, Julius Rosenberg. The information which Greenglass passed on was minor, though his confession led to one of the key cases in the history of the Cold War.

The other significant Soviet source was the American scientist, Theodore (Ted) Hall.[14] Hall was virtually the opposite of Fuchs in experience and personality. When war broke out in 1939, Hall was only 14 years old. A precocious child and student, Hall had completed high school and entered Queen's College in 1940. While still a teenager, he had rejected Judaism, his parents' religion, and set his heart on a scientific career. His rejection of religion was part of a rebellious nature which had also steered him towards left-wing politics while still a teenager. Unlike the reserved Fuchs, Hall was passionate, outspoken and played practical jokes.

By 1942, Hall had entered Havard University to study physics. By chance he roomed near two of Havard's leading left-wing students, further cementing his political stance. Another friend was a bohemian and eccentric literature student, Saville Sax, who was also a supporter of Soviet communism. Sax later assisted Hall in getting nuclear secrets to the Russians. Though Hall had troubles adjusting to university life, he again proved himself brilliant at physics and mathematics. Late the following year at the age of 19 he was recruited to work on the atom bomb project in New Mexico. When being recruited by the Russians, he was described as having 'an exceptionally keen mind and a broad outlook' and being 'politically developed'.[15] In light of his age, Hall was assigned the code name 'Mlad', meaning 'young', while Sax was code-named 'Star', meaning 'old'.

The courier who serviced Ted Hall (and conducted a number of other wartime industrial espionage assignments) was Lona Cohen, a young American communist.[16] She had carried out a number of assignments with her partner Morris Cohen and years later, in 1961, both were arrested in Britain for servicing another Soviet agent. In 1937 Lona

Petka's road to underground politics and espionage began when she met Morris Cohen at a rally in solidarity with Spanish republicans – six days later Morris sailed to fight himself. After being wounded in Spain he was selected to attend a school for underground party workers, set up by the head of the KGB in Spain, Alexander Orlov.[17] At the school, Cohen and other participants were taught the rules of conspiracy while two of its 'graduates' became radio operators for the Red Orchestra (see below). When he returned to the USA, Morris Cohen was equipped to work for Soviet intelligence but, unusually for a potential intelligence worker, he was openly employed at the Soviet pavilion at the World's Fair and later at Amtorg, the Soviet trade organisation.

In 1941 Lona Petka married Morris Cohen and shortly after he disclosed to her his life as a Soviet agent. After her initial disquiet, they carried out a number of operations, on one occasion jointly obtaining plans for a new American-designed machine gun mounted on an aircraft. Lona Cohen also became active as a courier collecting industrial and military information from many sources organised by her controller, 'Sam' Semyonov, a KGB officer in New York. Information came in the form of rolls of film collected from seamen or coded letters from a contact in the Office of Strategic Services (OSS).

By 1945 Lona Cohen was in 'cold storage', her agent work suspended for the time being and her husband Morris drafted into the army. At her job in an aviation factory, she had taken a public stance as a union militant and left-winger and been elected chair of the trade union branch. In spite of this overt activity, the New York KGB section, which was looking for an experienced courier, recruited her to help penetrate Los Alamos. Her task was to replace an unconventional courier who had obtained material from an unconventional source, Ted Hall.

The courier she replaced was Saville Sax, the former student at Havard who was by turns an aspiring writer and physicist. Sax was a supporter of Russian communism and a university friend of Ted Hall. When Hall was being recruited to the super-secret Manhattan Project he foresaw the political implications of a western monopoly on a nuclear bomb and, encouraged by Sax, resolved to pass information to the Russians.

To do this Hall and Sax had directly approached several Soviet officials in New York in October 1944, offering information on the nature of the new kind of bomb and the plan to build it. Although surprised at this approach, officers of the KGB made arrangements to keep in touch and in late 1944 Sax made his way to Albuquerque to collect information from Hall. Though the enterprise was well on its way, checks on the identities of Hall and Sax were only just beginning through a contact in the CPUSA.[18] As Albright and Kunstel point out, allowing the untrained Sax to be the courier with Hall was a risk according to the rules of conspiracy.[19] Hall may well have insisted on it, and as well, the Russians were worried about concentrating too many threads in the hands of another courier, Harry Gold. Another break with normalcy was the Russians' delayed background check on Hall and Sax, carried out in December 1944 after Hall had begun to pass information to them. In any case, Sax met Hall in New Mexico and carried back to New York vital material on the principles of the bomb. Its form was in keeping with the amateur security precautions: it was hand-written by Hall. Moreover, Hall's behaviour at Los Alamos was the opposite of the discreet low profile recommended by the rules of conspiracy. Instead he was a rebel, confronting the rules of the army which jointly controlled Los Alamos, and dressing unconventionally. He was the opposite of the colourless, reserved Fuchs. It may have been some of these things which prompted KGB headquarters in Moscow to issue a stern reprimand in July about the sloppy nature of the operation which may have endangered Hall.[20]

Nevertheless, Hall's secret activity was not blown and he continued to pass information to his new courier, Lona Cohen, including details of the planned test of the bomb at Almogordo. After the test came another meeting at Albuquerque between Hall and Cohen. The meeting almost failed because it was originally scheduled for a Sunday and did not occur. The fall-back was the following Sunday, then each Sunday after that. The meeting eventually took place on the fourth Sunday and more information was on its way to the USSR.

Years later Hall explained his rationale for his actions, fearing that an American monopoly of nuclear weapons would be dangerous, particularly in the context of a postwar depression. 'To help prevent that monopoly I contemplated a brief encounter with a Soviet agent, just to inform them of the existence of the A-bomb program.' He found the encounter was not brief, but maintained that some sort of nuclear balance may have resulted. It certainly appears to be the case that Soviet capability was advanced by at least several years due to the combined efforts of many pro-Soviet western sources and the apparatus which conveyed the information.[21]

THE RED ORCHESTRA

The Rote Kapelle or Red Orchestra was the name given to a series of anti-Nazi espionage groups in Europe established by Soviet military intelligence (GRU) from approximately 1936 onwards.

At its height the various arms of the Red Orchestra were drawing information from the German High Command, lower levels of the German army in France and Belgium, the Luftwaffe headquarters in Berlin, a variety of non-combatant diplomats and other sources. Within Germany itself several anti-Nazi groups functioned both as a political opposition and as espionage groups.

While the leading figures in these groups were Soviet intelligence officers, a number of participants were also militants from the French, Belgian, Swiss, German and Dutch communist parties. The meshing of the techniques of *konspiratsya* from both the fields of politics and espionage was nicely summed up by one of the leading figures in the group, a Polish communist, Leopold Trepper:

> Myths about espionage die hard. People imagine that a secret agent takes courses in some school where he is initiated into the arcana of the occult science of intelligence ... I have never taken a course in espionage ... My school was my life as a militant. Nothing could have better prepared me to lead a network like the Red Orchestra than the twenty tumultuous years of activity – often clandestine – before I entered Soviet intelligence.[22]

Trepper's life as a militant began as a worker activist in Polish coal-mines, for which he was jailed. Leaving for Palestine as a Zionist, he later joined the Communist Party of Palestine. Later in France, he organised Jewish workers for the French Communist Party. In 1937 he joined Soviet military intelligence, for whom he began to prepare an espionage network in Europe.[23]

Trepper's 'cover' for espionage was his involvement with a former Comintern militant, Leon Grossvogel, in a legitimate business, the Foreign Excellent Raincoat Company based in Belgium. Trepper's identity was that of 'Adam Mikler', a Canadian businessman whose business conveniently took him on journeys to a number of cities in different countries. His trips and business activity were not purely a façade, however. Reflecting on his role, he recalled 'the agent must not act, he must be ... the most attentive and persistent observer would not have noticed any difference between my life and the life of any of the other businessmen I met at the Stock Exchange or in a restaurant'.[24]

In fact he was the 'Grand Chef' of a series of espionage subgroups in Europe which fed their information to his overworked radio operators. When the company's premises were damaged by war in 1940, Trepper moved his base from Belgium to France, continuing his work by setting up another company, Simex, which financed its activities (and gathered information) through its dealings with the occupying German army. A series of arrests from mid to late 1942 led to the arrest of Trepper, who then convinced his captors that he would act as a double agent, deceiving Moscow. In fact he managed to alert Moscow to this and escaped in late 1943.[25]

Just prior to Trepper's establishment of his cover as a businessman in Belgium, another GRU officer, Alexander Rado, moved to Geneva to set up Geopress, a cartographic firm which provided cover for his activities. Rado operated at the head of three other subnetworks and at one stage had four or five radio transmitters in contact with Moscow.[26] Among those involved with the Swiss-based intelligence groups, several women stood out. The apparent founder of the network was a young GRU officer, Maria Josefovna Poliakova, who supervised Rado and also the functioning of the Swiss groups by coded radio messages from Moscow. Ursula Hamburger (Sonia Beurton) a GRU officer who was based in China in 1930–5 and after the Swiss episode lived in England where she was a contact of atom spy Klaus Fuchs. She fled in 1949 for East Germany. Another was Rachel Duebendorfer ('Sissy'), who maintained contact with Rudolf Roesseler ('Lucy'and who had very useful German military sources.

The Swiss group was the most productive of all Soviet wartime groups since it had made contact with anti-Nazi Germans of whom the key one was General Hans Oster of the military counter-intelligence, Abwehr. Oster was in turn in contact with a number of other highly placed anti-Hitler officers in the German High Command and elsewhere.[27] A stream of valuable information was thereby passed on to Moscow. A number of these sources in 1944 helped organise the unsuccessful attempt to assassinate Hitler and many later were executed.

At the heart of the functioning of the Red Orchestra was the co-operation between communist militants, trained in the political underground, and professional intelligence officers. Trepper noted:

180

the Red Army had at its disposal thousands of communists who regarded themselves not as spies but as fighters in the vanguard of the world revolution ... they never talked about salary or money. They were civilians who were devoting themselves to a cause, just as they might have done in a labor union.[28]

Differences and distance existed between the Comintern-based spies and the Russian 'professionals', some of whom looked down on the former.[29] But both groups expressed the continuity of the tradition of *konspiratsya* with the later refinements of espionage tradecraft – both spoke the same organisational language. For example, each espionage group was strictly centralised and organised in military fashion on the local level. In addition, the Moscow-based 'Director' insisted on being informed in the smallest detail of the work of each espionage group and issued instructions in a similar level of detail.[30] A study of these instructions and questions in radio messages to and from the Director shows remarkable similarity to Lenin's prescriptions (see chapter 1).

As well, each group was strictly compartmentalised. A British participant in Rado's Swiss group, Alexander Foote, noted: '[The local director] is usually unknown to his agents, couriers and radio-telegraphists, being in contact with them only through his "liaison agents" or "cuts-outs" who are the only people who are aware of his identity.'[31] Similarly, the time and place for some meetings between members of groups and the recognition signals or code words were laboriously organised through Moscow. Just as the 'The Rules for Party Conspiratorial Work' prescribed that emergency meetings should never be held in the same place twice, Trepper made a similar recommendation.[32]

The techniques of espionage communication were similar to those developed by the pre-revolutionary groups, as discussed, for example, by Krupskaya (see ch. 1 above). According to Foote:

In all agents' messages and in all enciphered texts only cover names are used for the sources and the messages are couched in a jargon which would make them not easily interpreted by anyone not 'in the net' ... [cover names] are employed indiscriminately without regard to sex; thus a male agent may easily have a female cover name ... a passport is 'a shoe'; a forger of false passports thus naturally becomes 'a cobbler', a prison was 'a hospital' and thus the police become 'the doctor'.[33]

The use of radio allowed more elaborate devices for preventing someone listening in:

> if I wished to call the Centre I would tap out my call sign in Morse on my fixed call wave – say, 43 metres. The Centre would be listening and reply on its fixed call wave, say 39 metres. On hearing the Centre reply, I would then switch to my working wave length – say 49 metres – and then with a different call sign send over my material.[34]

The main problem which proved the undoing of many of these groups was that the hours-long transmission, regardless of wavelength, allowed German radio direction-finding units to target them.

Another component of the Red Orchestra lay within the German government. It revolved around an economist, Dr Arvid Harnack, and his wife, an American, Mildred Fish.[35] Harnack was a secret communist who had little contact with the party after 1933 and operated independently, being recruited to intelligence in 1935. His position in the Ministry of the Economy allowed him access not only to trade and some military information on Germany's war preparations, but also social contact with businesspeople and diplomats, the latter through his wife's contacts. In a significant break with conspiratorial practice, Harnack insisted that he combine covert anti-Nazi political activity with espionage, in spite of initially agreeing to break off political activity.[36] Harnack did take precautions, however, joining the Nazi-sponsored Union of Lawyers and becoming active in its section in the ministry. The lack of compartmentalisation continued to concern the KGB. A 1940 assessment of his network of sources noted that 'Corsican's [Harnack] description of the way that they camouflage their operations is that, while not all members of the circle know one another, something of a chain exists. Corsican tries to remain in the background although he is at the heart of the organization. The aim of them all is to occupy administrative posts [in the government] after the *coup d'état*.'[37]

A significant source of intelligence for Harnack's group was a Luftwaffe officer who worked at the Air Ministry, Harro Schulze-Boysen, and his wife Libertas. Their activity broke all the rules of conspiracy and included holding meetings of the group and distributing anti-Nazi propaganda in Berlin. Perhaps his most valuable information, about the imminent German invasion of the USSR, was explicitly rejected by Stalin. Significant parts of both Harnack's and Schulze-Boysen's groups, including these leaders, were arrested and executed in 1942–3.

The contribution of the various parts of the 'Red Orchestra' to the ultimate Soviet victory is hard to judge and even today aspects of its operations are unclear. Nevertheless it represents most sharply the intermingling of the Comintern with Soviet intelligence and the common soil of *konspiratsya* which both adapted to their circumstances.

The espionage targets at the Manhattan Project and in Nazi-occupied Europe were clear and rather obvious. Less clear and more subtle was the work of Soviet intelligence oriented to the postwar world, predicated on the defeat of Germany. An example of this work occurred in Australia, a country remote from the sound of the European battle. It was because Australia was part of the British sphere of influence that its government officials shared a high degree of access to British secrets. As war turned into peace, Soviet intelligence began to obtain British government secrets from several civil servants in key positions. The KGB activity generated in the Australian capital of Canberra later greatly assisted the decryption of KGB cables in the Venona Project.

GETTING BRITISH SECRETS FROM AUSTRALIA

In their work on the American communist party, Klehr, Haynes and Firsov note that Soviet intelligence chose to work closely with the underground apparatus of the CPUSA.[38] It was through co-operation with the leader of that apparatus, Rudy Baker, that some of the technological and atomic espionage was initiated. A very similar arrangement existed in Australia, resulting in a steady stream of British Foreign Office material being conveyed to the Russians.

The story of these events began with the banning of the CPA under wartime defence powers in June 1940. The CPA had been preparing for an underground existence since January.[39] In March 1940 it had issued guidelines for looming illegality, which it said was based 'on the experience of our brother parties in countries under terror conditions'.[40] Much of it is based on practices similar to those outlined in the 'Rules for Party Conspiratorial Work'. The section on meetings urged party members, when arranging a meeting in writing, to use a time code for example, specifying a time two days and two hours ahead of the real time of the meeting. 'Always make two dates for the one purpose', it advised. Failure to arrive at the first date automatically meant a second time and place was arranged.

Anticipating arrests, the CPA urged its members to forget heroics: 'Don't try to take the blame to protect your friends. Experience has shown that this will merely give you away without giving your friends any real security.' 'Deny everything and let the police try to prove the truth of every accusation.' It signalled the 'old and dangerous' police interrogation techniques: 'Never believe police statements to the effect that it is no use your denying guilt as your friends have already told everything.' Some parts are almost identical to the 'Rules for Party Conspiratorial work':

> When you are released, remember that you are certain to be kept under observation for some time. Therefore don't think of meeting active comrades for some time. Find some indirect way of letting them know that you have been released and giving them all essential information.[41]

The person chosen by the party leadership to build the CPA underground, Wally Clayton, had moved from Melbourne to Sydney in 1939 to organise the sales of the national CPA newspaper *Tribune*. His success, his organising abilities and his relative anonymity in Sydney made him a logical choice to lead the underground work. On the night when the ban was declared, he was picked up in a series of sweeping police raids around Australian capital cities, but was soon released.[42]

Shortly after being banned, the CPA issued a set of directives to its leading cadres which set out the *modus operandi* of underground work.[43] Any postal communications would be sent to 'cover-addresses known only to one or two trusted comrades and which will be changed from time to time'. It clearly anticipated expert advice from the Soviet Union on conspiratorial methods and advised that

> the Party will use a transposition code for a few months for the communication by letter [of] most confidential material and the code will be changed from time to time and will be known only to leading executive members. This code, of course, can be decoded by experts but we will use it for a short time *until a more elaborate system can be obtained from abroad.* (emphasis added).

One of his first tasks was to find suitable cadres to work in the underground. These were, according to Clayton, 'people who could cut themselves off from society; who would leave their own homes and families and disappear'.[44]

Another task was to select a supportive periphery of people whose houses and farms would be used for meetings, for storing paper and petrol and hiding individuals. Such people were not necessarily members of the CPA, since most active members were known to the police and internal security. Rather they were relatives or friends who were judged utterly trustworthy. For this the CPA's contacts through its underground work in the Labor Party proved very useful (see ch. 6 above). Of these some were used immediately, others were kept as 'reserves' to take over after expected raids.[45] This period saw systematic fostering of a wide range of underground techniques, especially among the leadership who continued to meet, and among the rank and file who assisted in the printing and distribution of the *Tribune*. CPA members became acquainted with what was called 'the chain system'.[46] Essentially this referred to the compartmentalisation of the party structure along classical Russian underground lines. If any one of the activities was discovered by the police, the losses would be minimised since the discovery did not compromise the rest of the 'chain'.

The most secret part of the 'chain' was the operation of printing presses. During 1940–2 the CPA apparatus led by Clayton established a number of clandestine printeries. Copies of the *Tribune* were distributed in small parcels via the railway system all over the continent. The location of printeries was carefully selected. Large homes in wealthy suburbs were sometimes rented while at other times homes in secluded bushland were preferred. The location of each printing press changed every four to five months. Attention to detail was crucial. At all printeries a woman party member was employed to cook and to answer the door. Regular washing had to be hung on the clothes line to avoid arousing suspicion.[47]

A key figure in the underground apparatus in Sydney, Len Donald, worked as a barman in a Sydney hotel. The owner, Albert Sloss, was a close CPA sympathiser in the Australian Labor Party. As a barman Donald would receive documents, arrange rendezvous and act as a post box, particularly for connections with other states.[48]

The Nazi attack on the USSR in June 1941 and Soviet entry into the war radically changed the CPA's attitude which became pro-war. Communists opposed strikes and CPA members joined the armed forces. Because of their record, army authorities opposed their entry and guidelines were issued on how to conduct CPA political work within the army.[49] Six months later the Japanese bombing of Pearl Harbour changed the tasks of the CPA underground yet again. It now began to prepare for working underground during a Japanese military occupation of Australia. A military occupation meant that the apparatus would have to 'sit tight', cease the production of the *Tribune* and 'not be active until we could feel our way' in the new situation, recalled Clayton.[50] Such a situation, in which military terror would be widespread, would mean that the CPA would have to isolate itself even from its supportive periphery. Supporters would probably not be able to face up to the fatal consequences of hiding a person or a printing press, nor would it be right to ask them to do so, Clayton recalled. By late 1942 the danger of Japanese invasion had passed and the CPA was functioning almost openly as a group strongly in favour of the war effort. In December the Labor government lifted the ban on the CPA and the underground organisation wound down. Its connections and methods, however, remained among a small group of trusted activists centring around Clayton. These connections became central to Clayton's later organisation of espionage.

Following the alliance of the USSR with the anti-Nazi forces in World War Two, assistance from the West flowed to the USSR and diplomatic relations grew warmer. By May 1943 Stalin had decided that the existence of the Communist International was a 'hindrance' to the pursuit of the war.[51] But the dissolution of the Comintern posed problems for Soviet intelligence officials, particularly in countries like the USA, Canada and Australia. The dissolution was intended as a signal to the Allies that the Russians were reducing both the quantity and quality of their relations with local CPs. This meant that the very useful contacts cultivated by Russian intelligence bodies with local communists had to become more covert. The contact between Soviet intelligence and members of the CPA is revealed in a series of cables sent by Soviet intelligence during and after World War Two which were intercepted by British and American authorities and partially decoded.[52]

In September 1943, in the light of the dissolution of the Comintern, the head of the First Directorate (Foreign Intelligence) of the KGB, General Pavel Fitin ordered KGB officers in the United States, Canada and Australia to cease overt contact with the leaders of local communist ('Fellowcountryman') parties.[53] Covert contact continued, however:

> We propose ... (b) that meetings of our workers may take place only with the special reliable undercover contacts of 'Fellowcountryman' [organisations] who are not suspected by the [—] local authorities,

exclusively about specific aspects of our intelligence work [—] contacts, leads, rechecking of those who are being cultivated etc. For each meeting it is necessary to obtain our consent.[54]

In his role as organiser of the underground, Clayton was a 'special, reliable undercover contact' of the kind through whom liaison was to be maintained. He was also a member of the CPA's Control Commission, similar to the head of the American communist party's underground work, Rudy Baker.

The representative of the KGB's foreign intelligence directorate in Australia at that time was Semen Ivanovich Makarov, who arrived in Australia in 1943. His initial intelligence activities included meeting with the Consul General for France, Boris Eliachev ('Palm'), who had been recruited as an agent in 1943.[55]

Makarov, as 'resident' (senior official) for the KGB, did not conduct all the intelligence work himself, particularly when this involved regular travel from Canberra to Sydney. Working with him were 'cadre workers', one of whom was the *Tass* correspondent, Fedor Andreevich Nosov.[56] Based at an apartment in Sydney's bohemian district, King's Cross, Nosov was having regular meetings in early 1945 with his contact in the CPA, Walter Clayton. During one of these meetings Clayton mentioned that he was in contact with an officer of Australia's wartime Security Service, a comment that aroused the interest of Makarov and of the KGB Foreign Intelligence Directorate when it was reported to Moscow. The Security Service officer, Alfred Hughes, had been a left-wing police officer before the war and had been recruited as an investigator in the Security Service where he was regarded as an 'expert' on the CPA.[57] In March, Nosov raised the possibility of getting Hughes to use his position in some way to obtain information.[58]

Hughes was by no means the only CPA contact in the Security Service. Clayton may have had a relationship with a woman who worked as secretary to the NSW Police Commissioner, W. J. Mackay who, between March and September 1942, was the Director-General of the Security Service.[59] The most significant result of this contact between the CPA and the Security Service occurred in 1942 when Clayton obtained a copy of his own security file where he found details which enabled him to identify a well placed informer within the CPA.[60] The informer, James McPhee, had been responsible for CPA work in the Australian navy some years previously (see chapter 3). The source of the file was probably either the NSW director of the Security Service, Stanley Taylor, or Alfred Hughes, who was close to Taylor. Taylor himself had Labor sympathies and his brother, William Taylor, was a leading member of the Labor left while it was under the dominance of underground CPA members.

Clayton's contacts were of interest to Nosov and at a further meeting in April 1945, Clayton told the *Tass* correspondent about another undercover member of the CPA, Frances Bernie.[61] Bernie was working as a typist at the office of the Labor Minister for External Affairs, Dr H. V. Evatt. Clayton explained that he worked closely with her and 'was giving her detailed instructions on how to conduct herself in Evatt's outfit'. Makarov cabled the KGB in Moscow and with some surprise told them 'Secretary-typist Burny [*sic*] really does work at Evatt's. "Technician" [Nosov] has seen her a number of times in the secretariat.'[62]

Alerted to the espionage value of such a contact, Makarov was eager to hear more of this young woman and instructed Nosov to obtain a biographical sketch of her from Clayton and to ask him if he had obtained any confidential information from her. At about this time, the relationship between Clayton and his Soviet contacts underwent a change. Between March and April 1945, in the coded cables which Makarov sent to Moscow, Clayton was no longer referred to in plain text by his own name but was allocated a code name, 'Klod'. The security officer, Hughes became 'Ben' and Frances Bernie became 'Sestra' (sister). At this point it becomes clear that underground contacts of the CPA, whose purpose was local and political, were being drawn into the orbit of Soviet intelligence. Clayton himself was being drawn ever deeper into espionage, though he walked with eyes open. In May, Nosov gave him £15 'on the plausible pretext of compensating him for his personal efforts and the expenditure he incurs when he meets people on assignments of ours'.[63] Clayton was initially 'taken aback', Makarov reported, because he had 'always considered it his duty to help our country'. But Clayton then accepted the money and was carefully told it 'was intended for him personally and [that] no one should know of it'.

Clayton in many ways was the ideal recruit. He had practical experience in the tradecraft of conspiracy. He had painstakingly built an illegal apparatus in Australia and he was doggedly loyal to the ideals of the Comintern. Most of all, his work in the CPA underground meant that he was in contact with a broad range of members of the CPA whose openness about their membership varied from the discreet to the highly secret. Most were middle-class communists such as doctors, lawyers, journalists and scientists whose careers and social standing would be badly damaged by open activity.[64] In periods of relatively high popularity (such as the late 1930s) the CPA gathered many such members. This proved valuable in providing cover for an underground apparatus but was also of great interest to Soviet intelligence. In the late 1930s a relatively large number of scientists joined the CPA. The Soviet Union had always been interested in obtaining and copying scientific and technological information from the West and the cables sent by Makarov to Moscow in this period contain the names of many scientists, usually also identifying their political stance.[65]

But Clayton had also developed a small number of CPA members who were placed in sensitive positions in order to provide domestic political intelligence for the CPA.[66] An ideal 'listening post' would be a position on the staff of a government minister. Many official documents passed through these offices and people in such positions heard and saw all kinds of gossip and information. Such was the value of Frances Bernie. Just what material she provided to Clayton is not clear although it included private letters between Evatt and his personal secretary, Alan Dalziel, which dealt with domestic political matters.[67]

By July and August the Security Service officer, Alfred Hughes, was providing Clayton and through him, Nosov, with copies of files detailing the physical surveillance of the Soviet journalist Vladimir Mikeyev and of the structure of the Security Service. Clayton was also including details of right-wing political groups in Australia, a subject of little interest to Fitin's Foreign Intelligence Directorate. Fitin was more concerned with using Hughes to find out details of British intelligence.[68]

But in this period, Clayton's CPA contacts (or possibly his own diligent planning) turned up another welcome piece of news for Soviet intelligence. Clayton informed Nosov that two CPA members had obtained jobs in the small but significant Department of External Affairs. The first, Dr Ian Milner, had been a lecturer in political science at Melbourne University and had begun work in Canberra in February 1945. The other, James Hill, a young lawyer, began in June. Because of Australia's close relations with Britain, especially in wartime, External Affairs received a great deal of highly classified British information. This placed Milner and Hill in an extremely valuable position, in the eyes of Russian intelligence.

Ian Milner and James Hill became key figures in what followed and it is useful to discuss their backgrounds briefly. In the light of the risks they took for the USSR and the evidence from the Venona code-breaking, both were presumably undercover members of the Communist Party of Australia though it is not clear when they joined. Ian Milner was a brilliant young student in New Zealand when he won a scholarship to Oxford in 1933. Under observation by MI5 he was noted as a subscriber to the CPGB's *Daily Worker*. After graduating he held research fellowships at Columbia and California universities.[69] After a brief return to New Zealand, he was invited to apply for a lectureship in politics at Melbourne University in Australia. While there he became a committee member of the Australia–Soviet Friendship League in 1941. In late 1944 he successfully applied for a civil service position in the Department of External Affairs.

James (Jim) Hill began his working life as a bank clerk while studying law at night. He joined the Labor Party at the age of 20 in 1938, though there is some doubt whether this was genuine as Hill may have already been an undercover CPA member.[70] Hill attended Melbourne University, where he may have first met Clayton, who was responsible for the CPA branch at the university. Certainly Clayton had made contact with his brother, Ted Hill, who soon joined the CPA and later became one of its leaders.[71] Before he joined the army in 1941 Hill mixed with CPA members in a number of left-wing activities. In June 1945 he joined the Department of External Affairs and moved to the national capital, Canberra. One former CPA member in Canberra said that both Milner and Hill

> carefully refrained from mixing in ordinary Communist circles in Canberra. My judgement was that this was done to avoid drawing attention to some other activities in which they were engaged. I knew as a Communist Party member that Milner was a communist in Melbourne. It was common talk among Communist Party members in Canberra that Jim Hill had been a Communist Party member in Melbourne. Although at the time I concluded that they had left the party I now believe they were acting on instructions in not joining in the local Communist activities.[72]

Milner and Hill, an academic and a lawyer respectively, held the kinds of jobs that made them part of a class of CPA membership that was undercover.[73] In any case it is clear that by 1945, Jim Hill was one of

Wally Clayton's most valuable contacts from the point of view of Soviet intelligence. In late 1945, Clayton twice visited Milner and Hill in Canberra and at one meeting Hill gave him several cables from the British Foreign Office and a report drawn up for Australia's External Affairs Minister, Dr Evatt, on events in Greece, Bulgaria and Romania.[74]

In September, Clayton reported a young left-wing diplomat, Richard (Ric) Throssell, had just been appointed to the Australian embassy in Moscow.[75] Throssell was the son of the well-known novelist Katharine Susannah Prichard, who was also a member of the Central Committee of the CPA. His appointment to the department intrigued Makarov who described it as 'rather strange' given Prichard's CPA position which was well known to Evatt. (Indeed not only did Evatt know this, but Throssell's mother had personally approached Evatt and prevailed on him to have her son selected as a diplomatic cadet, according to an acquaintance of Prichard's.[76]) Clayton had tried to suggest to Throssell's mother that 'from the point of view of the party' it would be better for Ric to be posted in Europe, but his mother wanted him posted to Moscow and she prevailed.[77]

In Canada, meanwhile, events were occurring that had reverberations throughout Soviet intelligence. In September 1945, a cipher clerk of the Soviet embassy in Ottawa, Igor Gouzenko, defected bringing with him information on the work of Soviet military intelligence, the GRU, and of espionage concerning the atom bomb.[78] In Australia, the Canadian events sounded a distant warning bell to Milner, Hill and Clayton. In the wake of Gouzenko's defection, the Moscow Centre ordered extra precautions to be taken between Clayton and his contact, Nosov.

In November, Clayton's sources in External Affairs passed on an exchange of cables between the British prime minister, Attlee and the Australian prime minister, Ben Chifley, regarding the tense events during which the Dutch tried to reimpose their rule in the Netherlands East Indies (Indonesia).[79] Chifley supported the repatriation of nationalist Indonesians who had spent the war in Australia, a proposal attacked by the Dutch. In the cable Chifley estimated that Mountbatten (then the commander of Allied forces in south-east Asia) 'attached too much significance to the moods of the Dutch' and argued that 'to abandon the Indonesians, as M[ountbatten] proposed, was impossible, as this would arouse serious anxiety in Australia'. Also leaked were a number of British Foreign Office cables, relating to events in Poland where the Soviet Union was establishing its postwar order, and in Argentina.[80]

The amount of secret diplomatic traffic which Clayton and his contacts in the 'Nook' (code for the External Affairs Department) passed on to the Russians is unknown, since not all of the cables have been decoded. It was presumably substantial, especially given the ease with which Milner and Hill obtained material.

By February 1946 the details of Gouzenko's revelations about espionage in Canada were becoming public through his testimony before the inquiry. When Moscow enquired whether its Australian sources had been affected by the Canadian revelations, Makarov reported that Clayton was still confident and reported that his friends in the 'Nook' were 'in good spirits and are behaving with great caution'.[81] They had also noticed that an official of 'counter-intelligence' was now working in their department. This cable demonstrates by its references to the Gouzenko events and the consequent caution shown by Milner and Hill that they realised that the work they were engaged in was in the field of intelligence.

In this period, Milner had obtained access to British war cabinet planning documents, one entitled 'Security of India and the Indian Ocean' and another 'Security in the Eastern Mediterranean and the Eastern Atlantic'. Prepared by the Post-Hostilities Planning Staff for the war cabinet in London, the documents outline British strategic considerations just before the European war ended in May 1945. In mid-March 1946 Clayton travelled to Canberra from Sydney to organise the hand-over of the documents to Makarov who arranged for them to be photographed and handed back to Clayton 35 minutes later.[82] The contents, some thousands of words classified 'Top Secret', were then cabled to Moscow. The discovery of this leakage through the Venona decoding operation in late 1947 led the US to deny to the British the new rocket technology which Britain intended to share with Australia.[83]

Sometime in the middle of 1946, Ian Milner's career path changed. The newly founded United Nations Organisation was seen as a significant target by Soviet intelligence, who urged its local officers to identify potential 'recruiting possibilities' of local officers intending to work for the UN.[84] By this time Milner was deeply committed to assisting Soviet intelligence and it seems quite possible that his decision to apply success- fully for a post with the UN in mid-1946 was suggested by Moscow. After attending to some family matters in New Zealand, Milner began work for the secretariat of the UN Security Council in January 1947 and for the next few years worked on UN missions to Palestine and

Korea.[85] We now know from a file on Milner of the Czech secret police released in late 1996 that while working for the UN he had been formally recruited to Soviet intelligence.[86] A summary in the file dated 29 November 1960 notes that in 1950 'we received information about a possible repression against Milner [from] our agent in the American counter espionage agency. Therefore a decision was made to relocate Milner into one of the people's democracies.' (Milner entered Czechoslovakia in 1950 and lived there until his death in 1991.)

By July 1946 it was clear to Soviet intelligence that Clayton and his External Affairs contacts had opened a valuable window into the British Foreign Office. Britain, with its empire, navy and commercial power had been the pre-eminent foe of the young Soviet republic. That month, a senior official of the KGB, Petr Kubatkin, urged Makarov to 'state what opportunities [Klod] has for stepping up [his] work for us'.[87] In October 1946 the KGB tightened up the security of its intelligence operations world-wide, rejecting its previous policy of recruiting members of the local communist parties.[88] Shortly afterwards it warned of heightened surveillance in the British Commonwealth and ordered a 'temporary suspension' of contact between Makarov and Clayton with an agreed password to indicate when work was to be resumed.[89]

The break was to last until early 1948, but during this time Clayton tried to resume contact by having a woman intermediary pass a note to a Soviet Foreign Ministry official at a diplomatic reception. A concerned KGB agent then arranged for the Foreign Ministry to instruct the ambassador to avoid contact with the woman, probably the Canberra communist Doris Beeby.[90]

In early 1948 the KGB decided to reactivate Clayton and ordered Makarov to make personal contact with him. With even more emphasis than before, it ordered Makarov to take extreme care in choosing meeting places and to take other security measures. In May 1948 it was clear that Clayton's contacts were not as varied as they were in 1945–6. Moscow Centre asked: 'Among his old sources whose material he passed us formerly, whom does [Clayton] recommend that we should take on, apart from Professor and Tourist [James Hill]?'[91] A little later the Centre was anxious to see whether Alfred Hughes ['Ben'] or Frances Bernie ['Sestra'] could be 'used for our work' and asked whether it was advisable to involve the diplomat Ric Throssell, given that his mother was a well-known communist.[92] The last cable conveyed a sense of urgency: 'Hurry up with getting detailed character reports [*kharakteristiki*] on all candidates recommended by K[lod].' The final decoded fragments include the following words asking Makarov to 'Ascertain what experience with working with people under illegal conditions ...'

It is not clear whose experience is being referred to here, but the reference to experience in working under illegal conditions nicely illustrates the main theme of this work: that many communist parties shared an organisational heritage with Soviet intelligence. This in turn sheds new light on controversial Cold War espionage cases which involved British, American and Australian figures on the left.

NOTES

1. Trepper, *Great Game*, 139.
2. According to Albright and Kunstel only a minor and confusing role was played by the American technician David Greenglass, whose confession led to the execution of Julius and Ethel Rosenberg. (Albright and Kunstel, *Bombshell*, 284). Benson and Warner indicate that other sources in the bomb project are still unknown. (Robert Louis Benson and Michael Warner (eds.) *Venona: Soviet Espionage and the American Response 1939–1957*, National Security Agency, Washington, DC, 1996, xviii–xix.)
3. Fuchs' statement to British authorities, January 1950 in Norman Moss, *Klaus Fuchs: the Man who Stole the Atom Bomb*, Grafton Books, London, 1989.
4. Robert Chadwell Williams, *Klaus Fuchs, Atom Spy*, Havard University Press, Cambridge, MA, 1987, ch. 3.
5. Venona message, London to Moscow, 10 August 1941.
6. Williams, *Klaus Fuchs*, 59–61.
7. Radosh and Milton, *Rosenberg File*, 24–9.
8. Robert J. Lamphere and Tom Shachtman, *The FBI–KGB War: a Special Agent's Story*, W. H. Allen, London, 1987, 172.
9. Gold's statements to the FBI are reproduced in Williams, *Klaus Fuchs*, 195–220.
10. Venona message, 9 February 1944.
11. Venona message, 29 August 1944.
12. Lamphere and Shachtman, *FBI–KGB*, 103.
13. Radosh and Milton, *Rosenberg File*, 31.
14. Most of this summary is based on Albright and Kunstel, *Bombshell*.
15. Venona message, 12 November 1944.
16. Material on Lorna and her partner Morris Cohen is from Albright and Kunstel, *Bombshell*, chapters 3, 4 and 6.
17. Costello and Tsarev, *Deadly Illusions*, 275–6.
18. Venona message, 23 January 1945.
19. Albright and Kunstel, *Bombshell*, 112.
20. Venona message, 5 July 1945; see ibid., 140–5.
21. This is based on a reading of documents released by the KGB in 1992 and documents in the personal archive of Igor Kurchatov, the leading Soviet atomic scientist. These are reproduced as appendices two and three in Sudoplatov and Sudoplatov, *Special Tasks*.
22. Trepper, *Great Game*, 139.
23. Ibid., 87–95. A different but garbled and unreferenced account appears in the anonymous book *The Rote Kapelle: the CIA's History of Soviet Intelligence and Espionage Networks in Western Europe, 1936–1945*, University Publications of America Inc., Washington, DC, 1979, 367–73.

24. Trepper, *Great Game*, 139–40.
25. *Rote Kapelle*, 105–16.
26. Ibid., 212.
27. Ibid., 185–92.
28. Trepper, *Great Game*, 72.
29. Perrault, *Red Orchestra*, 116.
30. See for example the argument between Sissy and Moscow, discussed in *Rote Kapelle*, 180–2.
31. Foote, *Handbook for Spies*, 54.
32. *Rote Kapelle*, 248.
33. Foote, *Handbook for Spies*, 56–7.
34. Ibid., 63.
35. Costello and Tsarev, *Deadly Illusions*, ch. 4. Previous accounts have assumed all such operations were run by Soviet military intelligence (GRU) but as Costello and Tsarev point out the Harnack group was run by the KGB (79).
36. Ibid., 75, 81.
37. Ibid., 81.
38. Klehr *et al.*, *Secret World of American Communism*, ch. 6, esp. 217–18.
39. 'CC Minutes, 1936–40', box 4 (76). CPA Archives, ML MSS 5021, add-on 1936.
40. Untitled document headed 21/3/40 in 'Activities of Communist Party. Premiers' Correspondence.' AA (ACT) 467, item SF42/103.
41. This is similar to a statement by the CPA defector, Cecil Sharpley: 'Generally, party members who have been in the hands of the authorities have to prove themselves before they are completely in the confidence of the party.' AA (ACT) 6119, item 188.
42. Interview, Walter Clayton, 25 August 1993. Interview, Walter Clayton by Ken Mansell, MLOH, 202, 1–74.
43. 'To leading members of Party committees', in 'Activities of Communist Party. Premiers' Correspondence.' AA (ACT) 467, item SF42/103.
44. Clayton, Mansell interview.
45. Ibid.
46. This description was used by Laurie Aarons (interview, 26 Jan. 1995), who attributed it to a Comintern booklet on underground organising which was circulated in the CPA.
47. Interview, Claude Jones, 6 May 1995.
48. Interview, Bill Callan, 26 December 1991; a CPA defector, Cecil Sharpley also said this in a 1952 interview, Sharpley, Cecil vol. 4, AA (ACT) 6119, item 188.
49. 'CPA Interest in Armed Forces', AA (ACT) A6122, item 221, part 2, 366–78.
50. Interview, Clayton, 25 August 1993.
51. Natalya Lebedeva and Mikhail Narinsky, 'Dissolution of the Comintern in 1943', *International Affairs*, 8 (Moscow, English edition, 8/1994), 89–99.
52. These are part of a signals intelligence operation known by the code word 'Venona'. This operation began in February 1943 and was aimed at Soviet diplomatic communications, which used a number code and were sent over the normal cable system. The information derived from Venona was ultimately to reveal extensive Soviet espionage activity in the USA and other countries and lead, among other things, to the controversial execution of Julius and Ethel Rosenberg in 1953. In July 1995 the National Security Agency began the first stage of a series of releases of this material. Along with copies of the decoded documents, the NSA also released a pamphlet *Introductory History of the Venona and Guide to the Translations* by Robert Louis Benson. Copies of the decoded cables can be found on the NSA's Internet homepage at: www.nsa.gov.
53. The structure and names of Soviet intelligence bodies changed between 1943 and 1954 but the acronym KGB is used here to denote the apparatus designed to conduct foreign political intelligence.
54. Venona message, Moscow to Canberra, 12 September 1943. This message was also sent

to New York, San Francisco and Ottawa. The dashes within square brackets denote number groups which could not be decoded.

55. Venona message, Moscow–Canberra, 29 August 1944.

56. *Report of the Royal Commission on Espionage*, 92–3, 159.

57. Statement by one of Hughes' fellow officers, AA (ACT) A6119, item 1510, 7–13.

58. Canberra to Moscow, 17 March 1945.

59. Undated letter from an associate of Clayton's, Rupert Lockwood, to author, ibid. Lockwood claims that Clayton employed her as his secretary but that her previous role 'drew suspicion' on Clayton.

60. That this occurred was told to me by one of Clayton's associates: see McKnight, *Australia's Spies*, 82, 309.

61. Canberra to Moscow, 25 April 1945.

62. Ibid.

63. Canberra to Moscow, 5 May 1945.

64. In most undercover branches, one member would be a 'public' communist. For example, among CPA scientists, Dr R Makinson was an open member (and was later denied a professorship for 25 years) while others were covert.

65. Canberra to Moscow, 25 April 1945.

66. Laurie Aarons, a senior figure in the CPA, suggested that Clayton organised primarily in this way and that any documents which may have been given to the Russians were merely a 'spin off' and not the prime purpose. Interview, 15 June 1992.

67. Canberra to Moscow, 5 July 1945.

68. Moscow to Canberra, 15 September 1945.

69. Security file, AA (ACT) 6119, item 2020 [vol. IV]. A contrary, though flawed portrait of Milner is in Frank Cain 'The Making of a Cold War Victim', *Overland*, no. 134 (autumn 1994), 60–6.

70. Security file, Jim Hill, AA (ACT) 6119, item 91.

71. Statement by CPA defector, Cecil Sharpley, in AA (ACT) 6119, item 188.

72. Statement by Leslie White to ASIO, 8 January 1959, James Hill, AA (ACT) A6119, item 1243.

73. Interview, Edgar Ross, 7 May 1995. Ross, later a Central Committee member, names teachers, doctors and lawyers as typical covert members. Interview, Len Fox, 11 January 1995. Fox said that most communist journalists on major newspapers were not publicly known as communists.

74. Canberra to Moscow, 29 September 1945.

75. Canberra to Moscow, 30 September 1945.

76. Interview, Elfrida Morcom (Newbigin), 13 January 1995.

77. Canberra to Moscow, 30 September 1945.

78. Taschereau and Kellock, *Report of the Royal Commission*.

79. Canberra to Moscow, 16 November 1945.

80. Canberra to Moscow, cables of 8 November and 7 December 1945.

81. Canberra to Moscow, 8 March 1946.

82. Canberra to Moscow, 19 March 1946.

83. McKnight, *Australia's Spies*, 8–11.

84. Moscow to Canberra, 4 May 1946.

85. AA (ACT) A6119, item 342, Ian Milner, vol. 2, 120–2.

86. Phillip Deery, 'Cold War Victim or Rhodes Scholar Spy?', *Overland*, no. 147 (winter 1997). Milner's files are referenced as Personal File, Jan Frank Milner, Archival No. 621743, Archives of the Ministry of the Interior, Prague.

87. Moscow to Canberra, 1 August 1946. This cable, unlike most others, was signed by Kubatkin, not Fitin.

88. Moscow to Canberra, 9 October 1946.

89. Moscow to Canberra, 24 October 1946.

90. Moscow to Canberra, 9 January 1947. The likely identity of this intermediary can be

deduced from the fact that 'Biti' is a woman, is a close contact of Clayton (Clayton stayed with Beeby when in Canberra), and the difficulty for anyone other than a high official or CPA member to be invited to a diplomatic reception.

91. Moscow to Canberra, 16 May 1948.
92. Moscow to Canberra, 5 June 1948.

Conclusion

This book began by asking how it was that a number of communists in western countries were recruited to Soviet intelligence. It chose to provide part of the answer by exploring the tradition of underground or conspiratorial work. It seems unarguable that a continuity existed between the political underground and the tradecraft of espionage and that this gave the Soviet intelligence services a valuable edge and contributed to their own distinctive character. It is also clear that the use of local communists to carry out espionage proved very valuable to the Soviet Union, although this proved extremely damaging to the local communist cause, which was portrayed as treacherous.

An embodiment of this link between politics and espionage were the early officials of Soviet intelligence and those of the Communist International. They had direct personal experience in operating underground under Tsarism. They employed this experience and codified the 'rules of conspiracy'. They taught these 'rules' at schools for political activists and for intelligence workers.

But the notion of 'rules of conspiracy' can be misleading. In almost every case discussed in this book, there are examples of espionage and political practice that contradict or ignore the rules of conspiracy. In some cases, underground workers or couriers like the American communist Whittaker Chambers or the 'atomic spy' Harry Gold were allowed to accumulate documents which were later used by the authorities to prove espionage. In the case of the French Comintern courier in the Far East, Joseph Ducroux, a breach of the rules, carrying an address on a piece of paper, lead to the arrest of Ho Chi Minh and to the exposure of the Comintern group in Shanghai. In the case of both the Cambridge spies and the CPUSA group which operated around Chambers in Washington, the participants were known to each other, breaking the rule that people in an underground apparatus had to be compartmentalised. Perhaps the most remarkable breach was the recruitment of the flamboyant and indiscreet British spy, Guy Burgess, whose activity ultimately complicated the escape of the far more valuable spy, Donald Maclean.

But none of this should surprise us. In every human enterprise, concrete practice always confounds those who believe that events unfold according to a prearranged plan or theory. This does not disprove or deny the role played by careful but abstract plans (or conspiratorial rules), it simply means that many other factors come into play.

Assessing the theory in the context of the practice requires a concrete analysis of concrete situations. In a similar light and on a broader field, well grounded empirical studies will help us make sense and meaning of the historical era which closed in 1989–91.

In this regard, it is important that the new post-Cold War history is not the old anti-communist scholarship in new guise. It would be a mistake, for example, to see communist parties as mere extensions of Soviet espionage or even as a purely pro-Soviet phenomenon. This would be to gravely underestimate their effect on domestic policy, on the labour movement and on cultural and intellectual life. These spheres of influence were not only separate from any espionage, but were areas where Stalinism was grafted on to a pre-existing-130-year old tradition of radical socialist ideas. The political influence of communist parties was deeply affected by pro-Soviet ideas but not reducible to them alone.

THE FUTURE

New work on the Comintern is not common, which is surprising given the wealth of new archival sources that have suddenly become available in Russia and the drama which accompanied their release. We now know more about the inner functioning of the parties of the Comintern and about such specific topics as the 'Bolshevisation' of the 1920s, the Popular Front of the mid-1930s and the effects of Stalin's terror on the Comintern.[1] A debate has also started about the historiography of the Comintern in the light of the new sources.[2]

This book has been both broad and selective in the instances it describes of underground methods and associated events. A great deal more work can be done in filling out the 'underside' of many political parties affiliated with the Comintern. In even greater need of informed scholarly work is the field of intelligence studies. Hopefully this book has signalled a way to apply the methods of social and political history to the field, to supplement the more usual framework of diplomatic and military history.

A great deal is yet to be done in matching Russian archival sources with the decoded cables of Soviet intelligence known as Venona.[3] This will throw further light on the roots of espionage but may take some time. According to Warner and Benson, it may take 'a decade or two' before the Venona material is comprehended and 'a generation to produce its deepest and most lasting insights'.[4]

Another avenue for exploration is the effect of *konspiratsya* on the practice of communism in the West. In spite of working within far more liberal conditions than Tsarist Russia, the revolutionaries of the West seemed prone to suspicion and paranoia which was similar to that engendered within Russia under Stalin. *Konspiratsya* may be an unacknowledged source of what we call 'Stalinism'.

More needs to be done on one of the broader debates in the historiography of the communist movement. This concerns especially the debate between those who argue that after the 1920s communist parties were nothing more than creatures of the Soviet Union, and others who argue that such parties were merely an expression of the radical, socialist and populist tradition which predated 1917 and Stalinism.[5] Less polarised, more synthetic interpretations are surely needed.

Future scholarship devoted to the Comintern and its affiliated parties must draw on the strengths of each of the partisan camps. Historians need the sceptical and unsentimental perspective of the scholarship hostile to communism. They also need social and cultural insights of the scholarship sympathetic to communism to understand the human motivations in the tragic course of the communist movement.

NOTES

1. Klehr *et al.*, *Secret World of American Communism*; Klehr *et al.*, *Soviet World of American Communism*; Kevin McDermott and Jeremy Agnew, *The Comintern: a History of International Communism from Lenin to Stalin*, University of California Press, Berkeley, 1988.
2. Studer and Unfried, 'Beginning of a History'; Narinsky and Jurgen, *Centre and Periphery*.
3. A new work by Klehr and Haynes is forthcoming. Personal discussion, John Haynes, 28 May 1998.
4. Michael Warner and Robert Louis Benson, 'Venona and Beyond: Thoughts on Work Undone', *Intelligence and National Security*, vol. 12, no. 3 (July 1997), 11.
5. This point is discussed in Klehr *et al.*, *Secret World of American Communism*, 17–18.

Bibliography

PRIMARY SOURCES

The key primary source for this book is the files of the Communist International held at the Russian Centre for the Preservation and Study of Documents of Recent History, known by its Russian acronym RTsKhIDNI and situated in Moscow. This institution was founded in 1991 and was formerly the Central Party Archive of the Communist Party of the Soviet Union.

Another key repository is the Australian Archives in Canberra in the Australian Capital Territory which holds the files of the Australian government, including the Commonwealth Investigation Bureau and its successor the Australian Security Intelligence Organization. These are designated below by the prefix, AA (ACT).

The archives of the former Communist Party of Australia (CPA) held at the State Library of New South Wales in Sydney were extensively consulted. These are held in two separate entries, MSS 5021 and MSS 5021 (add-on 1936). In addition, several thousands of pages of CPA records are available on microfilm based on records at RTsKhIDNI in Moscow.

In chapter 4 I refer extensively to records of the Shanghai Municipal Police which are held at the National Archives in Washington, DC. Of particular use was a report by a British source (probably MI5, the Security Service), entitled 'Communist Activities in China, Federated Malay States, etc. (The "Noulens Case")'. These records are held in RG 263. A finding aid by Williamson (below) sets out these records.

In chapters 6 and 7, dealing with the Australian Labor Party, I consulted a series of personal papers deposited by J. R. Hughes at the University of Western Sydney, Macarthur. These have now been transferred to the

201

Mitchell Library within the State Library of New South Wales and are found under ML MSS 6381.

An important historical source for the final chapter is the group of documents known as the Venona collection. These documents consist of partially and fully decoded cables between Soviet intelligence personel in Russia and abroad. They derived from a project to decode encrypted Soviet diplomatic communications which were intercepted by American intelligence in the 1940s. Released in stages between 1995 and 1997 by the National Security Agency, the collection is found on its home page <http://www.nsa.gov/>.

INTERVIEWS AND LETTERS

I conducted a number of interviews or received letters from individuals as follows:

Laurie Aarons, interviews, 15 June 1992, 26 January 1995.
Eric Aarons, interview, 16 January 1995.
Audrey Blake, 10 October, 1995.
Simon Bracegirdle, interviews, 6–7 May 1995.
William Callen, interviews, 20 May 1992, 10 July 1996.
Walter Clayton, interviews, 25 August, 1993, 26 March 1995.
Len Fox, interview, 11 January 1995; letter 1 May 1995.
J. R. (Jack) Hughes, interviews, 9 May 1995, 30 June 1994, 25 September 1995, 16 November 1995; letter, 18 July 1996.
Claude Jones, interview, 6 May 1995.
Rupert Lockwood, interview, 21 June 1992, letter, 27 September, 1993.
Jack McPhillips, interview, 21 June 1995.
Dimitri Moiseenko, interview, 21 December 1996.
Elfrida Morcom (née Newbigin), interview, 13 January 1995.
Edgar Ross, interview, 7 May 1995; letters, 12 September 1995, 17 November 1995, 24 December 1995.
Betty Searle, letter, 30 July 1996.

PUBLICATIONS

Argus
Communist International (English language edition)
Communist Review

Daily News (Sydney)
International Press Correspondence (abbreviated as *InPreCorr*)
Pan Pacific Worker (Sydney and San Francisco)
Progress (Sydney)
Smith's Weekly
Sydney Morning Herald
Workers Weekly

BOOKS

VII Congress of the Communist International, Abridged Stenographic Report of Proceedings, Modern Publishers, Sydney, n.d.

Akimov, Vladimir, 'A Short History of the Social Democratic Movement in Russia', in Jonathan Frenkel (translation and introduction) *Vladimir Akimov on the Dilemmas of Russian Marxism, 1895–1903*, Cambridge University Press, Cambridge, 1969.

Central Committee of the CPSU (B), *History of the Communist Party of the Soviet Union (Short Course)*, Foreign Languages Publishing House, Moscow, 1943.

Engels, Frederick, 'Preface to the English Edition of 1888, Manifesto of the Communist Party', in Karl Marx and Frederick Engels, *Selected Works*, vol. I, Foreign Languages Publishing House, Moscow, 1958.

Engels, Frederick, 'On the History of the Communist League', in Karl Marx and Frederick Engels, *Selected Works*, vol. II, Foreign Languages Publishing House, Moscow, 1958.

Heckethorn, Charles William, *The Secret Societies of all Ages and Countries*, 2 volumes, George Redway, London, 1897.

Lenin, Vladimir, *Collected Works*, Progress Publishers, Moscow, 1978 (published in the United Kingdom by Lawrence & Wishart, London, 1978).

Marx, Karl and Frederick Engels, *The Cologne Communist Trial* (trans. with introduction by Rodney Livingstone), Lawrence & Wishart, London, 1971.

Trotsky, Leon, *1905*, Pelican Books, Harmondsworth, 1973.

Theses, Resolutions and Manifestos of the First Four Congresses of the Third International (trans. Alix Holt and Barbara Holland, introduction by Bertil Hessel), Ink Links, London, 1980.

PAMPHLETS

The Communist International: Between the Fifth and Sixth World Congresses, 1924–28, Dorrit Press, London, 1928.

Bauer, Otto, *Die Illegale Partei*, Editions 'La Lutte Socialiste', Paris, 1939.

Dixon, R., *Defend Australia?* Modern Publishers, n.d. but approx. 1936–7.

Kedrov, S., *Une Imprimerie Clandestine [A Secret Printery]*, Bureau d'Editions, Paris, 1932.

Les Questions d'Organisation au Veme Congres de l'IC, Librarie de l'Humanite, Paris, 1925.

Lozovsky, A., *The Pan Pacific Trade Union Conference*, RILU, Moscow, 1927.

Mif, P., *China's Struggle for Freedom: the Fifteenth Anniversary of the Communist Party of China*, Modern Books, London, n.d.

Piatnitsky, O., *The Bolshevisation of the Communist Parties by Eradicating the Social-Democratic Traditions*, Modern Books, London, c. 1932.

Wincott, Len, *The Spirit of Invergordon*, International Labour Defence, London, n.d.

ARTICLES

A major primary source has been the English language edition of *International Press Correspondence* (later changed to *World News and Views*) and the English language editions of the journal *Communist International*. Numbering and dating are irregular and sometimes omitted on originals. Major articles from here are indicated below. Articles are listed in chronological order.

O. Piatnitsky, 'Organisational Problems of Comintern Sections', *Communist International*, no. 4 (1924).

'Resolution on Reorganisation of the Party on the Basis of Shop Nuclei', *Communist International*, no. 7 (Dec. 1924–Jan.1925).

O. Piatnitsky, 'Party Construction in the Sections of the Communist International', *InPreCorr*, 5 February 1925.

D. Manuilsky, 'Bolshevisation of the Parties', *Communist International*, no. 10 (1925).

O. Piatnitsky, 'Conference of the Sections of the Comintern on Organisation', *Communist International*, no. 11 (1925).

'Report on the Organisation Conference,' *InPreCorr*, 15 April 1926.

'Decisions of the Second Org. Conference of Sections of the CI', *InPreCorr*, 5 May 1926.

O. Piatnitsky, 'Achievements and Immediate Tasks in Organisation', *Communist International*, 30 May 1927.

O. Piatnitsky, 'Achievements and Tasks in Factory and Trade Union Work', *Communist International*, 15 June 1927.

'The Struggle Against Imperialist War and the Tasks of the Communists', *InPreCorr*, 28 November 1928.

'Resolution of the ECCI on Communist Work in the Trade Unions of China', *InPreCorr*, 20 September 1929.

'Letter from the Org-Dept of the ECCI Confirmed by the Polit-Secretariat', *InPreCorr*, 31 December 1930.

'The Work of Factory Nuclei', *InPreCorr*, 24 December 1930 and 31 December 1930.

A. Lozovsky, 'The Trade Unions and the Coming War', *Communist International*, vol. 8, no. 14, August 1931.

A. Vasilyev, 'The Communist Parties on the Anti-Militarist Front', *Communist International*, vol. 8, no. 14 (August 1931).

B. Vasilyev, 'Organisational Problems in Underground Revolutionary Work', *Communist International*, vol. 8, no. 15 (1 Sept. 1931).

'The English Atlantic Fleet', *Communist International*, vol. 8, no. 17 (15 Oct 1931).

'War and the Immediate Tasks of the Communist Parties', *Communist International*, vol. 11, no. 6 (1 April 1932).

'The German Communist Party in the Struggle Against the Fascist Dictatorship', *Communist International*, vol. 10, no. 10 (1 June 1933).

'On the Question of Illegal Work', *Communist International*, vol. 10, no. 23 (1 Dec. 1933).

'Examples of the Work of the CP of Japan in the Army', *Communist International*, vol. 11, no. 1 (1 Jan. 1934).

'Fascism, the Danger of War and the Tasks of the Communist Parties', *InPreCorr* (Special Supplement), 5 January 1934.

'Some Experiences from the Activity of the CP of Japan in the Army,' *Communist International*, vol. 11, no. 14 (July 1934).

'The Lower Functionaries of the Communist Party of Germany', *Communist International*, vol. 11, no. 16 (20 Aug. 1934).

R. Cramm, 'Organisational Questions', in *Communist Review* (Australia), vol. 1, no. 8 (November 1934).

SECONDARY SOURCES

BOOKS

Albright, Joseph and Marcia Kunstel, *Bombshell: the Secret Story of America's Unknown Atomic Spy Conspiracy*, Times Books, New York, 1997.

Andrew, Christopher and Oleg Gordievsky, *KGB: the Inside Story of its Foreign Operations from Lenin to Gorbachev*, Hodder & Stoughton, London, 1990.

Andrew, Christopher and Vasili Mitrokhin, *The Mitrokhin Archive: the KGB in Europe and the West*, Allen Lane, Penguin Press, London, 1999.

Avtorkhanov, Abdurakhman, *The Communist Party Apparatus*, Henry Regnery Company, Chicago, 1966.

Ball, Desmond and David Horner, *Breaking the Codes*, Allen & Unwin, Sydney, 1998.

Barron, John, *KGB: the Secret Work of Soviet Secret Agents*, Hodder & Stoughton, London, 1974.

Benson, Robert Louis, *Introductory History of the Venona and Guide to the Translations*, Centre for Cryptologic History, National Security Agency, Maryland, n.d. [1995].

Benson, Robert Louis, *The KGB and GRU in Europe, South America and Australia*, Venona Historical Monograph 5, National Security Agency homepage, <http://www.nsa.gov>.

Benson, Robert Louis and Michael Warner (eds.), *Venona: Soviet Espionage and the American Response 1939–1957*, National Security Agency, Washington, DC, 1996.

Blobaum, Robert, *Feliks Dzierzynski and the SDKPiL: a Study of the Origins of Polish Communism*, East European Monographs, Columbia University Press, Boulder, 1984.

Bobrovskaya, Cecilia, *Twenty Years in Underground Russia: Memoirs of a Rank and File Bolshevik*, 2nd edition, Proletarian Publishers, Chicago, 1978.

Bonnell, Victoria E., *Roots of Rebellion: Workers' Politics and Organisations in St Petersburg and Moscow, 1900–1914*, University of California Press, Berkeley, 1983.

Borkenau, Franz, *World Communism: a History of the Communist International*, University of Michigan Press, Ann Arbor, 1962.

Borovik, Genrikh, *The Philby Files*, Warner Books, London, 1995.

Branson, Noreen, *History of the Communist Party of Great Britain: 1927–1941*, Lawrence & Wishart, London, 1985.

Braun, Otto, *A Comintern Agent in China 1932–1939* (trans. Jeanne Moore) Queensland University Press, St Lucia, (Queensland), 1982.

Braunthal, Julius, *History of the International, 1864–1914* (trans. Henry Collins and Kenneth Mitchell), Thomas Nelson, London, 1966.

Brimmell, J. H., *Communism in South East Asia: a Political Analysis*, Oxford University Press, Oxford and London, 1959.

Broido, Vera (trans. and ed.), *Eva Broido: Memoirs of a Revolutionary*, Oxford University Press, London 1967.

Buckley, Ken, Barbara Dale and Wayne Reynolds, *Doc Evatt: Patriot, Internationalist, Fighter and Scholar*, Longman Cheshire, Melbourne, 1994.

Cain, Frank, *ASIO: an Unofficial History*, Spectrum Publications, Richmond (Victoria), 1994.

Cain, Frank, *The Origins of Political Surveillance in Australia*, Angus & Robertson, Sydney, 1983.

Campbell, Ernest, *History of the Australian Labor Movement: a Marxist Interpretation*, Current Book Distributors, Sydney, 1945.

Carew, Anthony, *The Lower Deck of the Royal Navy, 1900–1939*, Manchester University Press, Manchester 1981.

Carr, Edward Hallett, *The Twilight of the Comintern, 1930–1935*, Macmillan, London, 1982.

Carr, Edward Hallett, *What is History?*, Pelican Books, Harmondsworth, 1967.

Chamberlin, William Henry, (introduction) *Blueprint for World Conquest: as Outlined by the Communist International*, Human Events, Chicago, 1946.

Chambers, Whittaker, *Witness*, André Deutsch, London, 1953.

Chan, Ming K., *Historiography of the Chinese Labor Movement, 1895–1949: a Critical Survey and Bibliography*, Hoover Institution Press, Stanford, 1981.

Cole, G. D. H., *A History of the Labour Party from 1914*, Routledge & Kegan Paul, London, 1969.

Coleman, Peter, *Obscenity, Blasphemy, Sedition: Censorship in Australia*, Jacaranda Press, Brisbane, n.d. [*c.* 1962].

Commonwealth of Australia, *Report of the Royal Commission on Espionage*, Sydney, 1955.

Cooksey, Robert, *Lang and Socialism*, Australian National University Press, Canberra, 1976.

Costello, John and Oleg Tsarev, *Deadly Illusions*, Century, London, 1993.

Crisp, L. F. *The Australian Federal Labour Party 1901–1951*, Hale & Iremonger, Sydney, 1978.

Crockett, Peter, *Evatt, a Life*, Oxford University Press, Oxford and Melbourne, 1993.

Dallin, David J., *Soviet Espionage*, Yale University Press, New Haven, 1955.

Davidson, Alistair, *The Communist Party of Australia*, Hoover Institution Press, Stanford, 1969.

Deakin, F. W. and G.R. Storry, *The Case of Richard Sorge*, Chatto & Windus, London, 1966.

Deacon, Richard, *A History of the Russian Secret Service*, Grafton Books, London, 1972.

Degras, Jane (ed.), *The Communist International, 1919–1943: Documents*, 3 vols., Oxford University Press, Oxford and London, 1960.

Dennis, Peggy, *The Autobiography of an American Communist: a Personal View of a Political Life 1925–1975*, Lawrence Hill & Co., Westport, 1977.

Divine, David, *Mutiny at Invergordon*, Macdonald, London, 1970.

Djilas, Aleksa, *The Contested Country: Yugoslav Unity and Communist Revolution, 1919–1953*, Harvard University Press, Cambridge, MA, 1991.

Drachkovitch, Milorad M. and Branko Lazitch (eds.), *The Comintern: Historical Highlights*, Frederick A. Praeger, New York, 1966.

Draper, Theodore, *The Roots of American Communism*, Viking Press, New York, 1957.

Dziak, John J., *Chekisty: a History of the KGB*, Lexington Books, Lexington, 1988.

Easson, Michael (ed.), *McKell. The Achievements of Sir William McKell*, Allen & Unwin, Sydney, 1988.

Elwood, Ralph Carter, *Russian Social Democracy in the Underground: a Study of the RSDLP in the Ukraine, 1907–1914*, International Institute for Social History, Amsterdam, 1974.

Farrell, Frank, *International Socialism and Australian Labour*, Hale & Iremonger, Sydney, 1981.

Firkins, Peter, *Of Nautilus and Eagles: a History of the Royal Australian Navy*, Hutchison, Richmond (Victoria), 1983.

Foote, Alexander, *Handbook for Spies*, Museum Press, London, 1964.

Freudenberg, Graham, *Cause for Power: the Official History of the NSW Branch of the Australian Labor Party*, Pluto Press, Sydney, 1991.

Gaddis, John Lewis, *The United States and the End of the Cold War: Implications, Reconsiderations, Provocations*, Oxford University Press, Oxford, 1992.

Gaddis, John Lewis, *We Now Know: Rethinking Cold War History*, Clarendon Press, Oxford, 1997.

Getzler, Israel, *Martov: a Political Biography of a Russian Social Democrat*, Melbourne University Press, Carlton (Victoria), 1967.

Gouzenko, Igor, *This was My Choice*, Eyre & Spottiswoode, London, 1948.

Hagan, Jim, and Ken Turner, *A History of the Labor Party in New South Wales 1891–1991*, Longman Cheshire, Melbourne, 1991.

Hall, Richard, *The Rhodes Scholar Spy*, Random House, Sydney, 1991.

Hardy, Deborah, *Land and Freedom: the Origins of Russian Terrorism, 1876–1879*, Greenwood Press, Westport, CT, 1987.

Hardy, George, *Those Stormy Years: Memories of the Fight for Freedom on Five Continents*, Lawrence & Wishart, London, 1956.

Hazell, Robert, *Conspiracy and Civil Liberties*, Occasional Papers on Social Adminstration, 55, Bell and Sons, London, 1974.

Hitchins, Keith, *Rumania: 1866-1947*, Clarendon Press, Oxford, 1994.

Hobsbawm, Eric, *Age of Extremes: the Short Twentieth Century*, Michael Joseph, London, 1994.

Hohne, Heinz, *Codeword: Direktor: the Story of the Red Orchestra* (trans. Richard Barry), Pan Books, London, 1973.

Hornstein, David P., *Arthur Ewert: a Life for the Comintern*, University Press of America, Lanham, 1993.

Hughes, Colin A. and B. D. Graham, *Voting for the Australian House of Representatives*, Australian National University Press, Canberra, 1974.

Johnpoll, Bernard K. and Harvey Klehr, *Biographical Dictionary of the American Left*, Greenwood Press, Westport, CT, 1986.

Keep, J. L. H., *The Rise of Social Democracy in Russia*, Clarendon Press, Oxford, 1963.

Kheng, Cheah Boon, *From PKI to the Comintern, 1924–1941: the Apprenticeship of the Malayan Communist Party*, Southeast Asia Program, Cornell University, Ithaca, NY, 1992.

Klehr, Harvey, John Earl Haynes, and Fredrikh Igorevich Firsov, *The Secret World of American Communism*, Yale University Press, New Haven, 1995.

Klehr, Harvey, John Earl Haynes, and Kyrril M. Anderson, *The Soviet World of American Communism*, Yale University Press, New Haven, 1998.

Klehr, Harvey and Ronald Radosh, *The Amerasia Spy Case: Prelude to McCarthyism*, University of North Carolina Press, Chapel Hill, 1996.

Knight, Amy W., *The KGB: Police and Politics in the Soviet Union*, Unwin Hyman, Boston, 1988.

Knightley, Phillip, *Philby: the Life and View of the KGB Masterspy*, André Deutsch, London, 1988.

Kovrig, Bennett, *Communism in Hungary: from Kun to Kadar*, Hoover Institution Press, Stanford, 1979.

Krivitsky, W. G., *I Was Stalin's Agent*, Hamish Hamilton, London, 1940.

Krupskaya, N. K., *Reminicences of Lenin* (trans. Bernard Isaacs), Foreign Languages Publishing House, Moscow, 1959.

Kuusinen, Aino, *The Rings of Destiny: Inside Soviet Russia from Lenin to Brezhnev* (trans. Paul Stevenson), William Morrow & Co. New York, 1974.

Lamphere, Robert J. and Shachtman, Tom, *The FBI–KGB War: a Special Agent's Story*, W. H. Allen, London, 1987.

Lane, David, *The Roots of Russian Communism: a Social and Historical Study of Russian Social Democracy 1898–1907*, 2nd edition, Martin Robertson, London 1975.

Lang, J. T., *The Turbulent Years*, Alpha Books, Sydney, 1970.

Lazitch, Branko and Milorad Drachkovitch (eds.), *Biographical Dictionary of the Comintern*, Hoover Institution Press, Stanford, 1973.

Leggett, George, *The Cheka: Lenin's Political Police*, Clarendon Press, Oxford, 1981.

Liebman, Marcel, *Leninism Under Lenin* (trans. Brian Pearce), Jonathan Cape, London, 1975.

Lockwood, Rupert, *War on the Waterfront*, Hale & Iremonger, Sydney, 1987.

Macintyre, Stuart, *The Reds: the Communist Party of Australia from Origins to Illegality*, Allen & Unwin, St Leonards, NSW, 1998.

MacKenzie, Norman (ed.), *Secret Societies*, Aldus Books, London, 1967.

McDaniel, Tim, *Autocracy, Capitalism and Revolution in Russia*, University of California Press, Berkeley, 1988.

McDermott, Kevin and Jeremy Agnew, *The Comintern: a History of International Communism from Lenin to Stalin*, Macmillan, London, 1996.

McKenzie, Kermit E., *Comintern and World Revolution 1928–1943: the Shaping of a Doctrine*, Columbia University Press, New York, 1964.

McKnight, David, *Australia's Spies and their Secrets*, Allen & Unwin, St Leonards, NSW, 1994.

McLane, Charles B., *Soviet Strategies in Southeast Asia: an Exploration of Eastern Policy Under Lenin and Stalin*, Princeton University Press, Princeton, 1966.

McNeal, Robert H., *Bride of the Revolution: Krupskaya and Lenin*, Victor Gollancz, London, 1973.

Manne, Robert, *The Petrov Affair: Politics and Espionage*, Pergamon, Sydney, 1987.

Markey, Raymond, *In Case of Oppression*, Pluto Press, Sydney, 1994.

Marquez, Gabriel Garcia, *Clandestine in Chile: the Adventures of Miguel Littin* (trans. Asa Zatz), Granta Books, London, 1989.

Masters, Anthony, *The Man Who Was M: the Life of Maxwell Knight*, Basil Blackwell, Oxford, 1984.

Mehring, Franz, *Karl Marx: the Story of his Life* (trans. E. Fitzgerald), George Allen & Unwin, London, 1951.

Milliss, Roger, *Serpent's Tooth*, Penguin Books, Ringwood (Victoria), 1984.

Modin, Yuri, with Jean-Charles Deniau and Agnieszka Ziarek, *My Five Cambridge Friends*, Farrar Straus & Giroux, New York, 1994.

Moore, Andrew, *The Secret Army and the Premier: Conservative Para-Military Organisations in New South Wales, 1930–32*, New South Wales University Press, Kensington, 1989.

Moss, Norman, *Klaus Fuchs: the Man who Stole the Atom Bomb*, Grafton Books, London, 1989.

Murray, Dian H. with Qin Baoqi, *The Origins of the Tiandihui: the Chinese Triads in Legend and History*, Stanford University Press, Stanford, 1994.

Naimark, Norman M., *Terrorists and Social Democrats, the Russian Revolutionary Movement Under Alexander III*, Harvard University Press, Cambridge, MA, 1983.

Nairn, Bede, *The Big Fella: Jack Lang and the Australian Labor Party*, Melbourne University Press, Carlton South, 1986.

Narinsky, Mikhail, and Jurgen Rojahn, *Centre and Periphery: the History of the Comintern in the Light of New Documents*, International Institute for Social History, Amsterdam, 1996.

Neuberg, A., *Armed Insurrection* (trans. Quintin Hoare), New Left Books, London, 1970.

Nollau, Gunter, *International Communism and World Revolution: History and Methods*, Hollis & Carter, London, 1961.

Oren, Nissan, *Revolution Administered: Agrarianism and Communism in Bulgaria*, Johns Hopkins University Press, Baltimore, 1973.

Orlov, Alexander, *Handbook of Intelligence and Guerrilla Warfare*, University of Michigan, Ann Arbor, 1972.

Penrose, Barrie, and Simon Freeman, *Conspiracy of Silence: the Secret Life of Anthony Blunt*, Grafton Books, London, 1987.

Perrault, Gilles, *The Red Orchestra*, Mayflower, London, 1970.

Petrov, Vladimir and Evdokia, *Empire of Fear*, André Deutsch, London, 1956.

Philby, Kim, *My Silent War*, Panther, London, 1980.

Piatnitsky, O., *Memoirs of a Bolshevik*, Martin Lawrence, London, 1932.

Pipes, Richard, *Russia Under the Old Regime*, Weidenfeld & Nicolson, London, 1974.

Radosh, Ronald, and Joyce Milton, *The Rosenberg File: a Search for the Truth*, Vintage Books, New York, 1984.

Roland, Betty, *Caviar for Breakfast*, Collins Publishers, Sydney, 1989.

Ross, E. *Of Storm and Struggle*, New Age Publishers, Sydney, 1982.

Ross, Edgar, *A History of the Miners' Federation of Australia*, Australasian Coal and Shale Employees' Federation, Sydney, 1970.

Ross, Lloyd, *John Curtin – a Biography*, Sun Books, Melbourne, 1983.

The Rote Kapelle: the CIA's History of Soviet Intelligence and Espionage Networks in Western Europe, 1936–1945, University Publications of America Inc., Washington, DC, 1979.

Schleifman, Nurit, *Undercover Agents in the Russian Revolutionary Movement: the SR Party, 1902–14*, St Martin's Press, New York, 1988.

Schneir, Walter and Miriam, *Invitation to an Inquest: Reopening the Rosenberg 'Atom Spy' Case*, 3rd edn, Penguin Books, Harmondsworth, 1974.

Selznick, Phillip, *The Organisational Weapon: a Study of Bolshevik Strategy and Tactics*, Free Press, Glencoe, 1960.

Serge, Victor, *What Everyone Should Know About State Repression*, (trans. Judith White), New Park Publications, London, 1979.

Shapiro, Leonard, *The Origin of Communist Autocracy: Political*

Opposition in the Soviet State: First Phase, 1917–1922, Havard University Press, Cambridge, MA, 1955.

Sharkey, L. L., *An Outline History of the Australian Communist Party,* Marx School, Sydney, 1944.

Straight, Michael, *After Long Silence,* W. W. Norton, New York, 1983.

Suda, Zdenek L., *Zealots and Rebels: a History of the Communist Party of Czechoslovakia,* Hoover Institution Press, Stanford, 1980.

Sudoplatov, Pavel, and Anatoli Sudoplatov, with Jerrold L. Schecter, and P. Leona, *Special Tasks: the Memoirs of an Unwanted Witness – a Soviet Spymaster,* Little, Brown, London, 1994.

Taschereau, Justice Robert and Justice R. L. Kellock, *Report of the Royal Commission to Investigate Facts relating to the Communication of Secret and Confidential Information to Agents of a Foreign Power,* Government Printer, Ottawa, 1946.

Thomas, S. Bernard, *Labor and the Chinese Revolution: Class Strategies and Contradictions of Chinese Communism, 1928–48,* Centre for Chinese Studies, University of Michigan Press, Ann Arbor, 1983.

Thomson, David, *The Babeuf Plot: the Making of a Republican Legend,* Greenwood Press, Westport, CT, 1975.

Thornton, Richard C., *The Comintern and the Chinese Communists 1928-1931,* University of Washington Press, Seattle, 1969.

Trepper, Leopold, *The Great Game: Memoirs of the Spy Hitler Couldn't Silence,* McGraw-Hill, New York, 1977.

Trotsky, Leon, *My Life: an Attempt at an Autobiography,* Charles Scribner, New York 1930.

Ulam, Adam B., *Lenin and the Bolsheviks: the Intellectual and Political History of the Triumph of Communism in Russia,* Secker & Warburg, London, 1966.

Ulyanovsky, R. A., *The Comintern and the East,* Progress Publishers, Moscow, 1979.

Utechin, S. V. *Russian Political Thought: a Concise History,* J. M. Dent & Sons, London, 1964.

Valtin, Jan [Richard Krebs], *Out of the Night,* William Heinemann, London, 1941.

Venturi, Franco, *Roots of Revolution: a History of the Populist and Socialist Movements in Nineteenth Century Russia,* Weidenfeld & Nicolson, London, 1960.

Walker, R. B. *Yesterday's News: a History of the Newspaper Press in New South Wales from 1920 to 1945,* Sydney University Press, Sydney, 1980.

Weeks, Albert L., *The First Bolshevik: a Political Biography of Peter Tkachev*, New York University Press, New York, 1963.

Weinstein, Allen, *Perjury: the Hiss–Chambers Case*, 2nd edn, Random House, New York, 1997.

Weller, Patrick, and Beverley Lloyd (eds.) *Federal Executive Minutes 1915–1955*, Melbourne University Press, Carlton, Victoria, 1978.

West, Nigel, *A Matter of Trust: MI5 1945–72*, Coronet Books, London, 1983.

Whitlam, Nicholas and John Stubbs, *Nest of Traitors: the Petrov Affair*, Jacaranda Press, Milton, Queensland, 1974.

Wicks, H. M., *Eclipse of October*, Holborn Publishing Co., London, 1958.

Williams, John R., *John Latham and the Conservative Recovery from Defeat 1929–1931*, Australasian Political Studies Association, Sydney, 1969.

Williams, Robert Chadwell, *Klaus Fuchs, Atom Spy*, Havard University Press, Cambridge, MA, 1987.

Williams, Robert Chadwell, *The Other Bolsheviks: Lenin and his Critics, 1904–1914*, Indiana University Press, Bloomington and Indianapolis, 1986.

Willoughby, Charles A., *Shanghai Conspiracy: the Sorge Spy Ring*, E. P. Dutton & Company, New York, 1952.

Wilson, Dick, *Chou: the Story of Zhou Enlai, 1898–1976*, Hutchinson, London, 1984.

Wincott, Len, *Invergordon Mutineer*, Weidenfeld & Nicolson, London, 1974.

Yong, C. F., *Chinese Leadership and Power in Colonial Singapore*, Times Academic Press, Singapore, 1992.

Young, Thom and Martin Kettle, *Incitement to Disaffection*, Cobden Trust, London, 1976.

ARTICLES AND CHAPTERS

ABC, 'The Making of an Australian Communist' (transcript), on *Sunday Night Radio Two*, Australian Broadcasting Commission broadcast, 16 September 1973.

Akimov, Vladimir, 'A Short History of the Social Democratic Movement in Russia', in Jonathan Frenkel (trans. and introduced), *Vladimir Akimov on the Dilemmas of Russian Marxism, 1895–1903*, Cambridge University Press, Cambridge, 1969.

Andrew, Christopher, 'The Growth of the Australian Intelligence Community and the Anglo-American Connection', *Intelligence and National Security*, vol. 4, no. 2 (April 1989).

Blake, Jack, 'The Australian Communist Party and the Comintern in the early 1930s', *Labour History*, no. 23 (1972).

Cain, Frank, 'The Making of a Cold War Victim', *Overland*, no. 134 (autumn 1994).

Carew, Anthony, 'The Invergordon Mutiny, 1931: Long-term Causes, Organisation, and Leadership', *International Review of Social History*, vol. 24 (1979).

Carment, David, 'Australian Communism and National Security September 1939–June 1941', in *Journal of the Royal Australian Historical Society*, vol. 65, pt. 4 (March 1980).

Churchward, Lloyd, 'An Early Alliance of the Left', *Australian Left Review* (Oct.–Nov. 1970).

Curthoys, Barbara, 'The Comintern, the CPA and the Impact of Harry Wicks', *Australian Journal of Politics and History*, vol. 39, no. 1 (1993).

Deery, Phillip, 'Cold War Victim or Rhodes Scholar Spy?', *Overland*, no. 147 (winter 1997).

Duncanson, Dennis J., 'Ho Chi Minh in Hong Kong, 1931–32', *China Quarterly*, no. 57 (Jan.–March 1974).

Elwood, Ralph Carter, 'Lenin and the Social Democratic Schools for Underground Party Workers, 1909–11', *Political Science Quarterly*, vol. 81, no. 3 (Sept. 1966).

Firsov, Fredrikh Igorevich, 'The Comintern and the Soviet German Non-Aggression Pact', *Bulletin of the CC CPSU from the Party Archives*, no. 12 (1989).

Firsov, Fredrikh Igorevich, 'The VKP(b) and the Communist International' (unpublished paper).

Gaddis, John Lewis, 'The Tragedy of Cold War History: Reflections on Revisionism', *Foreign Affairs*, 73, 1 (Jan.–Feb. 1994).

Haslam, Jonathan, 'Russian Archival Revelations and Our Understanding of the Cold War', *Diplomatic History*, vol. 21, no. 2 (spring 1997).

Lebedeva, Natalya and Mikhail Narinsky, 'Dissolution of the Comintern in 1943', *International Affairs* (Moscow, English edition), no. 8 (1994).

Litten, Frederick S., 'The Noulens Affair', *China Quarterly*, no. 138 (June 1994).

Lloyd, Clem, 'Evatt, Menzies, Latham and the Anti-Communist Crusade', in *Seeing Red: the Communist Party Dissolution Act and Referendum, 1951: Lessons for Constitutional Reform*, Evatt Foundation, Sydney, 1991.

Lloyd, Clem, 'Not Peace but a Sword – The High Court under J. G. Latham', *Adelaide Law Review*, vol. 11, no. 2 (Dec. 1987).

McDermott, Kevin, 'Stalin and the Comintern During the "Third Period", 1928–1933', *European History Quarterly*, vol. 25, no. 3 (1995).

McDermott, Kevin, 'Stalinist Terror in the Comintern: New Perspectives', *Journal of Contemporary History*, vol. 30 (1995).

McKnight, David, 'The Moscow–Canberra Cables: how Soviet Intelligence Obtained British Secrets Through the Back Door', *Intelligence and National Security*, vol. 13, no. 2 (1998).

Metzger, Laurent, 'Joseph Ducroux, a French Agent of the Comintern in Singapore (1931–1932)', *Journal of the Malayan Branch of the Royal Asiatic Society*, vol. 69, part 1 (1996).

Murphy, John, 'Interview with Bill Gollan', *Labour History*, no. 66 (Sydney, n.d.).

Orth, John V., 'The English Combination Laws Reconsidered', in Francis Snyder and Douglas Hay (eds.), *Labour, Law and Crime: an Historical Perspective*, Tavistock Publications, London, 1987.

Rao, Jingying, 'The Shanghai Postal Workers' Union: Sample of a Yellow Union', in E. J. Perry and J. N. Wasserstrom (eds.), *Chinese Studies in History: Shanghai Social Movements 1919–1949* (fall-winter 1993/4).

Radosh, Ronald, 'The Venona Files', *New Republic*, 7 August 1995.

Rawson, Don, 'McKell and Labor Unity', in Michael Easson (ed.) *McKell: the Achievements of Sir William McKell*, Allen & Unwin, Sydney, 1988.

Stranahan, Patricia, 'Editor's Introduction' to *Chinese Studies in History: A Journal of Translations* (special issue on the Communist Party in Shanghai) (winter 1994/5).

Schedvin, C. B. 'Sir Alfred Davidson', in R. T. Appleyard and C. B. Schedvin (eds.), *Australian Financiers: Biographical Essays*, Macmillan, Melbourne, 1988.

Starkov, Boris A., 'The Trial that was Not Held', *Europe-Asia Studies*, vol. 46, no. 8 (Dec. 1994).

Studer, Brigitte and Berthold Unfried, 'At the Beginning of a History:

Visions of the Comintern, After the Opening of the Archives', *International Review of Social History* 42 (1997).

Symons, Beverley, 'All Out for the Peoples' War: Communist Soldiers in the Australian Army in the Second World War', *Australian Historical Studies*, vol. 26, no. 105 (October 1995).

Tucker, Robert C. 'The Cold War in Stalin's Time: What the New Sources Reveal', *Diplomatic History*, vol. 21, no. 2 (spring 1997).

Utechin, S. V. 'Introduction', *What is to be Done?*, Panther, London, 1970.

Warner, Michael, and Robert Louis Benson, 'Venona and Beyond: Thoughts on Work Undone', *Intelligence and National Security*, vol. 12, no. 3 (July 1997).

Westad, Odd Arne, 'Secrets of the Second World: the Russian Archives and the Reinterpretation of Cold War History', *Diplomatic History*, vol. 21, no. 2 (spring 1997).

INDEXES AND FINDING AIDS

Getty, J. Arch and V. P. Kozlov, *Russian Centre for Preservation and Study of Documents of Contemporary History: a Research Guide*, Russian Archives Series, University of Pittsburgh, 1993.

Kahan, Vilem, (ed.) *Bibliography of the Communist International (1919–1979)*, (vol. I) E. J. Brill, Leiden, 1990.

Klein, Donald W., and Anne B. Clark, *Biographic Dictionary of Chinese Communism 1921–1965*, Harvard University Press, Cambridge, MA, 1971.

Parrish, Michael, *Soviet Security and Intelligence Organisations 1917–1990: a Biographical Dictionary and Review of Literature in English*, Greenwood Press, Westport, CT, 1992.

Symons, Beverley with Andrew Wells and Stuart Macintyre, *Communism in Australia: a Resource Bibliography*, National Library of Australia, Canberra, 1994.

Williamson, Jo Ann, *Records of the Shanghai Municipal Police, 1894–1949*, National Archives and Records Administration, Washington, DC, 1993.

Index

218